中國成語選粹

編者

司徒談

英譯者

趙書漢　湯博文

海峰出版社

Best Chinese Idioms

Compiled by

Situ Tan

Tr. into English by

Zhao Shuhan   **Tang Bowen**

Hai Feng Publishing Co.

© **Hai Feng Publishing Co., Ltd.**
ISBN 962-238-033-6

Published by
Hai Feng Publishing Company Limited
Rm. 1503 Wing On House,
71 Des Voeux Rd., Central
Hong Kong

Printed by
Friendly Printing Company Limited
Flat B1, 3/F., Luen Ming Hing Ind. Bldg.,
36 Muk Cheong St., Tokwawan, Kowloon
Hong Kong

Sixth Edition May 1990

出版：
海峰出版社有限公司
香港中環德輔道中71號
永安集團大廈1503室

印刷：
友利印刷有限公司
九龍土瓜灣木廠街36號
聯明興工業大廈4樓B1座

一九九〇年五月第六版

HF-51-P

前言

漢語有豐富的詞彙和各種形式的固定詞組。成語就是一種經常使用的固定詞組，在漢語詞彙中佔有重要的地位。

漢語成語形式簡潔、含義深刻。它們常被用來說明一件事實、一個道理或比喻一種形象，從而構成漢語的獨特風格。

漢語成語是在漢語的長期發展過程中形成的。大多數成語由四個字組成，在使用的時候實際上相當於一個詞。在談話、演講或寫作時，如運用得當，將會增强語言的感染力或說服力，產生其他方法所不能比擬的表達效果。

正確地運用成語，首要之點在於了解它的意義。有些成語的意義，從字面上不難了解；有些成語則不能按字面望文生義，而必須知道它的來源，才能準確掌握和運用。

漢語成語，數量龐大，除來自民間口語者外，相當大的部份來自古代典籍。這些來自古代典籍的成語，有的出自寓言故事，有的出自歷史事件或神話傳說，通常也叫典故。本書所選的大都屬於這一類。

中國的古代典籍記載了大量絢麗多彩的寓言故事和神話。這在先秦諸子的著作中尤為顯著，其中許多寓言故事和神話都有成語的概括形式。如"鷸蚌相爭"這一成語，是出自《戰國策》的一則寓言故事（參見第293－294頁）。"邯鄲學步"則見於《莊子》中的一段寓言（參見第124－125頁）。

歷史上的事件，也常常被概括為一個成語。如"一鼓作氣"，出自《左傳》，講的是公元前六八四年齊國侵犯魯國慘遭失敗的故事（參見第6－7頁）。"草木皆兵"則涉及東晉時的淝水之戰（參見第169－171頁）。這些來自寓言、神話和歷史事件的成語，有不少蘊含着深刻的哲理和寶貴的生活經驗，直到今天還有其現實意義。此外，還有一些成語，來源於古代作品中的名句。

本書選編了常用的和有故事性的成語二百零六條。在介紹成語故事時，一般按照古文直譯，但爲使讀者容易了解起見，有的地方做了一些刪節和修飾，增加了一點背景材料。許多中國成語並列有意義相近的英語成語。此外，還在成語條目的下面附加漢語拼音，不懂漢語的讀者，可以借助於"漢語拼音發音指南"（見書後），直接讀出漢語成語。

　　書前成語"目次"按首字筆劃順序排列。書末附有按漢語拼音字母順序排列的條目"索引"。

Foreword

The Chinese language is rich in vocabulary, phrases and idioms. As a form of set phrases, Chinese idioms are in wide use and occupy an important place in the language as a whole. Concise yet meaningful, they illustrate certain specific facts, carry certain moral teachings or suggest certain particular images, thus constituting a unique characteristic of the Chinese language.

Chinese idioms, which emerged and developed in the long years of Chinese history, mostly consist of four characters which go together and virtually function as a set term. When used properly and cleverly in everyday conversation, speeches or writings, they add to the appeal of the language and make it more to the point and achieve what cannot be achieved by other ways of expressing the same thought.

A correct understanding of their meaning is the key to the correct use of Chinese idioms. While some can be taken literally, others cannot be interpreted or used correctly without first delving into their real meaning and origin.

Being numerous and having backgrounds that can be traced back to ancient times, Chinese idioms are partly derived from oral language and partly — perhaps in the case of a greater percentage of them — from ancient historical records, literature and other writings. The latter category, with which this book chiefly deals, embraces those coming from parables or fables, historical stories or anecdotes, and fairy tales or legends.

Chinese historical records of the remote past abound in wise fables, didactic parables and thought-provoking tales. A case in point is the works of the philosophers of the various schools prior to the Qin Dynasty (221-207 B.C.). Many of the fables and tales contained in them are summarized in a few words which have since become popular idioms. The fable "The Fight Between the Snipe and the Clam" (see pp.293-294 of this book), for instance, first appeared in *Anecdotes of the Warring States* while "Imitating the Handan People in walking" (see pp.124-125) owes its origin to *The Book of Zhuang Zi.*

Some idioms deal with historical events or anecdotes. For example, "Plucking Up Courage with the First Drum" (see pp.6-7) comes from *Zuo Qiuming's Chronicles* and tells about the disastrous defeat suffered by the state of Qi in its invasion against the state of Lu in 684 B.C. "Every Bush and Tree Looks Like an Enemy" (see pp.169-171) is related to the famous Battle of the Feishui River during the Eastern Jin Dynasty (317-420).

Quite a number of Chinese idioms belonging to the above categories carry a philosophical note and draw on practical experiences, which make them significant even for contemporary life. There are also some idioms which have been taken from well-known ancient works and have thus become maxims.

The present book contains 206 Chinese idioms which are in common use and behind each of which there is a story or an anecdote. Generally speaking, the stories and anecdotes are based on the original versions in classical Chinese but, where necessary, abridgement and modifications are made and brief descriptions of their backgrounds given. Many of the Chinese idioms are accompanied by English equivalents. Chinese phonetic spelling (*pinyin*) is given to each title, and for readers who are not familiar with this system the appendix "Guide to Chinese Phonetic Alphabet" at the end of the book may prove useful.

The table of contents in this book has been arranged according to the number of strokes of the first Chinese character in each title. There is an index at the end of the book compiled alphabetically, using the *pinyin* system.

Contents
目次

一 丘 之 貉
yī qiū zhī hé

同一個山丘上的貉；比喻彼此一樣壞，沒有什麼區別。

　　西漢（公元前206－公元24）宣帝時，有個官吏叫楊惲。他熟讀史籍，評古論今，頗有卓見。有一次，楊惲聽到匈奴國王被人殺了，就發表議論說：「昏庸的君王不採納大臣的忠言，自然要得到這樣的下場。秦始皇的兒子秦二世也因這個原因亡了國。如果二世親近賢臣，他的王位是可以保持到現在的。這樣看來，那些昏庸的君王，不論是古代的，還是當今的，就如同生長在一個山丘上的貉一樣，都是蠢傢伙。」

出自《漢書》*

　　*《漢書》　歷史著作，記載西漢二百三十年間的歷史。東漢時人班固（32－92）作。

Jackals from the Same Hillock
All Tarred with the Same Brush
Birds of a Feather

Used in reference to persons who are of a kind.

DURING the reign of Emperor Xuandi of Western Han, there was an official named Yang Yun, who was noted for his wide knowledge of history and for his comments on weighty current affairs and events of the past.

Once Yang Yun was told that the ruler of the Xiongnu (Huns) was killed by somebody. "It's only natural," he commented, "that a fatuous ruler who was deaf to his ministers' advice would come to such an end. The same happened to the son of the First Emperor of the Qin

1

Dynasty, the Second Emperor. His empire would have endured down to the present day if the Second Emperor lent an ear to what his loyal ministers had to say. What I've said shows that stupid sovereigns, past and present, are like jackals from the same hillock."

*History of the Han Dynasty**

*Written by Ban Gu (A.D. 32-92) of the Eastern Han Dynasty, this book records the events of the preceding Western Han period.

一廂情願
yī xiāng qíng yuàn

單方面願意；指不顧有關方面的意見，只憑自己的願望去做事。

古時候，有個愚蠢的人，有一次他到都城裏去遊玩，偶然看見了國王的女兒，愛上了她。回家後，整天想和公主成婚，但是沒有辦法如願，最後竟害了相思病。親友們去看他，問他發病原因，他

2

如實相告，並說："要是娶不上公主，我的性命恐怕難保了！"親友們安慰他一番，又假意答應可以替他幫忙。幾天以後，親友們又去探望他，對他說："我們已經去說過了，只是公主不答應。"愚人一聽，很高興地說："這一下好辦了，只要我再去一趟，她就會答應的。"

出自 《百喻經》 *

*《百喻經》 佛教文學作品。

A Unilateral Wish

Referring to a person who acts completely according to his wishful thinking, disregarding the wishes of others concerned.

THERE was in ancient times a foolish person who, on his visit to the national capital, came across a princess and immediately fell in love with her. Back at home, he became lovesick, thinking of marrying her obdurately though he had no way of realizing his wish. When his relatives and friends came to see him, he told them everything, adding, "I'm afraid my days would be numbered if I could not have her as my wife." They comforted him and pretended to be willing to help.

Several days later, they came again and told him, "We've seen the princess and informed her of your wish. But she . declined." Elated, the foolish person said, "Now I'm more hopeful. She will certainly give me her hand if only I can go to see her in person."

*Sutra of One Hundred Parables**

*A collection of Buddhist stories publicizing the doctrine of Sakyamuni.

3

一葉障目
yī yè zhàng mù

　　一片樹葉遮住了眼睛；比喻被眼前細小事物蒙蔽，看不到遠處、大處。

　　從前，有一個人家裏很窮。他從一本古書上看到，螳螂捕蟬時隱蔽自己身體的樹葉，可以隱藏人的身體。他一心要找到這樣的樹葉。他從樹下撿回許多樹葉，然後逐個地檢驗。他拿着一片樹葉遮住自己的眼睛，問妻子："你能看見我嗎？"妻子起初總是如實地回答說："看得見。"幾天以後，妻子感到非常厭煩，就哄騙他說："看不見了。"他高興地拿着這片樹葉到市上去偷人家的東西。他當場被捉住。縣官審問他時，他把偷竊的經過告訴了縣官。縣官說："你這樣做不怕別人看見嗎？"他說："我用這一片樹葉遮住了眼睛，不是什麼東西也就看不見了嗎！"縣官聽了哈哈大笑，只好把他放了。

出自《笑林》*

*《笑林》　諷刺故事集，三國時（220－280）魏人邯鄲淳撰。

Covering One's Eyes with a Leaf
Seeing No Further Than One's Nose

Used to describe a person whose eyes are shaded by something trivial so that all things farther or more important are shut out.

ONCE upon a time, there was a poor man who read from a book that the tree leaves behind which a mantis hid while trying to catch a cicada could conceal a person from mortal eyes. So he made up his mind to find such leaves. He swept up a heap of leaves from under a tree and carried them home. Then he tested their worth one by one. Holding one of them

4

in front of his eyes, he repeatedly asked his wife, "Can you see me any more?" "Yes, I can" was her invariable answer. Tired of being unendingly bothered with the same stupid question, one day she tried to deceive him by saying, "No, I can't see you any longer."

Overjoyed, the poor man went to the market place with that "magic" leaf and helped himself to what he could lay his hands on. He was caught in the act. At the court, he told the magistrate his story. "But aren't you afraid of being discovered by others?" asked the magistrate. "No," the poor man confessed, "because once I cover my eyes with such a magic leaf, I won't be able to see anything before me."

The magistrate burst into laughter and ordered his release.

Collected Jokes*

*By Handan Chun of Wei of the Three Kingdoms Period (220-280).

一 鼓 作 氣
yī gǔ zuò qì

第一次擂鼓攻擊時，士氣最旺；比喻趁幹勁旺盛的時候，一口氣把事情幹完。

春秋時（公元前770－公元前476），齊國出兵侵犯魯國，魯莊公和曹劌帶領軍隊前去抵抗，兩國軍隊相遇後，齊國軍隊首先擂鼓衝鋒。魯莊公馬上要擂鼓迎擊，曹劌阻止了他。一直等到齊軍擂過三次鼓以後，曹劌才讓魯軍擂鼓衝鋒，結果把齊軍打得大敗。

戰鬥結束後，魯莊公問曹劌爲什麼要這樣做。曹劌回答道："打仗全憑勇氣。第一次擂鼓時，士氣最旺盛，第二次擂鼓時，勇氣已經衰退，第三次擂鼓時，勇氣全消失了。敵方三次擊鼓之後，士氣已經衰竭；這時，我軍才第一次擂鼓進擊，正當士氣旺盛，所以能一舉戰勝敵人。"

出自《左傳》＊

＊《左傳》 編年體歷史著作，記載春秋時期的重大歷史事件。作者左丘明，春秋末期魯國人。

Plucking Up Courage with the First Drum

THE soldier's morale is at its highest with the first beat of the battle drum. This idiom is used to encourage people to press on and finish something without let-up while their spirits are rising.

DURING the Spring and Autumn Period (770-476 B.C.), the state of Qi invaded the state of Lu. Duke Zhuanggong of Lu, accompanied by Cao Gui, personally commanded his troops in resistance against the enemy. When the battle was joined, Qi's army was the first to beat the drum for attack. The Duke was about to sound the drum and throw his men into action when Cao advised him not. Not until the other side had

drummed thrice did Cao advise the Duke to begin the
counter-attack during which the Qi army was routed.

After the victory, the Duke asked Cao why he had given
such advice. "It is the morale of men that counts in battle,"
replied Cao. "At the first drum, their courage is roused and is
at its highest. With the second drum, it begins to flag, and
with the third it runs out. When the enemy's courage ran out
with the third beat of the battle drum, ours was rising ever
higher with the first beat for charging forward. So we won at
one go."

*Zuo Qiuming's Chronicles**

*A classical history of the Spring and Autumn Period (770-476
B.C.). Its author, Zuo Qiuming of the state of Lu, lived during the
closing years of that period.

一 鳴 驚 人
yī míng jīng rén

一聲鳴叫就使人震驚；比喻平時默默無聞，突然作出了驚人的
事情。

戰國時（公元前475－公元前221），齊威王即位三年，沒有管
理過國家大事。臣子們看到國家日趨衰落，都很憂慮。

有個叫淳于髡（音昆）的人，他知道齊威王愛猜謎語，有一天，
對齊威王說："大王！我有謎解不開，請您猜一猜。"齊威王說：
"你就說吧！"淳于髡說："有一隻大鳥，棲息在大王的庭院裏，已
經三年了，牠不飛也不叫。大王知道這是為什麼？"齊威王聽了，
知道這是暗指他的，便笑笑說："這隻鳥三年不飛，是為了讓翅膀
長得堅強些，三年不叫，是為了察看周圍的情況。它雖然不飛，一
飛起來，就要衝上天去；牠雖然不叫，一叫起來，就使人震驚。"
此後，齊威王就親自管理起國家大事來，在不太長的時間裏，就把
國家治理好了。

出自《史記》*

*《史記》 中國第一部紀傳體歷史書籍，作者司馬遷（公元前145－？）西漢人。全書共50萬字，記述了從黃帝到西漢武帝三千年間的歷史。

Amazing People with the First Call

Startling the World
Coming as a Bombshell

Said of an obscure person who surprises the world with some spectacular achievement little expected by others.

KING Weiwang of Qi of the Warring States Period (475-221 B.C.) had been on the throne for three years, but he had never attended to state affairs. Seeing that the power and prestige of their country were steadily declining, his ministers were worried.

A man by the name of Chunyu Kun learned that King Weiwang was fond of solving riddles. So one day he said to him, "Your subject has been puzzled by a riddle. May I beg Your Majesty to solve it?" "Go ahead," consented the King, whereupon Chunyu said, "There is a big bird that has been staying in a courtyard of the imperial palace for three years. But not once has it tried its wings or sung. May Your Majesty enlighten your subject by telling him why?"

Fully aware that Chunyu was indirectly referring to him, King Weiwang replied, smiling, "The bird has not used its wings for three years because it wants them to grow stronger. It has not sung for three years because it wants first to size up the situation around. It may not have tried at flying, but once it does, it will storm the sky. It may not have sung, but once it does, it will amaze the world."

Shortly afterwards, King Weiwang began to take the reins of government into his own hands. The national affairs of Qi soon improved markedly.

*Records of the Historian**

*China's first history book written in a series of biographies. Produced by Sima Qian (145 — B.C.) of the Western Han Dynasty, it runs into half a million Chinese characters and covers a period of 3,000 years from the time of the legendary Emperor Huangdi down to the reign of Emperor Wudi of Western Han.

一 箭 雙 鵰
yī jiàn shuāng diāo

發出一支箭，射中兩隻雕；比喻做一件事得到兩種好處。

南北朝時（420－589），北周有個將官，名叫長孫晟。他精通兵法，並善於射箭。有一次長孫晟奉北周宣王的命令，護送公主到突厥國去和國王攝圖成婚。突厥國王想欣賞一下長孫晟高超的射箭本領，有次，他邀請長孫晟一塊兒出去打獵。這時，在空中有兩隻鵰在爭奪食物。攝圖拿了兩枝箭，交給長孫晟，請他將鵰射落。但長孫晟只發了一箭，就同時把兩隻鵰射落下來了。

出自《北史》*

* 《北史》 記載北魏到隋朝的歷史，唐人李延壽撰。

Shooting Two Hawks with One Arrow
Killing Two Birds with One Stone

Said of getting two separate results in one go.

DURING the Southern and Northern Dynasties (420-589 A.D.), there was a general in Northern Zhou, named Zhangsun Sheng. He was an expert in the art of war and was good at archery. One year, his sovereign King Xuanwang ordered him to escort a princess to the northwestern Turkish

9

kingdom where she was to marry its king Shetu. The Turkish ruler, who wished to see Zhangsun's skill, asked the Northern Zhou general to go hunting with him. Shetu saw two hawks contending for food in the sky. He gave Zhangsun two arrows, asking him to shoot down the birds with them. Zhangsun complied, but he killed the two hawks with only one arrow.

*History of the Northern Dynasties**

*A book recording the history of the period 386-618, i.e., from the Northern Wei to the Sui Dynasty. It was written by Li Yanshou of the Tang Dynasty (618-907).

一 擧 兩 得

yī jǔ liǎng dé

做一件事同時得到兩種收益。

10

有個叫卞莊子的人。一天，他和朋友去打獵，發現兩隻老虎吃一頭牛。卞莊子想立刻去刺殺老虎。他的朋友勸他說：「兩隻老虎爭吃一頭牛，最後必然會為爭奪牛肉而搏鬥，這樣一來，小老虎就會被大老虎咬死，大老虎也會受傷。那時，你再去刺殺受傷的大老虎，不是就可以得到刺殺兩隻老虎的好名聲嗎？」卞莊子採納了他的意見，果然沒有費什麼力氣，就得到了兩隻老虎。

出自《史記》

Achieving Two Things at One Stroke

Killing Two Flies with One Slap
Catching Two Pigeons with One Bean

ONCE a man named Bian Zhuangzi went hunting with a friend. They found two tigers eating a dead ox, whereupon Bian wanted to go forward and kill them. But his friend advised him to wait, saying, "The two beasts are bound to struggle against each other for the last morsel. In that case, the smaller tiger will be bitten to death by the bigger one, and the bigger one will certainly be wounded in the fight. Then you can kill the bigger tiger and make yourself widely known for having putting to death two tigers in one effort."

Bian followed his friend's advice and achieved what the latter had predicted.

Records of the Historian

入木三分
rù mù sān fēn

進入木頭三分深；形容書法極有筆力，現多用來比喻文章或言論深刻有力。

王羲之（321－379）是晉朝的一位大書法家。王羲之的字寫得秀麗而蒼勁。他寫的《蘭亭集序》是中國書法藝術的寶貴遺產。據說，有一次，他把字寫在木板上，叫刻字的工匠雕刻。當工匠刻木板的時候，發現他的字跡已透入木板三分深。這當然是一種誇張的說法，只是用以說明王羲之筆力強勁。

出自《書斷》*

* 《書斷》　一部關於書法史的著作，唐朝人張懷瓘撰。

Eating into the Wood by Three-Tenths of an Inch

Originally used to describe a calligrapher whose forceful strokes ate deeply into the wooden board on which the characters were written, this idiom now mostly alludes to incisive writings or views.

WANG Xizhi of the Jin Dynasty was a famous calligrapher whose penmanship was most graceful and yet forceful. The characters he wrote for "Preface to the Collection of Lanting Poems" are treasured as a great legacy of Chinese calligraphic art. It is said that once Wang Xizhi wrote a number of characters on a wooden board to be engraved by a craftsman who, when applying his tool, found that the calligrapher's strokes had already eaten into the wood by three-tenths of an inch. This was, of course, an exaggeration although Wang's calligraphy was of the most vigorous style.

*Commentaries on Calligraphy of Different Dynasties**

*A book on the history of Chinese calligraphy written by Zhang Huaiguan of the Tang Dynasty (618-907).

亡羊補牢
wáng yáng bǔ láo

丢失了羊，再去修補羊圈；比喻出了差錯，還可以設法補救，避免再次受損失。

戰國時，楚襄王寵信奸臣，朝政腐敗。大臣莊辛對楚襄王說："如果您只顧安樂享受，不關心人民生活，國家一定會滅亡的。"但楚襄王不聽從莊辛的忠告。莊辛不得已，就離開楚國到趙國去避難。

莊辛到了趙國才五個月，秦國就發兵進攻楚國，佔領了楚國的都城，楚襄王被迫流亡。這時，楚襄王才懊悔當初沒有聽信莊辛的話，於是派人到趙國把庄辛請回來。

莊辛回國後，見楚襄王情緒頹喪，就鼓勵他說："看見兔子才回頭找獵犬追捕，還不算晚；羊從圈裏跑掉了，再來修補羊圈，也不算遲。"

出自《戰國策》*

*《戰國策》 戰國時期的史料滙編，經西漢劉向校訂，按國別編成三十三篇。

Mending the Fold After Losing the Sheep
It is Better Late Than Never

This idiom alludes to the truth that something may go wrong, but it is not too late to take the necessary measures to prevent new mistakes and avoid further losses.

KING Xiangwang of Chu during the Warring States Period mistakenly trusted a group of crafty ministers and, consequently, government administration went from bad to worse. One day, an honest minister named Zhuang Xin said

13

to the King that the kingdom would certainly be ruined if he only indulged himself in pleasure and did not care for the well-being of the people. The King, however, lent a deaf ear to the advice. Zhuang Xin had to seek asylum in the state of Zhao.

Only five months later, the state of Qin mounted an attack on Chu. With the national capital occupied by the enemy, King Xiangwang had to go into exile. Events made him feel remorseful for not having listened to Zhuang Xin's advice. So he sent an attendant to Zhao to pursuade the virtuous minister to come back.

When Zhuang Xin returned to Chu and saw King Xiangwang dispirited, he encouraged him, saying, "It's not too late for the hunter to look for the hound and make it pursue a hare when he has spotted the game. Likewise, it's not too late to repair the fold even after some of the sheep have been found lost."

Anecdotes of the Warring States*

*A collection of historical data about the Warring States Period (475-221 B.C.). Containing 33 chapters each covering a state, it was collated by the Western Han historian Liu Xiang (77-6 B.C.).

三 人 成 虎
sān rén chéng hǔ

三人都説街上有老虎，結果就有人相信真有老虎來了；比喻謊言一再重複，聽的人就容易信以爲真。

戰國時，魏王爲履行和趙王簽訂的協定，決意把太子送到趙國去做人質，大臣龐葱奉命陪同太子前往。臨行前，龐葱對魏王說："如果有一個人向您報告說，大街上來了隻老虎，您相信嗎？"魏王說："我不信，老虎怎麼會跑到街上來呢？"龐葱接着問："如果有兩個人說，大街上來了隻老虎，您相信嗎？"魏王回答說："兩個人都這麼說，我倒半信半疑了。"龐葱又問："如果有三個人都這麼說，大王相信嗎？"魏王說："三個人都這麼說，我只好相信了。"龐葱接着說："老虎不會跑到大街上來，只因爲有三個人都這麼說，大王就信以爲眞了。我這次去趙國，背後說我壞話的人恐怕不止三個，希望大王仔細考察。"

魏王點點頭說："我明白了，你放心去吧！"

龐葱告別了魏王，陪太子到趙國去了。後來果然有不少人說龐葱的壞話，魏王聽了漸漸地相信了。

出自《戰國策》

A Tale About a Tiger Is Accepted as Truth When Told by Three Persons

A Thing Repeated Often Enough
Will Be Accepted as Truth

Used figuratively to mean that people may believe in a lie when it is repeated again and again.

IT happened in the Warring States Period. In compliance with a peace treaty signed with the king of Zhao, the king of the defeated Wei decided to send the Crown Prince to the other side as hostage. Minister Pang Cong, who was to accompany the prince on his journey to Zhao, had a talk with the king before departure.

"If somebody comes to report that there is a tiger in the street," said Pang, "would Your Majesty believe it?" "How can a tiger come to a busy street?" countered the king. "I won't believe it." Then Pang asked again, "Would Your Majesty believe it if two persons say that there is a tiger in the street?" "When two persons report to that effect," answered the king, "I may half believe it." "If three persons tell Your Majesty the same?" Pang asked the third question. "I have to believe it," replied the king, "if three persons give the same version."

15

"But no tiger will dare to come to a busy street," reasoned Pang. "Your Majesty will accept the hearsay as truth only because three persons allege that there is a tiger there. Now I'm going to Zhao with the prince. I believe that there would be more than three persons who would speak ill of me when I am away. I beg Your Majesty to consider carefully before you believe what they might say about me."

The king nodded, saying, "I've got what you mean. You can set out on your trip with an easy mind."

Sure enough, during Pang Cong's absence from Wei, there were really many people who made malicious remarks against him before the king. By and by, the king came to believe their words.

Anecdotes of the Warring States

三 令 五 申
sān lìng wǔ shēn

多次地命令告誡。

春秋時代的軍事家孫子把自己寫的兵法書獻給吳王。吳王看了非常滿意，問孫子："是否可以訓練一隊婦女士兵？"孫子說："可以。"

吳王從宮中選了一百八十名女子交給孫子。孫子把她們分成兩隊，叫吳王心愛的兩個妃子當隊長。隊伍站好後，孫子把操練的要求和方法作了詳細講解，又向她們三番五次地告誡要遵守命令。在眾女子都表示"明白"之後，孫子吩咐擺下刑具，然後傳令向右轉，她們却嘻嘻哈哈，大笑不止。孫子說："號令交待不夠清楚，這是主將的過錯。"於是又把號令重新向她們解釋一次，再次擊鼓傳令向左轉，可是她們還是嘻笑不止。孫子說："一切都交待清楚了，不服從命令，不聽從指揮，這就是隊長的過錯了。"下令把兩個隊長斬首。吳王得知後，急忙派人前去求情。孫子說："我既然接受

命令爲將，一切就得按照軍隊紀律辦事。"接着就把兩個隊長殺了，
另外指定了兩個人當隊長。這樣一來，衆女子在操練時沒有一個人
敢出聲音，都規規矩矩地按號令做了。吳王知道孫子善於用兵，就
任命他做了大將。

出自《史記》

Giving Three Orders and Five Injunctions

*Said of repeated orders and injunctions. (In Chinese language,
"three" and "five" going together mean "many times" or
"time after time".)*

IT happened during the Spring and Autumn Period. Strategist
Sun Zi presented the King of Wu with his book on the art of
war. Satisfied with the work, the King asked Sun Zi, "Can we
train a detachment of women fighters?" "Yes, we can," Sun
Zi replied. So the King put him in charge of 180 hand-picked
court ladies. Sun divided them into two groups headed by
two of the King's favourite concubines.

The strategist had the ladies line up and explained to them
in detail the requirements and methods of training,
repeatedly telling them that they must strictly obey orders.
When the ladies said that they had understood what was
demanded of them, Sun ordered for implements of punishment to be brought to the drill ground.

Then he barked the command, "Right turn!" But all the
trainees burst into laughter. "You haven't got the command
right," said Sun. "As the instructor, I am to blame." Having
explained once more the various commands, he shouted,
"Left turn!" But the ladies kept laughing. "I've already made
everything clear. It's now the group leaders who are to blame
for the soldiers' disobedience." Thus he gave order that the
two group leaders be executed.

Learning of this, the King sent people to intercede with
Sun on behalf of his two concubines. "Since I've been made
the instructor," reasoned Sun, "I've to act as required by
military discipline." Then the two ladies were put to death,

and another two chosen to fill their place.

After that, all the women soldiers kept quiet throughout the drill and did what they were ordered to. Convinced that Sun was an excellent strategist versed in the art of war, the King made him grand general.

Records of the Historian

大 公 無 私
dà gōng wú sī

做事公正，毫無私心。

春秋時，晉平公問祁黃羊："南陽縣缺個縣長，你看派誰去當？"祁黃羊回答說："叫解狐去最合適了。他一定能夠勝任的。"平公驚奇地又問他："解狐不是你的仇人嗎？你爲什麼推薦他呢？"祁黃羊說："您只問我誰能夠勝任，並沒有問誰是我的仇人呀！"於是平公就派解狐去南陽上任了。解狐到任後，替那裏的人民辦了許多好事，大家都歌頌他。

過了一些日子，平公又問祁黃羊說："現在朝廷裏缺個法官，你看誰可以担任這個職位？"祁黃羊說："祁午能夠勝任的。"平公又奇怪起來，問道："祁午不是你的兒子嗎？"祁黃羊回答說："您只問我誰可以勝任，您並沒有問誰是我的兒子呀！所以我推薦了他。"平公就派了祁午去做法官。祁午當了法官，也替人民辦了許多好事，受到人民的歡迎。

大學問家孔子聽到了這兩件事，十分稱讚祁黃羊。孔子說："祁黃羊推薦人，完全拿德才做標準，不因爲是自己的仇人，存有偏見，便不推薦他，也不因爲是自己的兒子，怕人議論便不推薦。像祁黃羊這樣的人，才是眞正的大公無私！"

出自《呂氏春秋》＊

18

* 《呂氏春秋》　戰國末期秦相國呂不韋（？－公元前235）召集門客編寫。

Selflessness

To be impartial and act without thought of self.

IT happened during the Spring and Autumn Period. Duke Pinggong of Jin asked Qi Huangyang, "Nanyang County needs a new magistrate. Who do you think is fit to fill the vacancy?" Qi answered, "Xie Hu would make the best choice. He is equal to the post, I'm sure." Surprised, the Duke said, "Isn't Xie Hu an enemy of yours? Why should you recommend him, of all persons?" "Yes, he is," rejoined Qi. "But Your Grace has only asked me who is fit to be the new magistrate. I'm not supposed to say who my enemy is." So Duke Pinggong made Xie Hu magistrate of Nanyang County, where the latter did many good things for the people, winning praises from all quarters.

Some time later, Duke Pinggong asked Qi Huangyang again, "A new judge is needed in the imperial court. Whom, in your opinion, should be chosen for the post?" Qi replied, "Qi Wu, I think." Again surprised, the Duke said, "But isn't Qi Wu your son?" "Your Grace only asked me who should be made the judge," came the answer. "That's why I've suggested Qi Wu. I don't think Your Grace wants to know who my son is." So Qi Wu was made the new judge, and as such he performed many good deeds, much to the acclaim of all.

Hearing of how Qi Huangyang had behaved in this two cases, Confucius spoke highly of him. The Master had this to say: "In recommending people for official posts, Qi Huangyang was only guided by the criteria of virtue and abilities. He had no prejudice against anyone or refrained from recommending anyone even though the latter might be his enemy. Nor was he afraid of being gossiped about and so he did not hesitate in recommending his own son. Qi Huangyang can be said to be truly selfless."

19

*A work written by proteges of Lu Buwei (? -235 B.C.), Prime Minister of the state of Qin towards the end of the Warring States Period.

大 材 小 用
dà cái xiǎo yòng

大的材料用在小處；比喻用人或用物不當，造成浪費。

　　南宋傑出的詞人辛棄疾（1140－1207），一生堅決主張抗金，多次向朝廷建議出兵北伐收復被金侵佔的土地。由於受到主和派大臣的排擠，他的主張始終未被採納。1201年，當辛棄疾在紹興任職時，宋朝皇帝下令召見他。他的朋友，另一愛國詩人陸游（1125－1210）認為這是辛棄疾向皇帝當面陳述主張的好機會，於是寫了一首詩贈給他，詩中有＂大材小用古所嘆＂的句子。陸游惋惜辛棄疾雖有卓越的政治才能，但無法施展。

出自《劍南詩稿》*

*《劍南詩稿》　詩集，南宋陸游作。

Large Material for Small Use

Referring to waste or misuse of fine materials or talents.

THE famous poet Xin Qiji (1140-1207) of the Southern Song Dynasty, who all along stood for resistance against the Kin invaders, repeatedly petitioned the throne that troops be used to recover the lost territories. His proposal, however, was turned down by the reigning emperor due to the opposition by ministers who advocated   unprincipled peace.

When Xin Qiji served as an official in Shaoxing of present-day Zhejiang Province in 1201, however, the emperor planned to grant him an audience. His friend, another patriotic poet by the name of Lu You (1125-1210), regarded this as a good opportunity for Xin to present his views to the throne. So Lu wrote a long poem to Xin, which contained the lines "Large material being put to petty use,/At this people have sighed from ancient times." Lu deeply regretted that Xin could not put his outstanding talent to better use.

*Poems from Jiannan**

*By Lu You (1125-1210).

大 義 滅 親

dà yì miè qīn

爲維護正義，殺掉親人；形容對犯罪的親屬不徇私情。

春秋時，衞國國王的弟弟州吁和石厚同謀，殺死自己的哥哥做

21

了國王，人民十分不滿。州吁担心王位不鞏固，於是就派石厚向他父親石碏請教，石碏原是衞國的大臣，現告老在家，見兒子來問，便對他說：“周王是諸侯的最高領袖，如果能去朝見周王，得到他的許可，州吁的王位就可以鞏固了。”石厚又問怎樣才能見到周王。石碏說：“周王很寵信陳桓公，陳、衞兩國又很和睦，如果州吁親自去請陳桓公向周王懇求，周王一定會答應的。”

當石厚跟隨州吁到陳國去的時候，石碏秘密派人告訴陳桓公說：“州吁和石厚是殺死我國國王的兇手，現在他們就要到貴國來，請您把他們捉住。”陳桓公聽了石碏的話，逮捕了州吁和石厚。之後，衞國派人到陳國殺死州吁。對於石厚，大家認爲是石碏的兒子，應從輕處理。石碏說：“像石厚這樣的壞人，應當殺掉。我雖然有愛子之心，但也不能徇私情而忘大義。”於是派人到陳國殺了石厚。

出自《左傳》

Killing One's Blood Relations to Uphold Justice

Said of a person who places justice and righteousness above family considerations even by executing his own guilty relatives.

DURING the Spring and Autumn Period, Prince Zhou Xu of the state of Wei, colluding with Shi Hou, usurped the throne by murdering his elder brother, the reigning sovereign. This aroused popular discontent. Worried that his position was insecure, Zhou Xu sent Shi Hou to consult the latter's father, Shi Que, on measures that should be taken.

Now a retired court official, Shi Que told his son, "Zhou Xu's position as sovereign would be secure if he could win approval of the King of the Zhou Dynasty who is above all the lesser kings or dukes." Asked how to seek an audience from the Zhou king, the elder Shi said, "Now Duke

Huangong of Chen enjoys the King's special trust. Zhou Xu can approach the Duke who may be willing to help since his state is on excellent terms with Wei. If the Duke can put in a good word on your sovereign's behalf, I'm sure the King of Zhou will grant him an audience."

When Zhou Xu and Shi Hou were on their way to Chen, Shi Que secretly informed Duke Huangong, "Zhou Xu and Shi Hou are the culprits who murdered the former ruler of Wei. Now they are heading for Chen in order to see Your Grace. I beg you to arrest them on their arrival."

The Duke did as was requested. Then the state of Wei sent men to Chen to have Zhou Xu executed there. As for Shi Hou, it was suggested that he should be dealt with leniently on account of his being Shi Que's son. The old man, however, was firmly opposed to this, saying, "A villain like Shi Hou should be executed without fail. I might be fond of my son, but how can I let personal considerations prevail over the cause of justice and righteousness?" So he sent an attendant to Chen to put his son to death.

Zuo Qiuming's Chronicles

□ 蜜腹劍
kǒu mì fù jiàn

口有蜜，腹有劍；形容狡詐陰險。

唐玄宗時，有個宰相李林甫，為人陰險奸詐，善於阿諛奉承。他對那些有才能、有聲望的人十分嫉妒，總要想方設法加以排擠、暗害。他還專門結交宦官，要他們幫他在唐玄宗面前說好話。因此，他很得唐玄宗的寵信，一直在朝中做了十七年的大官。

李林甫和人交往，表面上總是裝得很謙恭、和善，說出話來十分動聽，而肚子裏却懷着害人的壞主意。日子久了，人們終於識破了他的這種偽善面目，於是就說他："口有蜜，腹有劍。"

出自《資治通鑑》 *

　*《資治通鑑》　編年體通史，記載從戰國到五代（公元前403－公元959）的歷史，主編人爲北宋司馬光（1019－1086）

Honey in Mouth but Dagger in Heart

A Honey Tongue, a Heart of Gall

Said of treachery and craftiness.

LI Linfu, Prime Minister during the reign of Emperor Xuanzong of the Tang Dynasty, was a cunning and sinister person who knew how to curry favour with those above him. Jealous of those who were talented and prestigious, he racked his brains to elbow them aside and even murder them. He fawned on the influential eunuchs so that they might put in a good word on his behalf in Xuanzong's presence. Consequently, he wormed himself into the good graces of the emperor and held a high official post for 17 years running.

　Li Linfu always feigned humbleness, politeness and kindness and　spoke cajolingly,　but he was vicious inwardly, always ready to harm others. By and by, people saw through his hypocrisy.　"Li Linfu has honey in his mouth," they said, "but dagger in his heart."

*History as a Mirror**

　*A book of general history written in the annalistic style, this work records the events of the years 403 B.C.－A.D. 959, that is, from the Warring States Period to the Five Dynasties. Its chief compiler was Sima Guang (1019-86) of the Northern Song Dynasty.

千里送鵝毛

qiān lǐ sòng é maó

千里送鵝毛，比喻禮物雖輕，但含有深厚的情意。

　　唐朝時，有個地方官吏派一名差人向皇帝進貢天鵝。差人經過一片湖水時，給天鵝洗澡，不小心讓天鵝飛走了，只落下了一根鵝毛。他只得把鵝毛獻給皇帝，並且作了一首歌。歌中有"千里送鵝毛，禮輕情意重"的句子。

出自《路史》*

*《路史》　主要記載傳說中的歷史故事，南宋（1127－1279）羅泌撰。

A Swan Feather from a Thousand *Li* Away

Said of a gift which may be small but, coming from afar, carries with it the sincere wishes of the sender.

DURING the Tang Dynasty, a local official ordered an attendant to take a swan to the emperor as a gift. The attendant gave the swan a bath in a lake en route. But the bird flew away in the process, leaving behind only a feather. He could do nothing but present the remaining feather to the emperor, attaching to it a slip of paper bearing a poem which said, among other things, "However insignificant the gift may seem, it conveys the deep feeling of the sender."

*Historical Legends**

*By Luo Mi of the Southern Song Dynasty (1127-1279).

千金買骨

qiān jīn mǎi gǔ

用一千兩金子買回馬骨頭；比喻渴望得到有才能的人。

從前，有一個國王貼出告示，說願出一千兩金子買一匹千里馬。三年過去了，沒有一匹千里馬送來。國王悶悶不樂，有個侍臣對國王說："王啊，請您給我一千兩黃金，我要親自出去尋求千里馬。"國王同意了。

侍臣花了三個月的時間打聽到了一匹千里馬，可是等他上門一問，那匹千里馬已經死了。侍臣拿出五百兩黃金，把那匹馬的骨頭買了回來。國王見了怒不可遏，高聲訓斥他說："我要的是活馬，你把馬骨頭弄來有什麼用處？白白浪費了我五百兩黃金。"侍臣說："這幾年您沒買到千里馬，是百姓怕您不肯真出黃金。現在，我花了五百兩黃金買了千里馬的骨頭，這個消息一傳開，很快就會有人把千里馬送來給您的。"果然，不出一年，就有好幾匹千里馬送到了國王手中。

出自《戰國策》

Buying a Horse's Bones for One Thousand Ounces of Gold

Used to describe a person who is anxious to enlist the services of talented people.

ONCE upon a time, there was a king who put up a notice saying that he would pay 1,000 ounces of gold for a horse capable of covering 1,000 *li* (500 kilometres) a day. Three years had elapsed without response. This made the king unhappy. So one of the palace attendants said to him, "May I beg Your Majesty to give me one thousand ounces of gold and permit me to travel round in search of such a fine horse?" The king consented.

Three months had passed before the court attendant got to know about a thoroughbred that could run 1,000 *li* per day. Unluckily, by the time he came to its owner the horse had already died. He bought, instead, the horse's bones for 500 ounces of gold.

When the attendant reported back to the king, the latter flew into a rage and reprimanded him, saying, "I want a live, good horse. What's the use of buying me a heap of horse bones? You've spent 500 ounces of gold for nothing." The attendant explained, "Your Majesty has not been able to buy the fine horse you want all these years because the people are afraid that Your Majesty might not pay the amount of gold promised. Now that I've bought the horse's bones for 500 ounces of gold, they would bring the excellent horse to Your Majesty when they have heard the news."

Just as expected, several fine horses capable of 1,000 *li* a day were presented to the king in less than one year.

Anecdotes of the Warring States

王顧左右而言他
wáng gù zuǒ yòu ér yán tā

齊王左右張望把話題扯開；比喻迴避正在討論的問題。

孟子對齊宣王說道:" 有個人把妻室兒女托付給一個朋友照顧，自己到楚國去了。等他回來的時候，他的妻子兒女却在挨凍受餓，對待這樣的朋友應該怎麼辦呢?"齊王說:"和他絕交。" 孟子說:"如果管刑罰的長官不能管理他的下級，那應該怎麼辦呢?" 齊王說:"撤掉他！"孟子說:"如果一個國家政治搞得不好，那又該怎麼辦呢?"

齊王回過頭來，左右張望，把這個話題岔開了。

*《孟子》 儒家經典著作，戰國時人孟軻（公元前372－前289）著。

The King Looked Left and Right and Talked of Other Things

Used in reference to a person who tries to evade the point at issue by going into some other subject.

"SUPPOSE," Mencius said to King Xuanwang of Qi of the Warring States Period, "there is a person who, before going on a journey to the state of Chu, entrusts his wife and children to a friend and, on his return, finds his family suffering from hunger and cold. What, then, would Your Majesty do?" The King replied, "I would no longer call him a friend."

"What if an official in charge of the administration of justice is incapable of managing his subordinates?" Mencius asked again. The King's reply was: "I would have him discharged."

"What if the affairs of a state are badly run?" Mencius asked the third question. Thereupon the King looked left and right, trying to change the topic of conversation.

*The Book of Mencius**

*A Confucian classic by Meng Ke (Mencius, 372-289 B.C.) of the Warring States Period.

天 衣 無 縫

tiān yī wú fèng

天上的衣服是沒有線縫的;比喻文章或講話十分周密,找不出什麼毛病。

傳說有個叫郭翰的人,在一個夏天的夜晚,獨自一人在庭院乘涼,忽然看見一個女子從天而降,自稱是天上的織女。郭翰發現這個女子穿的衣服沒有一點縫合的痕跡,便問她爲什麼能做成這樣。那女子答道:「天上織女做衣服不用針線,當然就沒有線縫了。」

出自 《靈怪錄》 *

* 《靈怪錄》 唐 (618－907) 牛嶠著,內載奇異傳聞。

Heavenly Robe Is Seamless

Fit to a T
Fit Like a Glove

Used to describe an essay or speech which is flawless or perfectly convincing.

ACCORDING to legend, there was a man by the name of Guo Han. One mid-summer evening, he was relaxing in the cool when, all of a sudden, he saw a maid descending from the sky. She introduced herself as the fairy Girl Weaver in heaven. Noticing that her robe was seamless, he ventured to ask why. "We in heaven make garments without using needles or thread. They are naturally without seams."

Stories of Supernatural Beings *

*By Niu Qiao of the Tang Dynasty (618-907).

29

太公釣魚，願者上鉤
tài gōng diào yú, yuàn zhě shàng gōu

太公釣魚，願者上鉤，比喻明知是圈套，却自願上當。

太公姓姜，名尚，西周時人，曾輔佐周武王滅了商朝。據民間傳說，太公在出仕之前，隱居於渭水（在今陝西省境內）之濱。他常拿一根不帶魚餌的直鉤釣竿，在水面上懸空垂釣。一些樵夫看到他這樣釣魚都發笑。太公說："我不是想釣真的魚，而是想釣一位賢明的君主。"太公就這樣期待了幾十年，到他快八十歲的時候，周武王的父親周文王得知太公有治國才能，親自請他出來做了丞相。

出自,《武王伐紂平話》 *

* 《武王伐紂平話》 關於周武王討伐商代最後一個統治者商紂的故事集。

Willing Fish Rising to Lord Jiang's Hookless Line

Said of a person who willingly plays into the hands of somebody else.

LORD Jiang, whose real name was Jiang Shang, lived in the Western Zhou Dynasty. He assisted King Wuwang of Zhou in over-throwing the Shang Dynasty. Legend has it that for years before he became an official, he led a secluded life somewhere along the Weishui River (in present-day Shaanxi Province). He often angled with a baitless and hookless line which hung in mid-air. Some woodcutters who were passing by laughed at him when they saw his peculiar way of fishing.

"What I aim at is not real fish at all," Lord Jiang

explained, "but some virtuous sovereign."

Lord Jiang lived as a hermit for scores of years before his dream came true. Learning of his outstanding statecraft, King Wenwang of Zhou, King Wuwang's father, made him Prime Minister when he was nearing eighty.

*King Wuwang's Expedition Against King Zhou**

*A collection of stories about the punitive expedition launched by King Wuwang of Zhou against the last ruler of the Shang Dynasty.

井底之蛙
jǐng dǐ zhī wā

井底下的蛙；比喻見識淺薄。

廢井裏住着一隻青蛙。有一天，青蛙在井邊碰見了一隻從海裏來的大鱉。青蛙就對海鱉誇口說："你看，我住在這裏多快樂！高興時，就在井欄邊跳躍一陣；疲倦時，就回到井裏，睡在磚洞裏休息一會。有時把身子泡在水裏，只露出頭和嘴巴；有時在軟綿綿的泥地裏散一會步。那些螃蟹和蝌蚪，誰也比不上我。而且我是這口井唯一的主人，在這裏十分自由自在，請到井裏來看看吧！

那海鱉聽了青蛙的話，倒真想進去看看。但牠的左脚還沒有全伸進去，右脚就已經被井欄絆住了。牠連忙後退了兩步，才站住脚，然後把大海的情形告訴青蛙說：「你見過海嗎？海的廣大，哪止千萬里，海的深度，哪止千萬丈。古時候，十年有九年大水，海裏的水，並沒有漲了多少；後來，八年裏有七年大旱，海裏的水，也不見得淺了多少。可見大海是不受旱澇影響的。住在那樣的大海裏，才是真的快樂呢！」

青蛙聽了海鱉的話，吃驚地呆在那裏，再沒有話可說了。

出自《莊子》*

* 《莊子》 莊周（公元前369－前286）及其弟子撰寫。莊周爲道家學派的創始人。

A Frog at the Bottom of a Well

Said of a person with a limited outlook.

A frog lived at the bottom of a well. One day, he saw a big turtle at the well side, who had come from the sea. "What a good time I'm having here in this well!" he told the turtle. "When I'm in good humour, I can hop along its coping, and I'll go back for a rest by a crevice in the bricks when I get tired. I can swim for fun with only my head and mouth above water, or stroll through the soft mud. The crabs and tadpoles all envy me, for I'm master of this well where I can do what I like. Why don't you come in and see for yourself what a nice place this is?"

The turtle accepted the invitation. But before he could get

his left foot into the well, his right one was caught on something. He halted and stepped back and then began to describe the sea to the frog. "Have you ever seen a sea?" he asked. "It's tens of thousands of *li* broad, and thousands of feet deep. There were floods in ancient times nine years out of ten, yet the sea water never swelled much. Later, there were droughts seven years out of eight, yet the sea water never grew much less. This is because no floods or droughts can do much with the sea. It's really wonderful to live in it."

Hearing this, the frog fell silent, staring at the turtle, dazed.

*The Book of Zhuang Zi**

*By Zhuang Zhou (369-286 B.C.), founder of the Taoist school of philosophy, and his disciples.

五十步笑百步
wǔ shí bù xiaò bǎi bù

　　向後敗退五十步的人，譏笑敗退一百步的；比喻都犯了錯誤，只是程度不同。

　　戰國時，梁惠王很喜歡和別國打仗。有一天，他問孟子："我對於國家的事情，總算盡了心了；河北年成不好，我就把河北的災民移到河東去，或把河東的糧食調到河北來。假如河東年成不好，我也同樣設法去救濟。我看看鄰國，實在都不及我那樣的愛護百姓；可是，鄰國的百姓，並未減少，而我國的百姓，也不加多。這是什麼道理呢？"

　　孟子說："大王喜歡打仗，我就拿打仗的事情打個比方吧！戰鼓咚咚的一敲起來，雙方的士兵，就揮舞着刀槍，交了鋒。打敗的一方，不免丟了盔甲，拖着刀槍，爭相逃命。如果有一個人逃了一百步，另一個人只逃了五十步，這個逃了五十步的，却嘲笑那個逃了一百步的，您看對不對呢？"

　　梁惠王說："這當然不對，逃了五十步的那個人只不過是還沒有逃到一百步罷了，但他也是同樣逃跑了的。"

　　孟子說："大王既然知道這個道理，您怎能希望您的百姓比鄰國的多呢！"

出自《孟子》

One Who Retreats Fifty Paces Laughs at Another Who Does a Hundred
The Pot Calls the Kettle Black

Referring to two persons who have both made mistakes, though the mistake of one may be less serious than the other's.

KING Huiwang of Liang of the Warring States Period enjoyed fighting with other states. One day he told Mencius, "I think I've done all I can for my country. When there is crop failure north of the Huanghe River (Yellow), I would have the local people moved east, or have grain transported there from the east. If crops fail east of the river, I would do likewise to relieve the people there. None of the rulers of the neighbouring states love their people as much as I do mine, yet their populations have not decreased and mine has not increased. Would you please tell me why?"

Mencius replied, "Since Your Majesty loves fighting, I might as well explain the matter by taking an example from it. Once the war drum is sounded, soldiers of both sides will join battle, sword in hand. Then those who are defeated will abandon their armour and flee, trailing their weapons behind them. Suppose there is one soldier who has retreated a hundred paces, and another who has retreated fifty. Now the latter is mocking the former. Is it right, Your Majesty?"

"Of course not," replied the King. "The second soldier may not have fled a hundred paces, but he has turned tail just the same."

"Well," said Mencius, "if Your Majesty understand this, how can you expect that your population should grow more quickly than that of any of the neighbouring states?"

The Book of Mencius

不入虎穴，焉得虎子
bù rù hǔ xuè, yān dé hǔ zǐ

不進老虎洞，怎能捉到小老虎；比喻敢於冒險，敢於迎接困難，克服困難，才能獲得成功。

西漢明帝時，班超奉命出使西域（今新疆一帶）。他先到鄯善國。鄯善國王熱情地接待他，但過了不久，忽然變得冷淡起來。原來是匈奴也派來了使者。國王正在猶疑不決，不知道應該和哪一方友好。班超得知後，就把同來的人召集在一起研究對策。班超說："不入虎穴，就捉不到小老虎。現在面臨險境，唯一的辦法就是把匈奴使者殺掉。只有這樣，才能把鄯善國王投靠匈奴的念頭打消。否則連我們自己的性命也難保了。"

當天夜裏，班超率領同來的人攻入匈奴人的營地，並乘風放火，殺死了匈奴使者。鄯善國王大為震驚，於是，表示決心和漢朝友好。

出自《後漢書》*

* 《後漢書》 記載東漢歷史的著作，南北朝時人范曄（398—445）作。

How Can One Catch Tiger Cubs Without Entering the Tiger's Lair?
Nothing Ventured, Nothing Gained

This idiom alludes to the truth that one can succeed only by taking risks and defying and overcoming difficulties.

DURING the reign of Emperor Mingdi of Western Han, Ban Chao was sent to the Western Regions (around modern Xinjiang) as head of a good-will mission. He first came to the state of Charklik whose king received him warmly. Before long, however, the king began to cold-shoulder him because an envoy had come from the Xiongnu (Hun) tribe.

When Ban Chao learned that the Charklik king could not decide which side to ally with, the Han emissary discussed the matter with his colleagues. They put their heads together and worked out a plan to cope with the situation. Ban Chao said, "No one can ever obtain tiger cubs without entering the tiger's lair himself. We're now in a dangerous situation. The only way out for us is to get rid of the Xiongnu envoy. Only this can prevent the Charklik king from throwing in his lot with the Xiongnu. Unless we act resolutely, we would even be unable to go back alive."

That very night, Ban Chao and his men stormed the camp of the Xiongnu party and, aided by a favourable wind, set fire to their tents. Taken unawares, the Xiongnu ran for life and their leader was killed. This shocked the Charklik king, who thus made up his mind to enter into friendly relations with the Han court.

*History of the Later Han Dynasty**

*Recording the events of the Eastern Han Dynasty (25-220), this history book was compiled by Fan Ye (398-445) of the Southern Dynasties.

不爲五斗米折腰
bù wèi wǔ dǒu mǐ zhé yāo

不願爲了五斗米的微薄薪俸，而向別人彎腰行禮；比喻爲人清高。

陶淵明（365－427）是東晉時的著名詩人。他四十一歲時做了彭澤縣（在今江西省）縣令。到任後十八天，上級派了個官吏到縣裏來視察。這個官吏一向傲慢自大，縣裏的官吏建議陶淵明穿戴整齊去迎接。陶淵明說："我不願爲五斗米向這種人彎腰行禮。"他於是辭官而去，並寫了著名的《歸去來辭》一文，表示隱退的決心。

出自《晉書》*

*《晉書》，記載晉代歷史的著作，唐朝人房玄齡等撰。

Not Bowing for Five Pecks of Rice

Loss of Honour Is Loss of Life

Used with reference to a person who is aloof from pursuits of material gains.

TAO Yuanming, a famous poet of the Eastern Jin Dynasty, was made magistrate of Pengze County (in modern Jiangxi Province) at the age of 41. Eighteen days after he had assumed office, the higher authorities sent a petty official to inspect work in the county. Because this man was notoriously arrogant, Tao Yuanming's colleagues advised him to have himself neatly dressed for greeting the coming inspector. "I'm not going to bow to his like for a monthly salary of five pecks of rice," Tao said. He tendered his resignation the very day the inspecting offical arrived. To show his determination to return to his home village and live in seclusion, he wrote a descriptive prose entitled *Home-Going.*

History of the Jin Dynasty *

*By Fang Xuanling (579-648) and others of the early Tang Dynasty.

不 恥 下 問

bù chǐ xià wèn

不以向學問或地位比自己低的人請教爲可恥；形容謙虛好學。

春秋時，衞國大夫孔圉（音羽）死了，按照謚法（給死者一定稱號的規定）被稱爲"文"，孔子的學生子夏問孔子道："老師，孔圉的稱號爲什麼叫'文'？"孔子說："孔圉天資聰明而又勤奮好學，他不認爲向地位比自己低、學問比自己差的人請教，是件羞恥的事，所以他死後給他'文'的稱號。"

出自《論語》*

* 《論語》 儒家經典著作，是孔子的弟子關於孔子言行的紀錄。

Not Feeling Ashamed to Consult One's Inferiors

Bow Down Thine Ear

Said of a person who is very modest, always ready to learn from those inferior to himself.

KONG Yu, a high minister of Wei of the Spring and Autumn Period, was posthumously conferred the title "Wen" (meaning "Ready to Learn") in the light of his deeds. Zi Gong, one of Confucius' disciples, asked his teacher, "Master, why was Kong Yu given the posthumous title 'Wen'?" Confucius replied, "Kong Yu was clever and he learned hard. He did not deem it a shame to consult his inferiors and those who were less learned than he. That is why he was conferred the posthumous title 'Wen'."

Confucian Analects*

*A Confucian classic describing Confucius' words and deeds as recorded by his disciples.

日暮途窮
rè mù tú qióng

天已黑，路已走到了盡頭；比喻面臨末日，前途無望。

　　春秋時代，楚國楚平王聽信了讒言，將伍子胥的父親和哥哥殺害了，伍子胥逃到了吳國。為了借助吳國的兵力替自己報仇，他幫助吳王闔閭奪得了王位。後來，伍子胥同吳王闔閭領兵攻楚，打進了楚國的國都。這時楚平王已經死了，伍子胥便把楚平王的墳墓掘開，挖出屍體，親自用鞭子狠狠打了三百下。伍子胥的一個好友申包胥寫信責備他太過份了。伍子胥對送信人說："你替我告訴申包胥，就說我好比一個行路的人，天已黑了，而距離目的地還很遠（後演變為：天已黑了，路已走到了盡頭——編者註），我為了趕路，只好顛顛倒倒地疾行，不能按常理行事了。"

出自《史記》

40

The Day Is Waning and the Road Is Ending

At the End of One's Tether
On One's Last Legs

Said of a person who is approaching the end of his days or heading for doom.

INFLUENCED by slanderous talk, King Pingwang of Chu of the Spring and Autumn Period killed Wu Zixu's father and elder brother. Wu Zixu himself fled to the state of Wu where, in order to use its army in his future effort to avenge his relatives, he helped king of Wu.

Years later, Wu Zixu assisted He Lü in attacking Chu and occupying its capital. By then, King Pingwang of Chu had died, but Wu Zixu dug out his corpse which he whipped, with a vengeance, 300 times as a sign of taking revenge.

Hearing of this, Shen Baoxu, a good friend of Wu Zixu's, sent him a letter criticizing him as having gone too far. But Wu Zixu told the messenger, "Tell your master Shen Baoxu that I may be likened to a traveller who finds the sun setting while he still has a long way to go. (The latter part of this comparison was later corrupted into "the road is ending" — *Editor.*) Unable to wait any longer in my urge to avenge my father and brother, I had to act against conventions."

Records of the Historian

以 卵 擊 石
yǐ luǎn gī shí

用鷄蛋去碰石頭；比喻不自量力。

有一天，墨子從魯國動身往北到齊國去，在路上遇到一個卜卦

的人。那人對墨子說，從我卜卦的兆頭看，今天北方忌黑色，你的
臉很黑，往北去一定不吉利。墨子不相信，和他爭辯起來。最後墨
子駁斥說："你所說的是迷信，我所說的是真理，用你的話反對我
的話，就好像用雞蛋去碰石頭，即使將天下所有的雞蛋投來，石頭
也不會受到絲毫損傷。"

出自《墨子》 *

* 《墨子》 戰國時人墨翟（約公元前468－前376）著，墨翟是墨家學派
的創始人。

Hurling an Egg at a Stone
Kick Against the Pricks

*This metaphor is used with reference to a person who grossly
overrates his own strength.*

IT happened in the Warring States Period. One day, Mo Zi
left the state of Lu and headed northward for the state of Qi.
He met a diviner en route, who told him, "As I can foretell
from all the omens, it is inauspicious for you to go further
north. This is because your face looks dark, a colour which is
taboo in the north today."

Unconvinced, Mo Zi argued with him. "What you've said is
superstition," he said finally, "while what I've said is truth.
Using your argument to refute mine is like hurling an egg
against a rock. The rock will remain intact even if all the eggs
under heaven are thrown at it."

The Book of Mo Zi *

*The author of this work, Mo Di (c. 468-376 B.C.), lived in the
Warring States Period. He was the founder of Mohism.

以鄰爲壑
yǐ lín wéi hè

把鄰國當作排泄水的溝壑；比喻只圖自己一方的利益，把困難或禍害轉嫁給別人。

戰國時，有一個名叫白圭的人，他採用築堤的辦法排除水患。一天，白圭向孟子誇耀說，他治水的本領比大禹還高明。孟子反駁他說："你錯了，大禹治水，是順着水流的方向把水引導到海裏去。而你却把水引向鄰國，拿鄰國來做你排水的溝壑。這種做法是有道德的人所厭惡和反對的。"白圭聽了啞口無言。

出自《孟子》

Using a Neighbour's Field as Drain

This idiom alludes to the act of safeguarding one's own interests by shifting one's difficulties onto others.

THERE was, during the Warring States Period, a man named Bai Gui, who tried to combat floods by building river dykes. One day, he boasted to Mencius that he was even more clever than Yu the Great of the remote past in taming the unruly rivers. Mencius, however, rebuked him, saying, "Yu the Great tried to divert the floodwaters into the sea while you plan to make them flow into the neighbouring states whose territories you want to use as drains. This is something all noble-minded persons are above doing."

Mencius' disarming argument made Bai Gui speechless.

The Book of Mencius

毛遂自薦

máo suì zì jiàn

毛遂自己推薦自己；比喻自告奮勇或自我推薦。

戰國時，秦國出兵進攻趙國的都城邯鄲，趙王派他的弟弟平原君到楚國求援。平原君決定挑選二十個文武全才的人跟他一塊去，但挑來挑去只選中了十九人。這時，門客毛遂來到平原君面前說："那就讓我去吧！"平原君問他道："先生在我門下幾年了？"毛遂回答說："三年了。"平原君說："有才能的人，好像一把錐子放進布袋裏，它的尖兒很快就會露出來。先生來了三年，沒有人提起您，我看您還是留下吧！"毛遂答道："您從來就沒有像錐子那樣把我放進您的口袋裏，要是早放進去了，它就早會整個兒挺出來，何止露出一點尖鋒呢！"平原君見他說得有道理，答應了他的請求。

到了楚國，平原君就跟楚王商談聯合抗秦的事。由於楚王拒絕，談了半天也沒有得出結果。這時，毛遂挺身而出，走到楚王面前，陳述利害，楚王終於被毛遂說服，答應了趙國的要求。

出自《史記》

Mao Sui Recommending Himself

Used to describe a person who volunteers his services for a post or task.

DURING the Warring States Period, the state of Qin launched an attack on Handan, capital of Zhao. The king of Zhao decided to send his younger brother, the Prince of Pingyuan, to seek help from Chu. The Prince wanted to pick twenty men well versed in both polite letters and martial arts to go with him. He could, however, find only nineteen such men.

"Let me go, then," Mao Sui, one of the Prince's retainers, recommended himself. "But how long have you been with me?" asked the Prince. "Three years" was the answer, whereupon the Prince held forth. "A man of ability is like an awl in a cloth bag — its point will soon pierce through for all to see. You've been here for three years, yet nobody has ever mentioned you before me. You'd better stay behind." "But you've never regarded me as an awl and put me in your bag. If you have, the whole — and not merely the 'point' — of me would have pierced through." Convinced, the Prince granted Mao Sui's request.

When he arrived in Chu, the Prince of Pingyuan held talks with its king on uniting to resist Qin. The meeting dragged on for a long time and no agreement was reached because of the Chu king's reluctance to help Zhao. His patience taxed, Mao Sui walked up to the king. He analysed the pros and cons of the whole issue and finally convinced the Chu ruler to comply with the request of Zhao.

Records of the Historian

反覆推敲
fǎn fù tuī qiāo

反覆推敲，形容認眞修改文字，也指對問題的再三研究。

唐朝時，有位詩人叫賈島。他早年騎着毛驢到京城參加科舉考
試。見路上風景優美，賈島詩興大發，做得"鳥宿池邊樹，僧敲月
下門"的詩句。但對僧的動作是用"敲"字還是用"推"字，一時
拿不準。他騎在驢上，一邊吟哦，一邊伸手做推門和敲門的姿勢。
正在這時，大詩人韓愈路過，賈島把自己的難處對他說了，韓愈沉
吟了一會說："我認爲還是用'敲'字好。"從此，這兩位詩人結
下了友誼。

出自《苕溪漁隱叢話》*

* 《苕溪漁隱叢話》 一部討論詩的著作，南宋胡仔撰。

Repeatedly Weighing the Words "Push" and "Knock at"
Careful Deliberation

Said of a person who racks his brains to find the right words in writing a sentence, or who deliberates on a problem over and over again.

IN his early years, Jia Dao, a poet of the Tang Dynasty, went on donkey back to the nation's capital to take part in civil-service examinations. Inspired by the charming land-scape on the way, he composed a verse containing these two lines:
"Birds fall silent for the night in lakeside trees
And a monk knocks at a moon-lit door."

But he was uncertain whether to say *"knock-at* a door" or *"push* a door".

So, while reciting the two lines on the donkey's back, he imitated the monk first pushing and then knocking at a door. Just then, he met another famous poet Han Yu, who was going the same way. Jia Dao told his friend his problem. Han Yu recited the lines a few times before he said, "I think 'knock at' is better than 'push'." This incident helped to seal their friendship.

*Poems Reviewed by the Shaoxi Fishing Hermit**

*Written by Hu Zai of the Southern Song Dynasty (1127-1279).

打 草 驚 蛇
dǎ cǎo jīng shé

打草驚動了蛇；原比喻懲辦某個犯法的人，而使有同樣行爲的人受到震動，現用來比喻做事不慎密、行爲不謹慎，致使對方有所戒備。

唐朝時，有個縣令叫王魯，貪贓枉法，搜刮民財。他的下屬官吏也都和他一樣。當地百姓怨聲載道。有一天，王魯批閱訟狀，發現他的一名官吏被人控告貪贓枉法，所列罪欵都和他自己有牽連。因此，他一面翻閱，一面不免發慌。心想，幸好這紙訟狀落在自己手中，否則就會惹出麻煩。看完，順手在訟狀上慌亂地批了幾個字：「你雖然打的是草，可我像藏在草叢裏的蛇一樣，感受到震驚了。」

出自《開元天寶遺事》*

*《開元天寶遺事》 五代時（907－960）王仁裕撰，記述唐玄宗時的民間傳說。

48

Beating the Grass and Startling the Snake

Waking a Sleeping Dog

This idiom originally meant punishing an evil-doer as a warning to others of his like. It is now used to describe a reckless act which has alerted an opponent.

A Tang Dynasty magistrate called Wang Lu was a corrupt official who raked in a huge amount of money. His subordinates followed suit, taking bribes and doing all kinds of evil. This caused widespread resentment among the local people.

One day, when going over the file, Wang Lu discovered a joint complaint against one of his subordinates who was accused of corruption and breach of law, which involved himself. Thumbing through the file, he was flustered. "I must be more careful in the future," he said to himself. "It's lucky that this case has been referred to me." After reading the material, he flurriedly wrote on the file these words as they came to his mind: "You may only have beaten the grass, but I've been frightened like the snake hiding in it."

Anecdotes of the Kaiyuan and Tianbao Reigns*

*Written by Wang Renyu of the Five Dynasties (907-960), this book relates stories from the period of the Tang Dynasty Emperor Xuanzong (Minghuang), who reigned between 712 and 756.

世外桃源
shì wài taó yuán

與世隔絕的桃花源；指理想中的生活安樂的地方。

《桃花源記》是晉朝文學家陶淵明（365－427）寫的一篇文章。文章描述在東晉時有一個漁夫，迷失了路途。他沿小河而行，在河

49

的盡頭發現了一處山青水秀，充滿桃花芬香的地方。那裏人們過着和平愉快的生活。人們告訴漁夫說，他們的祖先爲了逃避秦朝的戰亂，來到這裏，從未外出，於是就與世隔絕了。他們殺了鷄、鴨，熱情地歡待漁夫。漁夫返回後很懷念這個地方，待他再去尋找時，却找不到了。

The Land of Peach Blossoms Beyond This World

Referring to a utopian land of peace and happiness away from the turmoil of the world.

THE land of Peach Blossoms was written by the Jin Dynasty man of letters Tao Yuanming. It tells of a fisherman of Eastern Jin who, having lost his way, proceeds along a stream at the end of which he finds a place of beautiful hills and rivers and fragrant peach blossoms. The people there live a peaceful, happy life. Seeing the fisherman, they tell him that their ancestors came to that place to flee from the recurring wars during the Qin Dynasty. They decided to live there for ever and stay away from the troubling world. The fisherman is made guest of honour at a feast featuring chicken and duck. Back at home, he always thinks of this Land of Peach Blossoms, which, however, can no longer be found when he makes a second trip there.

目 無 全 牛
mù wú quán niú

像有經驗的屠夫那樣，看見的不是整個的牛；現用以比喻技巧高明，工作效率高。

戰國時， 梁惠王看見 庖丁正在宰割一頭牛， 他的動作是那麼熟練和美妙。 梁惠王讚嘆道： "你的技巧怎麼能熟練到這個程度啊！"庖丁放下刀，回答說："是的。我的技術能夠超過一般水平，這是由於我不斷地努力鑽研的結果。回想我初學宰牛的時候，我眼睛所見的無非是一頭一頭的牛而已；三年以後，我就不見整牛了，所見的是一塊塊肌肉和筋骨的組合，是一個個可以解剖分析的許多部件。只要順着肌肉筋骨的空隙之處下刀，就很方便地一件件分開了。"

接着，他又說："不過，在筋骨交錯比較複雜的地方，我總是特別小心，集中精神，對準關鍵仔細地下刀，等輕輕一割開，牛肉就土崩瓦解似地撒開來。這時，我心情輕快極了。我直起腰來，擦一擦刀，愉快地結束了我的工作。"

梁惠王聽了，高興地說："好！從你這番話中，學到了很多道理。"

出自《莊子》

Seeing No Ox as Whole

Originally referring to a master butcher who saw an ox only as parts and joints to cut, this idiom is now used to describe excellent skills and most efficient work.

KING Huiwang of Liang of the Warring States Period saw his cook cutting up a slaughtered ox. He worked so expertly and harmoniously that the sovereign could not help asking him in admiration, "How have you become so skilled?" Laying down his chopper, the cook answered, "My above-the-average skill is the result of persistent, diligent study and work. I recall that when I first learned butchery, what I saw before me was only individual oxen. After three years' practice, however, I saw no more whole oxen but merely the sum total of their muscles, tendons and bones to cut, merely parts for dissection. I cut by following such openings or cavities as there may be, according to the ox's natural constitution.

After a while, the cook added, "Nevertheless, each time I come upon a complex part where tendons and bones meet, I always work most cautiously, focusing all my attention on it. I gently apply my blade on the key point until the part yields like crumbling earth. Then, with a light heart, I straighten my back and wipe my chooper clean. That's how I cheerfully finish my task."

"Well said," cried the King. "I've learned quite a lot from what you've said."

The Book of Zhuang Zi

四 面 楚 歌
sì miàn chǔ gē

楚人的歌聲從四面八方傳來；比喻孤立無援，四面受敵的處境。

秦王朝滅亡後，項羽的楚軍和劉邦的漢軍發生了戰爭。楚軍敗退到垓下（今安徽靈壁縣南），被漢軍團團圍住。這時，項羽的兵已經很少，糧食也快吃完了。爲了動搖楚軍軍心，夜裏，漢軍故意唱起了楚國的歌曲。項羽不知是計，聽後十分驚異，心想：漢軍裏爲什麼會有這麼多的楚國人，難道楚國地方已被漢軍佔領了嗎？他驟然感到大勢已去，和愛妾虞姬訣別後，就帶領八百騎兵，突破重圍往南逃走。當逃到烏江的時候，只剩下二十多人了，而後面追趕的漢軍却有好幾千人。項羽自知失敗已成定局，於是就自刎了。

出自《史記》

Hearing the Chu Songs on Four Sides

Said of a person who finds himself besieged by the enemy on all sides, or utterly isolated and cut off from outside help.

FOLLOWING the overthrow of the Qin Dynasty, war broke out between Xiang Yu, the king of Chu, and Liu Bang — king of Han — for national supremacy. The Chu army suffered defeat and retreated to Gaixia (south of modern Lingbi County, Anhui Province) where it was surrounded by the Han army. By then, Xiang Yu had few troops left and provisions were running out.

To shake the morale of the Chu army, one night the Han army sang songs of Chu. Xiang Yu was taken in and wondered why there were so many Chu natives in Liu Bang's army. "Could it be that all the Chu territory has been occupied by Liu Bang?" he asked himself, nonplussed.

Realizing that the other side was getting the upper hand of him, Xiang Yu bid farewell to his favourite concubine, Yu Ji, and, after effecting a breakthrough, fled south at the head of 800 men. By the time he had reached the bank of the Wujiang River, only a little more than twenty men were still with him while the pursuing Han soldiers numbered several thousand. Knowing that defeat was a foregone conclusion, Xiang Yu committed suicide.

Records of the Historian

出奇制勝

chū qí zhì shèng

出奇計以取得勝利；比喻用別人意想不到的方法制服了對手。

戰國時，燕國國君昭王派大將樂毅率兵攻打齊國。樂毅足智多謀，很快就打下了齊國的七十多個城。只有即墨城和莒城未被攻下。即墨城居民推選一個叫田單的人擔任守城指揮。這時燕昭王已去世，他的兒子惠王繼承了王位。田單想，燕軍強大，光憑勇敢是難以取勝的。於是他就派人到燕國，散佈樂毅看不起惠王的流言。惠王得知後，非常生氣，撤換了樂毅。田單利用這一時機，襲擊燕軍。他徵集了一千多頭牛，在牠們的背上，披上畫有龍紋的紅綢，在牛的角上綁上鋒利的尖刀，在牛的尾巴上扎上用油浸過的蘆葦。一天夜間，田單挑選了五千名精壯的士兵，讓他們跟在牛的後面，點起火來。這羣牛帶着烈焰，向燕軍兵營狂奔而去。燕軍兵營頓時火起。燕軍驚恐萬狀，四處潰逃，齊軍大勝，收復了失去的土地。

西漢司馬遷在他撰寫的《史記》中，認爲田單的這次勝利，是軍事上出奇兵的典範。

出自《史記》

Winning by Novelty or a Surprise Attack

KING Zhaowang of Yan of the Warring States Period dispatched General Yue Yi at the head of an army to attack Qi. The resourceful general quickly took more than 70 cities, leaving only Jimo and Jucheng still unoccupied. The people of Jimo selected Tian Dan as commander of the troops defending their city. By then, King Zhaowang had already died and his son had succeeded him as King Huiwang.

Tian Dan reckoned that, since Yan was much stronger than Qi, it would be impossible for his men to win merely by dint of courage. So he sent some of his subordinates to Yan where they spread the rumour that its general Yue Yi was acting in defiance of King Huiwang's orders. Taken in, the King removed Yue Yi from commandership.

Tian Dan seized this opportunity to spring a surprise attack on the Yan troops. He requisitioned more than 1,000 oxen, which were then bedecked with scarlet dragon-patterned silk on the back, daggers on the head, and fat-soaked reeds on the tail. One night, Tian Dan hand-picked 5,000 soldiers who drove the decorated oxen to the Yan camp. When fire was set to the animals, the burning beasts dashed towards the enemy camps, causing them to burst into flames. The panicking Yan soldiers fled for all they were worth. The Qi army won smartly and recovered the lost territory.

In his *Records of the Historian,* the famed Sima Qian highly appraised the role of Tian Dan in this campaign, which he regarded as a classic example of defeating the enemy by a novel stratagem.

Records of the Historian

出 爾 反 爾
chū ěr fǎn ěr

你怎樣對待人家，人家也怎樣對待你；現用來比喻言行前後矛盾，反覆無常。

戰國時，鄒國同魯國打仗，鄒國被打敗了。鄒穆公對孟子說："這次戰鬥，我的官吏死了卅三人，而百姓却沒有一個去援救的，這些百姓實在可恨極了。殺了他們吧，殺不了那麼多；不殺吧，他們又是那樣仇恨長官，坐視不救。你看，該怎麼辦才好呢？"

孟子回答說："在饑荒的歲月裏，你的百姓有的餓死了，有的逃荒在外，可是在你的穀倉裏堆滿了糧食，庫房裏堆滿了財物。你的官吏也不來報告，這是官吏們不關心人民疾苦的表現。曾子曾經說過："當心啊！當心啊！你怎樣對待人家，人家也怎樣對待你。"

你們平時不管百姓死活，遇到機會，他們自然要報復。您不要責怪
他們吧！如果做國君的愛護百姓，百姓就會愛護他，並且願意為他
出力，甚至犧牲性命。"

出自《孟子》

Getting What One Has Given

Originally meaning that a person is dealt with by others in the way he has dealt with them, this idiom is now used in reference to inconsistency or self-contradiction.

DURING the Warring States Period, the state of Zou was defeated in a war with the state of Lu. Duke Mugong, ruler of Zou, complained to Mencius, "I've lost thirty-three of my officers in this campaign, but not a single one of the common people offered to come to their help. I am thinking of killing them, but they are too many to kill. On the other hand, how can I let them live when they are so hateful of my officers and did nothing at all to help them? What do you think I should do, Master?"

"During the last famine," Mencius replied, "some of your subjects were starved to death, others became homeless refugees. But Your Grace's granaries overflowed with grain, and your store houses were filled with all kinds of treasures. Unmindful of the people's sufferings, your officials did not report to Your Grace the tragic life of the masses. As one of Master Confucius' disciples, Zeng Zi, cautioned, 'Beware! You shall be dealt with in the way you have dealt with others.' As you do not care about the well-being of the common people, they will naturally reply in kind. How can Your Grace blame them for what they have done? Surely, if a sovereign loves his people, the people will unfailingly love him and be ready to do whatever they can for him, even at the risk of their very lives."

The Book of Mencius

56

失斧疑鄰
shī fǔ yí lín

丟失了斧子，懷疑被鄰居偷去；比喻主觀臆斷、胡亂猜疑。

　　有人丟失了一把斧子。他懷疑是鄰居的兒子偷去了。他就留心
觀察那青年的神態，果然發覺大為可疑。不論那青年一言一行，都
是像偷過斧子的樣子。他就斷定，一定是他偷的。可是，第二天，
他上山去打柴，在一棵樹旁，忽然發現了他失去的那把斧子。原來
是打柴的時候，他忘記把斧子帶回去。他很後悔錯疑了鄰居的兒
子。回家以後，再留心觀察那青年的神態，果然毫無可疑之處，不
論那青年一言一行，都不像是偷過斧子的樣子。他對自己說："小
小的斧頭，哪家沒有？誰願意來偷！我早就說過，這青年決不會幹
那樣的事的。"

出自《列子》*

*《列子》　相傳是戰國時（公元前475－前221年）人列禦寇所作，其中
保存了大量的古代寓言故事。

Losing an Axe and Suspecting a Neighbour

This idiom alludes to conjectures or ungrounded conclusions

A man lost an axe and suspected his neighbour's son of
having stolen it. He watched the boy's expression and
behaviour which now, sure enough, looked suspicious to him.
The youngster's words and actions were all like a thief's.
"Yes, it is he who stole my axe," the man concluded.

　　The second day, he went to gather wood in a mountain
where, unexpectedly, he found his axe lying beside a tree. He
remembered that he forgot to take it back the other day. He
felt sorry for having wronged his neighbour's son.

57

After this, he found that the boy's expression and hehaviour were no longer suspicious at all. And what the youngster said and did were now unlike those of a thief. "It is, after all," he thought, "but a small axe. Who will steal such a cheap thing? Didn't I say long ago that this boy wouldn't do that at all?"

*The Book of Lie Zi**

*Attributed to Lie Yukou of the Warring States Period (475-221) B.C.), this book contains a large number of ancient fables.

皮之不存，毛將焉附
pí zhī bù cún, máo jiāng yān fù

皮沒有了，毛也就長不住了；比喻兩種事物的互相依存關係。

戰國時，魏國的國君文侯出外巡遊，在路上遇見一個樵夫，身上穿着一件羊皮襖，毛向裏，皮向外，肩上搦着柴草。文侯覺得奇怪，便問他："你爲什麼反穿了皮衣搦柴呢？"（古時，穿皮襖的習慣，總把羊皮露在外面——編者註）那人回答："我爲了愛護羊毛，不讓它給柴草擦壞了呀！"文侯聽了笑了笑，告訴他說："你可曉得，毛是附在皮上的。把羊皮擦壞了，羊毛怎能保得住，還不是要掉下來嗎？"

出自《新序》*

*《新序》 西漢劉向（公元前77年－前6年）撰，書中記載了許多歷史故事。

58

With the Hide Gone, What Can the Hair Adhere to?

Said of two things that depend on each other for existence.

WHILE on an inspection tour, Marquis Wenhou, ruler of Wei of the Warring States Period, met a woodcutter wearing a sheepskin with the hide outside, carrying a bundle of straw. "Why do you wear your sheepskin inside out to carry straw?" asked the Marquis, puzzled. (People in ancient China always wore a sheepskin with the hair outside.) "To protect the fur," answered the woodcutter. "But don't you realize," said the Marquis, "that the hair adheres to the hide? When the hide wears out, what can the hair adhere to? Wouldn't it fall off all the same?"

New Discourses *

*Written by Liu Xiang (77-6 B.C.) of the Western Han Dynasty, this book records many historical episodes.

守 株 待 兔
shǒu zhū dài tù

守在樹下等待兔子；比喻妄想不勞而獲，坐享其成。

古時候宋國有個農夫，有一天，他在田地耕作，看見一隻兔子疾跑過去，正好碰上了田邊的一棵大樹，把頸子折斷了，死在樹下。那個農夫就這樣不費一分氣力，拾得了一隻兔子。

從此，這個農夫就不耕田了。他只坐在那棵大樹底下，等待着跑來碰在樹上的兔子。可是，再也沒有第二隻兔子跑來碰樹，他的田地也都荒蕪了。

出自《韓非子》*

59

*《韓非子》 戰國末，法家的主要代表人物韓非（公元前 280－前 233 年）作。

Waiting by a Tree for a Hare to Turn Up

Referring to a person who waits for gains without pains.

THERE was, in ancient times, a farmer in the state of Song. One day, when he was working in the fields he saw a hare running past him, only to break its neck on a tree and fall dead. So he got a hare without paying anything.

Thenceforth, the farmer abandoned his hoe and waited by the tree all day long, hoping to get another hare in the same way. But no more hares appeared, and in time his land became choked with weed.

The Book of Han Fei Zi*

*By Han Fei (280-233 B.C.) of the late Warring States Period, who was the chief representative of the Legalist school of philosophy.

妄自尊大
wàng zì zūn dà

狂妄地誇大自己。

公元25年，劉秀雖然在洛陽即帝位，建立了東漢政權，但全國尚未統一。當時公孫述在成都（在今四川）稱帝。隗囂佔領着隴西（今甘肅一帶）。隗囂部下有個叫馬援的人，受隗囂的委派，到成都去訪問公孫述。馬援想，自己和公孫述是同鄉，原來又相識，公孫述定會熱情接待。誰知完全出乎意料，公孫述竟擺出皇帝氣派，高坐殿上，並在階下排列着很多衞士，然後叫馬援上殿相見，而且還沒有說上幾句話，就把他打發走了。馬援很不高興，回去對隗囂說："公孫述見識淺薄，像井底的蛤蟆一樣，傲慢自大。我們還是到洛陽劉秀那裏找個出路吧！"

出自《後漢書》

Having Too High an Opinion of Oneself
Proud as a Peacock

CHINA remained divided even after Liu Xiu ascended the throne in Luoyang and established the Eastern Han Dynasty in the year A.D. 25. Gongsun Shu occupied Chengdu and called himself emperor while Wei Xiao made Longxi (in modern Gansu Province) his kingdom.

Wei Xiao had under him a general named Ma Yuan, who went to see Gongsun Shu as Wei's representative. Being a fellow villager and an old acquaintance of Gongsun's, Ma reckoned that he would be warmly received at Chengdu. But he was wrong, for Gongsun Shu put on the airs of an influential emperor. Gongsun sat imperiously on his throne and had an array of guards displayed below him in the audience hall. Then he sent for Ma Yuan, who was, however, dismissed after a few words.

Very disappointed, Ma Yuan told Wei Xiao on his return, "Gongsun Shu is as ignorant as a frog living at the bottom of a well, yet he is ludicrously arrogant. We'd better go to join Liu Xiu at Luoyang and try our luck there."

History of the Later Han Dynasty

羊 質 虎 皮
yáng zhì hǔ pí.

羊身上披着虎皮；比喻外表威武，而內心怯弱。

有一隻羊在山林裏拾到一張老虎皮。牠把虎皮披在身上，神氣十足地在山崗上走來走去。羊雖然披着老虎的皮，但看到鮮嫩的青草，就貪婪地吃起來。有一次，一隻豺狼走來，羊忘掉了自己身上披着虎皮，嚇得趕忙跑了。

羊始終沒有忘掉自己還是一隻羊。

出自《法言》*

* 《法言》 西漢揚雄（公元前53－公元18年）撰。

A Goat in Tiger's Skin
An Ass in a Lion's Skin

Said of a person who is outwardly mighty by inwardly timid.

ONCE a goat found a tiger's skin in the woods. Clothing itself in this skin, it strutted along on the hillside. At the sight of some tender grass, it began to eat avidly as usual. One day, it saw a wolf in the distance. Forgetting the tiger's skin on itself, the goat fled for all it was worth.

The goat never forgot for a moment that it was a goat, after all.

*Confucian Discourses**

*By Yang Xiong (53 B.C.–A.D. 18) of the Western Han Dynasty, this was an exposition of Confucianism modelled after *Confucian Analects*.

老 馬 識 途
lǎo mǎ shí tú

老馬熟悉自己走過的道路；比喻富有經驗的人善於處理事情。

春秋時，齊桓公帶兵打敗了山戎國，接着又打敗了孤竹國。孤竹國離齊國很遠，齊國的軍隊是春天出去的，凱旋回來已是冬天，景物變了，軍隊在中途迷失了道路。這時，相國管仲對齊桓公說："老馬能夠認得走過的路，爲什麼不利用牠們的智慧呢？"於是挑選了幾匹老馬，讓牠們在前頭走，人們跟着老馬後面，終於找到回去的路。

出自《韓非子》

An Old Horse Knows the Way
An Old Ox Makes a Straight Furrow

Said of an experienced person who knows how to cope with different situations.

DURING the Spring and Autumn Period, Duke Huangong of Qi conquered the states of Shan Rong and Gu Zhu successively. Gu Zhu was far away from Qi. It was spring when the Qi troops left their country, but winter had set in when they began their triumphant return journey. They lost their way because the natural landscape was now vastly different. All were much worried.

"But old horses know the way they have traversed," said Guan Zhong, Qi's Prime Minister, to Duke Huangong. "Why not use their wisdom and make them serve as guide?" So several old horses were picked to lead the way, followed by the Qi soldiers who finally returned to their homeland in triumph.

The Book of Han Fei Zi

再 作 馮 婦
zài zùo féng fù

比喻再幹一次自己說過不再幹的事。

古時候，晉國有位勇士，名叫馮婦。他能赤手空拳打死老虎，後來他發誓不再殺生，因此，打虎的行當也就不幹了。

有一天，馮婦駕着馬車來到郊外，看到許多人拿着器械，正在追逐一隻老虎，這隻老虎被逼到山脚下的一個角落裏，無路可逃，回過頭來，張牙舞爪，嚇得追趕牠的人遠遠地呆立着，都不敢近前。

馮婦看見這種情景，就跳下車來，捲起袖子，奔上前去把老虎打死了。

出自《孟子》

To Be Feng Fu Again

Used to describe a person who does something which he once said he would never do again.

THERE was in ancient China a warrior named Feng Fu in the state of Jin. He won fame for being able to beat a tiger to death barehanded. Later he vowed not to kill any living creatures, and so gave up killing tigers.

One day, when he was travelling to the wild country on a carriage, Feng Fu saw many people, armed with weapons, pursue a tiger. The beast retreated to a spot on the hillside where, cornered，it turned about, baring its fangs and ready to attack. Frightened, the pursuers stopped in their track and no one dared to get near the animal.

Seeing this, Feng Fu descended from his carriage, rolled up his sleeves and killed the threatening tiger.

The Book of Mencius

夸 父 追 日
kuā fù zhuī rì

夸父追太陽；比喻硬要做自己力量達不到的事。

古時候，有個巨人叫夸父，他不僅力氣大，而且步行如飛。他為了要征服灼熱的太陽，邁開飛快的腳步朝着太陽的方向追趕下去。當他越來越接近太陽時，夸父口渴得要命。當他離開太陽只有幾里路時，渴得再也支持不住了。他急忙趕到黃河去喝水，黃河的水被他喝乾了。他又趕到渭河去喝水，渭河的水也被他喝乾了，還是不能解渴。他決定到北方的大湖裏去喝個痛快，可是極度乾渴的夸父，還未等走到那兒，便在途中渴死了。

出自 《山海經》＊

＊《山海經》　戰國時代作品，它保存了大量古代神話傳說。

Kua Fu Chasing the Sun

Biting Off More Than One Can Chew

Said of a person who tries to do something beyond his ability.

THERE lived, in ancient times, a giant named Kua Fu. He not only had extraordinary physical power but also could walk almost as fast as a flying arrow.

To overcome the scorching sun, Kua Fu started to chase it in gigantic strides. When he was nearing the blazing ball, he felt utterly thirsty, and when he was only a few *li* away from it, his thirst became unbearable. So he rushed to the bank of the Huanghe (Yellow) River whose water he drank up. Then he emptied the water of the Weihe River. Still parched with thirst, he decided to go to the north and drink his fill from the water of a big lake there. Unfortunately, he died of thirst en route.

*Classic of Mountains and Waters**

*Containing a large number of ancient mythological stories, this is a work of the Warring States Period (475-221 B.C.).

死 灰 復 燃
sǐ huī fù rán

灰爐重新燃起來；比喻失勢者重新得勢。

西漢武帝時，有個叫韓安國的官員，因犯法被送進監獄。獄吏田甲常常侮辱他。韓安國氣憤地說："誰能料定死灰就不能重新燃起來呢？"田甲聽了說："燃吧，如果再燃起來，我就撒泡尿澆滅它。"不久，韓安國被釋出獄，重新做了官。田甲得知後，怕受到報復，逃走了。這時，韓安國揚言："田甲若不趕快回來，我就要把他全家殺掉。"田甲只好自動回來向韓安國請罪。韓安國笑着道："現在你可以撒尿了。"田甲嚇得面無人色，連連叩頭求饒。韓安國說："起來吧！像你這樣的人，才不值得報復呢！"

出自《漢書》

Dying Ashes Burn Again

Said of a person who falls from power but later gains the upper hand again.

DURING the reign of Emperor Wudi of the Western Han Dynasty, there was an official called Han Anguo. When he was imprisoned for some criminal offence, the jailor, Tian Jia, often insulted him. "Who can say for certain," Han said indignantly, "that dying ashes would never be able to burn again?" Tian shot back, "Well, they might burn again, but I can piss and put them out. That's all."

Not long after that, Han Anguo was released and became an official again. Tian Jia, who learned of what had happened, fled to some other place for fear that Han might retaliate against him. "If Tian Jia does not come back," Han said after the former jailor's flight, "I would have his whole family exterminated."

Tian Jia could not but return to his home village and went to Han Anguo to apologize. "Now you can piss," Han joked, laughing. At this, Tian's face turned ghastly pale with fright. He kowtowed again and again, begging for mercy. "Rise to your feet," Han said. "I'm above retaliating on a person like you."

History of the Han Dynasty

百發百中
bǎi fā bǎi zhòng

射一百次中一百次；形容神槍手的射擊技術，或用來比喻料事很有把握。

春秋時，楚共王手下有個名叫養由基的人，善於射箭。有一次，他站在離柳樹百步以外的地方，張弓搭箭，連發數箭，都射中了柳樹的葉子。大家看了讚嘆不絕。之後，輾轉相傳，就把他的箭術稱爲"百發百中"。

出自《戰國策》

A Hundred Arrows, a Hundred Hits

Said of superb marksmanship, and of a person who can unmistakenly foresee what is to happen.

KING Gongwang of Chu of the Spring and Autumn Period had under him a man named Yang Youji, who was versed in archery. One day, Yang Youji demonstrated his skill by repeatedly shooting through a willow leaf 100 paces away. All the onlookers gasped in admiration. News spread and, in due course, Yang Youji became known as an archer who could "score a hundred hits for a hundred arrows shot".

百聞不如一見
bǎi wén bù rù yī jiàn

聽了一百次，不如親眼看見一次；形容聽得再多，也不如自己看到的可靠。

西漢宣帝時，西北的羌人（當時少數民族之一）侵擾邊境。宣帝得報後，立即召集羣臣商討對策。大臣們都主張派遣大軍，前去攻剿。可是當宣帝徵詢誰可以率軍前往的時候，誰也不作聲了。

有個名叫趙充國的老將，七十六歲了。他自告奮勇，表示願意担任這個職務。宣帝很高興，並問他，要帶多少兵馬。趙充國說："情況究竟如何，現在還不清楚，因此無法提出要求。百聞不如一見，我要親自到邊境去看一看，了解了情況，再向聖上詳細奏報。"

趙充國到了邊境以後，實地進行了調查了解，又從俘虜口中，

問明羌人各部首領之間的關係。於是他定出了駐兵屯守的計劃，主
張對羌人採取分化瓦解，爭取和好的政策。實施後，效果很好，漢
人和羌人一時的緊張關係隨即緩和下來。

出自《漢書》

Seeing Once Is Better Than Hearing a Hundred Times

Seeing Is Believing

This idiom alludes to the truth that, no matter how much one may hear, it is not as reliable as what one sees for himself.

DURING the reign of Emperor Xuandi of Western Han, a northwestern minority nationality, the Qiang, intruded into the border areas of the empire. The sovereign called a meeting of his ministers to discuss what measures to take. All were for sending troops to annihilate the intruders. When the emperor asked who should command the punitive army, however, no one uttered a word.

A 76-year-old general, Zhao Chongguo, volunteered to go at the head of the Western Han army. Pleased, Emperor Xuandi asked him how many troops he wanted to take. "I can't say definitely before I've familiarized myself with the real situation," replied the veteran general. "Hearing a hundred times is not as good as seeing once. I beg first to go to the borders and size up the situation there for myself. Then I'll report everything to Your Majesty and raise my specific demand."

On his arrival at the frontier regions, the General made an on-the-spot investigation and, through the captured Qiang soldiers, found out about the actual relationships between the leaders of the various Qiang groups. He then proposed to the court the policy of stationing troops at the borders and dividing and demoralizing the Qiang chiefs so as to realize *rapprochement* between the Han empire and the Qiang nationality. When it was approved by the throne and put into effect, this policy proved fruitful and helped to ease the tense Han-Qiang relations.

History of the Han Dynasty

有 備 無 患
yǒu bèi wú huàn

有了準備，就可以避免禍患。

　　春秋時，晉悼公採用大臣魏絳的策略，做了中原各諸侯的盟主。後來鄭國背棄盟約降服了南方的楚國。晉悼公極爲不滿，於是聯絡了十一個盟國的軍隊去攻打她。鄭國自知抵禦不了，便向晉國求和。晉國答應了。鄭國爲了感謝晉國，派使臣送給晉國大批禮物。晉悼公把一部份禮物分給魏絳，魏絳不肯接受，並且趁機對晉悼公進行了一番勸告，說：“您做了許多國家的盟主，這是您個人的才幹。我個人沒有什麼功勞。不過我奉勸您：當您順利的時候，應該想到將來可能碰到的困難和危險，要事先作好應付的準備，有了準備就可以避免禍患。”晉悼公說：“你說得很對。”

出自《左傳》

Preparedness Forestalls Calamities
Having a Second String to One's Bow

DURING the Spring and Autumn Period, Duke Daogong of Jin acted on the proposal of his minister Wei Jiang and became leader of an alliance of the ducal states on the Central Plains. Soon afterwards, the state of Zheng surrendered to the southern state of Chu in violation of the oath of alliance. The resentful Duke Daogong allied with other states in preparation for an attack on Zheng. Too weak to resist, Zheng sued for peace and Jin agreed to the specific terms.

To express its thanks to Jin, the state of Zheng sent to it an envoy bearing quantities of gifts. Duke Daogong gave some of the gifts to Wei Jiang, who refused them and took the opportunity to tell his sovereign: "It's the outstanding capabilites of Your Grace that have made you the acknowledged leader of the multi-state alliance. I've done nothing to deserve Your Grace's reward. I would like, however, to offer a piece of advice: When circumstances are favourable, never forget that difficulties and dangers might crop up any time. One should always be prepared to cope with any situation and all eventualities."

"Well said," commented Duke Daogong.

Zuo Qiuming's Chronicles

至 死 不 悟

zhì sǐ bù wù

到死都不覺悟；現比喻為人頑固不化。

從前，有個人在打獵時捉到一隻小鹿，家裏養的幾隻狗見了小鹿就想把牠吃掉。於是主人有意每天把鹿拖到狗的身邊，讓牠們在一起玩耍。小鹿逐漸長大，竟認為狗是牠的好朋友，對待狗越來越隨便了。一天，小鹿跑出門外，看見路邊躺着一羣別人家的狗，小鹿也跑上去和牠們玩耍。這羣狗又驚又喜，隨後一齊撲上去，把小鹿吃了。這隻小鹿到臨死也沒醒悟過來，狗為什麼把牠吃掉。

出自《柳河東集》 *

＊《柳河東集》 唐柳宗元（公元773－819年）著。

72

Unable to Understand Till Death

Now used to describe a person who is incorrigibly stubborn.

ONCE upon a time, a man captured a fawn. His dogs very much wanted to eat it. Every day, their master took the little deer among them and make them frolic with it. As the fawn grew, it came to regard dogs as its friends, with whom it played as it wished.

One day, the young deer ran outside the gate and saw a pack of strange dogs lying in a street corner. It went up and tried to play with them. Happily surprised, the dogs fell upon the deer and devoured it.

Even when it was gasping its last, the poor thing was still at a loss why the dogs would eat it.

Collected Works of Liu Zongyuan*

*Liu Zongyuan (773-819) was a famous scholar of the Tang Dynasty.

此地無銀三百両
cǐ dì wú yín sān bǎi liǎng

此地沒有三百両銀子；比喻想隱瞞和掩飾某事，結果反而暴露了。

從前，有個叫張三的，喜歡自作聰明。他積了三百両銀子，怕別人偷去，便趁黑夜把銀子埋在牆脚下，上面寫了一張字條："此地無銀三百両"。此事，他的鄰居王二看得一清二楚，等他走後，便把銀子偷走。怕張懷疑，王二也自作聰明，寫了一張條子貼在原地："隔壁王二不曾偷"。

出自　民間故事

73

"No Three Hundred Taels of Silver Buried Here"

Used to describe a person who tries to conceal or cover up something but gives himself away by the act.

ONCE upon a time, there was a man named Zhang the Third who fancied himself clever. One day he stole 300 taels of silver. Fearing that the money might be stolen by others, he buried it beneath a wall under cover of night and put up a sign there, which said, "Nobody buried 300 taels of silver here."

Zhang's neighbour, Wang the Second, who had seen what Zhang did that night, helped himself with the hidden silver afterwards. Afraid that Zhang might become suspicious of him, Wang also posted a note over the place where he had found the money. The note read, "Your neighbour Wang the Second never stole the silver buried here." He thought he had acted cleverly.

(A folk tale)

因 勢 利 導

yīn shì lì dǎo

順着事物發展的趨勢加以引導。

戰國時，魏國派龐涓帶領軍隊去攻打韓國。韓向齊國求救，齊威王命田忌和孫臏領兵去攻打魏國以解韓國之圍。孫臏對田忌說："魏國的軍隊一向強悍，輕視齊國。善於用兵的人就要利用敵人這種輕敵的思想，引誘他們中計。"他建議採用減灶的辦法引誘魏軍深入。他們命令部隊在撤退的第一天築十萬人煮飯用的灶，第二天減至五萬，第三天減至三萬。龐涓見齊軍的灶數一天天減少，以為齊軍大量逃亡，不敢應戰，不由得欣喜若狂。於是便只帶一部份騎兵，日夜兼程追趕。一天夜晚，龐涓進入形勢險要的馬陵道，受到齊軍的伏擊。魏軍潰敗，龐涓因而自殺。

出自《史記》

Guiding Something Along Its Course of Development

THE state of Wei of the Warring States Period sent Pang Juan at the head of a big army to attack Han. The latter state sought help from Qi whose King Weiwang ordered Tian Ji and Sun Bin to launch an attack against Wei on Han's behalf.

"The Wei troops have been known for being fierce and tough," Sun Bin said to Tian Ji. "They always be little Qi. He who knows the art of war will make use of this characteristic of theirs and defeat them by a clever ruse." Sun Bin proposed a stratagem to lure the enemy in, a strategem whereby the Qi troops would fein retreat and build fewer and fewer stoves as the days wore on. Stoves for cooking 100,000 soldiers' meals were put up on the first day of the "retreat", for half the number of soldiers on the second, and 30,000 soldiers on the third.

Mistaking the decreasing number of stoves on the other side for massive desertion and lack of courage on the part of the Qi army, Pang Juan was overjoyed. He pursued the Qi troops, taking with him only a small number of mounted soldiers. He advanced nonstop until, one night, he reached a strategically important place, Malingdao, where he fell into an ambush laid by Sun Bin and Tian Ji. The Wei troops were routed and Pang Juan ended up by committing suicide.

Records of the Historian

曲 突 徙 薪
qū tū xǐ xīn

把烟囪改砌成彎的，把柴草搬走；比喻在災難發生之前，把發生災難的原因消除掉。

有家人家新造了一座房子，主人請了許多客人來參觀。有個客人看見烟囪是筆直的，灶邊堆了不少柴草，他就對主人說：" 烟囪這樣筆直，灶裏火星容易冒出來，您應趕快把烟囪改成彎的，把柴草搬走，不然就會發生火災。" 主人聽了沒有吭聲。過了不久，這家人家果然失火了，幸虧鄰居們都來救援，才把火撲滅了。主人爲了酬謝幫他救火的鄰居，就屠了牛，備了酒席，宴請他們。在救火中被燒傷的人被讓在上座，其餘的人按照出力大小挨次入座。可就是沒有請那個勸他改建烟囪的人。這時，有人就對主人說：" 要是你早聽了那位客人的話，就不至發生火災了，更不必費錢來辦這桌酒席。今天旣然論功請客，你怎能把那位客人忘了呢！"主人聽了，恍然大悟，立即派人去把那位客人請來。

出自《漢書》

76

Bending the Chimney and Removing the Firewood

Used in reference to precautionary measures that should be taken to eliminate the cause of a possible danger.

A man built a new house, and invited many of his friends to have a look at it. Noticing that the kitchen chimney was straight and much firewood was piled beside the stove, one of the guests said to the host, "With the chimney as straight as that, it is easy for sparks to fly out. You'd better build another chimney which is curved. And move the firewood away from the stove. Otherwise, your house might catch fire." But the master of the house ignored this advice.

Not long afterwards, the house did catch fire. Luckily, the neighbours came and helped to put it out. To express his thanks, the householder killed an ox and prepared a feast to entertain them. Those who had received burns were seated in places of honour, and the others according to their merit. But the man who had advised the host to rebuild the chimney had not been invited.

"If you had acted as advised by that friend," someone said to the host, "the fire could have been avoided and, of course, you could have saved the expense for this party. Now you're entertaining us for what we did, how could you ignore that man who suggested that a new chimney be built and the firewood be removed?"

Realizing his mistake, the householder invited the man who had given him wise advice.

History of the Han Dynasty

曲 高 和 寡

qǔ gāo hè guǎ

樂曲的格調越高，能唱和的人就越少；比喻論說或作品不通俗，不能爲一般人所了解。

宋玉是戰國時楚國的文學家。有一天，楚襄王聽到有人說宋玉行爲不好，就把宋玉召來，對他說：“先生的行爲有不檢點的地方吧？爲什麼有些人在背後議論你呢？”宋玉回答說：“大概是有的，但請大王先不要責備我，讓我把話說完。前些天有個人去街上唱歌，先唱的是《下里巴人》(指民間歌曲)，跟着他唱的有好幾千人；後來他唱《陽春白雪》(指高深的樂曲)，跟着他唱的有幾十個人。唱到最後，他又一再變調，能跟着他唱的只剩下幾個人了。可見，曲調越高深，能跟着唱的人就越少。那些平凡的人，怎麼能夠理解我的行爲啊！”

楚襄王聽了宋玉這番話，眞以爲他行爲出衆，也就不再追究他了。

出自《文選》*

* 《文選》 一部自先秦到梁的文學選集，南北朝梁代蕭統 (501—531)編。

Highbrow Songs Find Few Singers

The higher the level of a song is, the fewer people will it find to join in the chorus. Said of a speech or book which is too abtruse for ordinary people to understand.

SONG Yu of Chu was a man of letters who lived during the Warring States Period. One day, King Xiangwang hearing that Song Yu was too careless in his conduct, summoned him to his presence and said, "Sir, is there anything in your conduct which is not unblamable? Don't you know people are gossiping about you?"

"Yes," rejoined Song Yu, "what Your Majesty has said might be true. But I beg Your Majesty to hear me out before criticizing me. A few days ago, I saw a person singing in the street. He first sang a folksong named *Song of the Rustic Poor,* which was joined by several thousand others. Then he sang a highbrow song called *Song of the Spring Snow,* which only a few score of others could follow. Towards the end, he changed to a more elite song, which only half a dozen people could sing. This shows that the more select a song, the fewer the people who know it. And how can the average person understand what I do?"

*Selected Writings**

*A collection of literay works of the period from before the Qin Dynasty to the Liang Dynasty (502-557), this book was edited by Xiao Tong (501-531) of the Southern and Northern Dynasties.

合 浦 珠 還
hé pǔ zhū huán

珍珠回到合浦來了;比喻丟失了的東西重新歸還到原主手裏,或流落到異地的人終於回到了故鄉。

東漢時,廣西南部合浦沿海一帶出產珍珠,當地人民都靠採集珍珠為生,以珍珠向鄰邦交趾換取糧食。後來由於合浦的官吏營私舞弊,殘酷剝削採珠者,而毫不注意養護、繁殖,使得合浦珍珠的產量日益減少。人們紛紛傳說:海裏的珍珠不願住在合浦境內,都跑到交趾去了。後來有個叫孟嘗的人做了合浦太守,他對採珠辦法進行了改革,廢除過去搜刮勒索採珠者的規定。不到一年,海裏的珍珠又多起來,產量連續上升。人們又紛紛傳說:"珍珠又從交趾回到合浦來了。"

出自《漢書》

The Return of Hepu Pearls

Pearls of Hepu came back to where they were produced. Said of something which has been lost but which later returns to its rightful owner, or of a person who returns to his native place after years of wandering far from home.

DURING the Eastern Han Dynasty, the people of the coastal prefecture of Hepu in southern Guangxi earned a living by gathering pearls which they exchanged for grain from China's neighbour Cochin-China. But, due to corruption of the local officials who cruelly exploited the pearl fishers and neglected pearl culture, yield decreased more and more. People said, "The pearls do not like Hepu any more. They've moved to Cochin-China."

Later, a man named Meng Chang was made prefect of Hepu. He introduced reforms in pearl fishing and abolished all the extortionate measures against the pearl divers. In less than one year, the local peasants were able to gather more pearls from the sea, enabling the yield to increase steadily. So people said, "The pearls have returned to Hepu from Cochin-China."

History of the Han Dynasty

牝牡驪黃

pìn mǔ lí huáng

以母爲公，以黑爲黃；今比喻觀察事物只注重表面，拘於外形而忽略其實質。

春秋時，秦穆公對善於相馬的伯樂說："你的年紀大了，你的兒孫裏有沒有能接替你的人？"伯樂說："我們的子孫都是些平庸的人，只能辨別一般的馬。我有個朋友叫九方皋，識馬的本領比我強多了，我想把他推薦給大王。"秦穆公聽了很高興，召見了九方皋並打發他去找千里馬。"過了三個月，方九皋回來了，說："千里馬找到了。"秦穆公問："你找到的是一匹怎樣的馬呢？"九方皋說："是一匹黃色的公馬。"

秦穆公派人去領馬。去的人回報說："是一匹黑色的母馬。"穆公聽了，很不高興，責備伯樂說："糟透了！你推薦的人連公母黑黃都分不清，怎麼還能找到千里馬呢？"伯樂嘆了一口氣答道："這正是九方皋相馬技術比我高明的證據啊！他對馬的觀察，已經深入到馬的內部。他看到的是別人眼睛所看不到的本質的東西，而不去注意一些外表的、次要的東西。我這位朋友的相馬技術真是難能可貴啊！"

秦穆公聽後，派人去把那匹馬牽回來，果然是匹珍貴的千里馬。

出自《列子》

Taking a Black Mare for a Yellow Stallion

Said of a person who sees only the appearance of a matter and neglects its essence.

DUKE Mugong, ruler of Qin during the Spring and Autumn

81

Period, told Bo Le, who was widely known for his ability in judging horses, "You are getting old. Is there anyone among your children who can take over your job?" Bo Le replied, "All my children are of ordinary cut. They can only judge ordinary horses. But I would like to recommend to Your Grace a friend of mine by the name of Jiu Fanggao, who is much better than me in appraising horses." ·

Elated, the Duke summoned Jiu Fanggao to the court and ordered him to go and find an excellent steed capable of running 1,000 *li* a day. Jiu returned from his trip three months later. "I've found the horse Your Grace wants," he reported to the Duke. "What horse have you found?" queried the sovereign. "It's a yellow stallion," answered Jiu.

Duke Mugong sent someone to take the horse, but on his return the latter reported, "It's a black mare." Unhappy on hearing this, the Duke said to Bo Le reproachfully, "It's too bad. Your friend can't even tell a black female animal from a yellow male one. How can he find me a good horse for me?"

"But that's where my friend is more qualified than me in judging horses. He proceeds from the outside to the inside and sees the essential parts of a horse which others can't see. He doesn't pay so much attention to what is superficial and secondary. He is really a most capable horse judger."

Thereupon, the Duke had that horse taken to him and, sure enough, it proved a valuable animal that could cover 1,000 *li* per day.

The Book of Lie Zi

先 斬 後 奏
xiān zhǎn hòu zòu

先殺了再去報告皇帝;指對某個問題未經請示就處理了,造成既成事實,然後再向上級報告。

東漢時，洛陽縣令董宣剛到任，就遇到一件難辦的案子：皇帝劉秀的姐姐湖陽公主的家奴仗勢殺人，逍遙法外。有一天，湖陽公主外出，那個殺人的家奴也陪着同行。董宣知道後親自帶人前去捉拿。董宣數說了公主窩藏罪犯的罪狀後，當場把兇手處死。公主大怒，立即進宮告狀。皇帝聽後大發雷霆，責問董宣爲何殺人不先報告，並要判處董宣死刑。董宣據理力爭，皇帝無奈，只好不予追究。

出自《後漢書》

Execution First, Report Later

Said of a person who acts without first getting the approval of his superior, or who reports to the higher authorities only after his action has become an accomplished fact.

DONG Xuan of Eastern Han was made magistrate of Luoyang County. He had before him a difficult case the very day he assumed office: A servant of Princess Huyang, sister of the reigning emperor, Liu Xiu, killed somebody but remained at large on the strength of his powerful connections.

One day, the Princess was out on a trip, accompanied by a number of attendants including the murderer servant. Dong Xuan, who got news of this, went with his yamen runners to arrest him. The magistrate accused the Princess of sheltering a criminal and then had her guilty servant executed on the spot.

When his angry sister told him what had happened, the emperor flared up and blamed Dong Xuan for failing to seek imperial instruction for his action beforehand. The Son of Heaven was ready to have the Luoyang magistrate executed. But the honest official argued his case, reasoning things out the best he could. Unable to justify himself, the emperor had to drop the matter at that.

History of the Later Han Dynasty

先發制人
xiān fā zhì rén

先下手爭取主動，以制服對方。

　　秦末，陳勝、吳廣起義反抗秦朝。會稽郡守殷通想起兵響應，便把曾任楚國將領的項梁請來商議，項梁說：“現在很多地方都起兵反秦，這正是滅秦朝的時機。我聽說，先發動的就能制服敵人，後發動的就要被敵人所制服。”殷通說：“你是楚國將帥的後代，只有你才能統帥起義軍隊。”項梁早有割地為王的野心，便借機先下手殺了殷通，接着佔領了會稽所屬各個縣，宣佈起兵反抗秦王朝。

　　　　　　　　　　　　　　　出自《史記》

He Who Strikes First Gains the Upper Hand

The Best Defence Is Offence

TOWARDS the end of the Qin Dynasty, Chen Sheng and Wu Guang rose in revolt against the imperial rule. Yin Tong, prefect of Guiji who was ready to respond, sought the advice of Xiang Liang, a general of the former state of Chu.

"There have been armed anti-Qin uprisings in many places," said Xiang Liang. "This presents the best opportunity to overthrow the Qin house. I've been told that he who strikes first gets the better of others while the late starter will be the looser." Yin Tong said, "You're a descendant of a famous general of Chu. Only you are qualified to command the insurgent troops."

Xiang. Liang, who had long been ambitious of seizing enough territory to become king, struck first and killed Yin Tong. He occupied all the counties in Guiji Prefecture and raised the anti-Qin standard.

Records of the Historian

多行不義必自斃
duō xíng bù yì bì zì bì

壞事做多了，就要自取滅亡。

春秋時，鄭武公死後，長子莊公做了國君。但莊公的母親武姜偏愛次子共叔段，想幫助共叔段奪取君位。她向莊公請求把一個最大的城——京邑　封給他，莊公同意了。

共叔段在京邑不斷擴充勢力，引起鄭國大臣們的不安。有個叫祭（音宰）仲的大臣提醒莊公說，共叔段的封地太大，將來一定無法控制。莊公說："他壞事幹多了，一定會令自己走上死路。"後來，共叔段果然準備向鄭國都城發動襲擊，武姜準備和他裏應外合，

85

開城接應。莊公知道後，就派大將領兵前去討伐，共叔段不敵，只好逃亡到國外去了。

出自《左傳》

Too Many Evil Deeds Ruin the Doer

This idiom alludes to the truth that, if a person keeps on doing evil, he is bound to bring ruin to himself.

DURING the Spring and Autumn Period, Duke Zhuanggong of the state of Zheng ascended the throne as the eldest son of the deceased sovereign. But the Duke's mother, Wu Jiang, had partiality for her second son, Gong Shu Duan, and tried to help him seize the throne. She asked the Duke to give Gong Shu Duan the city of Jingyi, which was the largest in the country. The Duke complied.

Then Gong Shu Duan expanded his territory more and more, and this worried the court ministers. One of them, by the name of Zai Zhong, reminded Duke Zhuanggong of the fact that Gong Shu Duan's fief was so large that he was bound to rise in revolt some day. "If he does too many evil deeds," said the Duke, "he would surely head for doom."

Some time later, Gong Shu Duan planned to launch a surprise attack on the national capital and his mother promised to co-ordinate from inside and open the city gate to let him in. But Duke Zhuanggong stole a march on his younger brother by ordering one of his generals to attack him. Gong Shu Duan was defeated and had to flee abroad.

Zuo Qiuming's Chronicles

多多益善
duō duō yì shàn

越多越好。

韓信是漢高祖劉邦手下的一員大將，可是劉邦對他並不信任，韓信對劉邦也頗爲不滿。後來，劉邦借口韓信陰謀造反，把他軟禁了起來。

有一次，劉邦和韓信談論各個將領的才能，劉邦問："像我這樣的人，能夠帶多少兵？"韓信回答說："您不過能帶領十萬兵罷了。"劉邦又問："那末你又能帶多少兵呢？"韓信說："我麼，越多越好。"劉邦哈哈大笑，說："既然你帶兵越多越好，那爲什麼被我軟禁了呢？"韓信說："您雖然不能帶兵，但善於駕馭將領。這就是我被您軟禁的道理！"

出自《史記》

The More, the Better

LIU Bang, known in history as Emperor Gaozu of Western Han, distrusted his general Han Xin, who thus nursed a grievance against the sovereign. On the pretext of Han Xin plotting a revolt, Liu Bang had him placed under house arrest.

One day after this incident, Liu Bang had a talk with Han Xin about the ability of the Han Dynasty generals. "How many soldiers can a general like me command?" Liu Bang asked. "Not more than a hundred thousand," the latter replied. "And how many can you command?" Liu Bang asked again. "As for me, the more the better," Han Xin said.

Liu Bang roared with laughter. "Well," he contended, "if that is the case, why have you been put under house arrest by me?" Han Xin's answer was: "Although Your Majesty is not good in commanding troops, you know how to make your

generals serve your cause. That's why you've got the upper
hand of me now."

Records of the Historian

危如累卵
wēi rú lěi luǎn

像堆鷄蛋那樣危險；比喻形勢危急。

　　春秋時，晉靈公命令工匠爲他造一座九層的高台。大臣們議論
紛紛，認爲這樣做太浪費資財了。靈公知道了很生氣。有一個叫荀
息的大臣進宮對靈公說："王啊！聽說您的心情不好，我來給您耍
個把戲逗逗樂。我能把十三個棋子搭成一張枱，再在上面堆九個鷄
蛋。"靈公讓他表演，荀息先把十三個棋子鋪在地上，然後小心翼翼
地把九個鷄蛋放上去。靈公連聲驚叫："危險！危險！"荀息說："這
不算什麼，還有比這更危險的呢！"靈公說："那是什麼事呢？"
荀息說："蓋九層高台，得花三年時間。在這三年裏，男人不能耕
地，女人不能織布。這樣，國家就會衰弱，要是鄰國趁機來攻打，

88

必然遭到國破家亡的危險，那時，建成的高台對您還有什麼用處呢！"晉靈公聽了，當即收回了建造高台的命令。

出自《左傳》

As Precarious as Piled Eggs

Used in reference to an extremely dangerous situation.

IT happaned in the Spring and Autumn Period. Duke Linggong of the state of Jin ordered that a nine-storey decorated terrace be built for his enjoyment. This caused much controversy among his ministers who considered the project too expensive. The Duke was very angry when he learned of their attitude.

"Your Grace," said Xun Xi, an official who was given an audience by the Duke, "I've heard that you are unhappy these few days. So I'm here to amuse you. I can make a terrace of thirteen chessmen and pile nine eggs on it." The Duke asked him to go ahead.

Xun Xi spread thirteen chessmen on the ground and proceeded to place the eggs on them. "It's too dangerous," cried the Duke. But Xun Xi said, "No, there's something much more dangerous than this." The Duke asked what he was driving at. "Now, it takes three years to build a nine-storey terrace. During these years, men will be too busy with the project to till the land and women will have to give up weaving cloth altogether. The country will be weakened this way, and should a neighbouring state take the opportunity to attack us, Jin would be facing the danger of extinction. What's the use of your high terrace, by then?"

Hearing this, Duke Linggong cancelled the building project.

Zuo Qiuming's Chronicles

89

自知之明
zì zhī zhī míng

自己了解自己，對自己有正確的估計。

戰國時，齊國大夫鄒忌，長得很漂亮。一天早晨，他穿戴完畢，照着鏡子，問妻子說："我和城北的徐公相比，誰漂亮？"妻子回答說："你漂亮，徐公怎能比得上你呢！"徐公是齊國的美男子，鄒忌對妻子的回答不大相信，於是他又問他的妾道："我和徐公相比，誰漂亮？"妾也說："徐公怎能比得上你！"第二天，來了一位客人，鄒忌和他聊天，就問他："我和徐公誰漂亮？"客人說："徐公不如你漂亮！"

又隔了一天，正好徐公來訪。相比之下，鄒忌感到自己確實不如徐公漂亮。事後，鄒忌想：本來我不如徐公漂亮，可是妻子、妾、客人都說我比徐公漂亮，這原來是因為：妻子偏愛我，妾懼怕我，客人有求於我。

出自《戰國策》

The Wisdom of Knowing Oneself

Used to describe a person who has a correct appraisal of himself.

ZOU Ji, a senior official in the state of Qi during the Warring States Period, was a fine figure of a man. One morning, having dressed, he studied himself in the mirror. "Who is more handsome," he asked his wife,"Lord Xu in the north city or me?" "You, of course," replied the woman. "How can Lord Xu compare with you?"

Knowing that Xu was the most handsome man throughout the state, Zou Ji could not quite believe his wife. So he asked his concubine, "Who is more handsome, Lord Xu or me?"

"How can Lord Xu compare with you?" answered the concubine.

The next day, a friend of his came to see him. Zou Ji asked the visitor during their conversation, "Would you tell me who is more handsome, Lord Xu or me?" "Xu is not nearly as handsome as you," the friend replied.

On the third day, Lord Xu himself called. Comparing his looks with Xu's, Zou Ji concluded that he himself was by far the plainer of the two.

"The fact is that I am not as handsome as Lord Xu," Zou Ji thought afterwards. "But my wife, my concubine and my friend all said that I *am* more handsome than Lord Xu. This is because my wife is biased, my concubine dares not offend me, and my friend wants me to do him a favour."

Anecdotes of the Warring States

自 相 矛 盾
zì xiāng máo dùn

用自己的矛攻自己的盾；比喻說話、做事前後抵觸，不能自圓其說。

有一個賣矛和盾的人，他舉起盾向人叫賣說："我的盾呀！非常牢固，無論怎樣好的矛，也戳不穿它！"說完，又舉起矛誇口說："我的矛呀！十分鋒利，無論怎樣堅硬的盾，也能戳進去！"

站在旁邊的人聽了，暗暗地發笑。有一個人問他："照這樣說來，你的矛是挺鋒利的，你的盾又是那樣堅固。如果用你的矛來戳你的盾，結果怎樣呢？"那人窘得答不上話來了。

出自《韓非子》

Using One's Own Spear to Strike One's Own Shield

Said of a person who argues or acts in such a way that he cannot justify himself.

THERE was a man who sold spears and shields. Holding one of his shields in hand, he cried, "My shields are so strong that nothing can pierce them." Then, he picked up one of his spears and shouted, "My spears are so sharp that there is nothing they cannot pierce."

The onlookers sniggered at him, and one of them said, "So your spears are the sharpest and your shields are the strongest. But what if one should use your spears to pierce your shields?"

The man could give no answer.

The Book of Han Fei Zi

如 魚 得 水
rú yú dé shuǐ

像魚得到水；比喻得到適合發展才能的條件或十分重要的助手。

東漢末年，劉備在軍事上多次失利，最後帶着剩下的幾千人馬到處奔逃，沒有自己的地盤。這時劉備已經年近半百。他渴望得到人才圖謀發展。他聽說隱居的諸葛亮很有才能和抱負，就決心請諸葛亮放棄隱居生活，出來幫助自己。他冒着隆冬嚴寒親自去拜訪諸葛亮。他接連去了三次，終於在第三次見到諸葛亮。諸葛亮向他分析了形勢，指明出路，確定了戰略。從此，劉備便拜諸葛亮做他的重要謀臣。兩人感情深厚，相處得非常融洽。劉備的結義兄弟關羽和張飛對此十分不滿。劉備向他們解釋說："我得到諸葛亮，就像魚得到了水一樣。希望你們不要再多講了。"關羽和張飛聽了很慚愧，就改變了態度。

出自《三國誌》*

* 《三國誌》 紀傳體史書，分魏、蜀、吳三誌，西晉時人陳壽（公元233－297年）作。

Like Fish in Water
Being in One's Element

Said of a person who has the necessary conditions for developing his talent, or of a person who has found the right assistants.

IN the closing years of the Eastern Han Dynasty, Liu Bei, who later built the Shu Kingdom, suffered one military defeat after another and had to rove with the remaining several thousand men under him. Nearly fifty years old now, he eagerly hoped that he could find a talented man to help him turn the tide. He heard that there was an aspiring man of talent named Zhuge Liang who was living in seclusion. So Liu Bei decided to request Zhuge to come out and assist him in improving his position.

Thrice Liu Bei visited Zhuge Liang in a severe winter, seeing him only the last time. Zhuge analysed the situation, pointed the way out and outlined the strategy that should be followed. Then Liu Bei made him his chief counsellor. The two got on well with each other and became fast friends.

Liu Bei's sworn brothers, Guan Yu and Zhang Fei, however, resented the growing friendship between Liu and his adviser. "With Zhuge Liang working with me," Liu Bei explained, "I'm like a fish that has been let into water again. Please say nothing more in complaint." Feeling quite ashamed, Guan Yu and Zhang Fei changed their attitude.

*History of the Three Kingdoms**

*By Chen Shou (233-297) of the Western Jin Dynasty, this work records the history of Wei, Shu and Wu kingdoms mainly through biographies.

完璧歸趙

wán bì guī zhào

把璧完好地歸還趙國；比喻把原物無損傷地歸還本主。

戰國時，秦昭襄王聽說趙惠文王有一塊寶玉，想把它騙取過來，便寫信給趙王，願意以十五座城池交換。趙王想，送去會受騙；不送去又怕秦國進犯趙國。後來，他決定派藺相如到秦國去獻璧，藺相如到了秦國，當面把寶玉獻給秦王。秦王看了以後，又把它交給左右的人看。藺相如見秦王沒有交付城池的意思，就假說玉中有點小毛病，需要指給秦王看，趁機把玉收了回來。藺相如捧着玉，靠在柱子上，怒冲冲地大聲說："趙王派我來時，齋戒了五天才將寶玉交給我。現在大王却這樣隨便接受它，顯然沒有交付城池的誠意。現在我已經把玉收回來了，如果你想強奪，我寧願把我的頭同玉一齊在柱子上碰碎。"秦王怕玉碰碎了，同意齋戒五天再受玉。藺相如知道秦王不可能交付城池，就趁機派人把玉送回了趙國。

出自《史記》

Returning the Jade Intact to Zhao

Said of giving something back to its rightful owner in good condition.

DURING the Warring States Period, King Zhaoxiang of Qin learned that King Huiwang of Zhao had a piece of precious jade. He thought of cheating it out of the hands of Zhao's ruler. So he wrote a letter to him, expressing his wish to exchange fifteen cities for the jade.

This placed King Huiwang in a dilemma. "The Qin sovereign might be trying to get the treasure by deception," he thought. "But if I do not send the jade to him, he may attack Zhao on some pretext." Finally King Huiwang decided to dispatch Lin Xiangru to Qin and present the matchless jade to its ruler.

Lin Xiangru personally handed the jade to King Zhaoxiang, who examined and passed it round to his ministers. Seeing that the Qin king had no intention of parting with his fifteen cities, the Zhao envoy demanded the jade back on the pretext that he had to point to King Zhaoxiang some flaw that was in it. Having regained the precious stone, he rushed towards a decorative column in the reception hall and shouted in towering anger: "When my sovereign decided to send me here with this piece of jade, he gave it to me only after five days of fasting. But Your Majesty has just now accepted it in such a casual manner. This shows that you are not sincere in exchanging fifteen cities for our jade. With it now back in my hands, I am ready to hit myself together with this jade against the column, should you try to grab it from me."

Afraid that the rare stone might really be broken to pieces, the Qin king agreed to fast for five days before accepting it. Seizing this opportunity, Lin Xiangru, who was now perfectly certain that King Zhaoxiang would never give Zhao the fifteen cities he had promised, had someone take the much treasured jade back to his country.

Records of the Historian

96

宋襄之仁
sòng xiāng zhī rén

宋襄公的仁慈；比喻對敵人講仁愛。

　　春秋時期，宋襄公攻伐鄭國，在泓水岸邊與趕來救援鄭國的楚軍相遇。當宋軍已經排列好陣勢的時候，楚軍還在渡河。一名叫子魚的軍官對宋襄公說：“敵軍的人數多，我軍人數少，趁敵軍正在渡河的時候，發動攻擊，一定可以取得勝利。”宋襄公搖搖頭說：“你急什麼？我聽說，當別人有困難的時候，採取行動，是不道德的。”子魚說：“請大王好好想想，如果等楚軍渡過河再進攻，時機就錯過了。請您為宋國人民着想，不要怕違背什麼道德吧！”宋襄公聽了，十分氣惱，大聲斥責子魚道：“滾回去！你再說一句，就按軍法從事。”子魚無奈，只好退出，不久，楚軍列陣完畢，宋襄公才下令攻擊，結果被楚軍打敗，宋襄公腿部挨了一箭，三天以後就死去了。

出自《韓非子》

Kindness of the Type of Song's Duke Xianggong

Said of kind-heartedness or benevolence to the enemy.

IT happened in the Spring and Autumn Period. In his attack on the state of Zheng, Duke Xianggong of Song found his troops confronted across the Hongshui River by the army of Chu that had come to Zheng's rescue. When the Song army was already in battle array, the Chu army was still in the course of crossing the river.

"We're outnumbered by the Chu army," Zi Yu, a Song officer said to the Duke. "We shall certainly win if we spring an attack while the enemy soldiers are still crossing the Hongshui." The Duke shook his head, saying, "What's the hurry? I've been told that it is immoral to take actions against anyone who is in difficulty." Zi Yu insisted by saying, "I beg Your Grace to reconsider it. Should we start the attack after the Chu soldiers have got to this side of the river, we would have missed the opportunity. Please think again, in the interests of our people instead of morality so called."

This angered the Duke, who chastised Zi Yu, saying, "Out of here! You shall be court-martialled if you don't stop your jaw." Zi Yu had to give up and go.

Soon after this incident, the Chu army completed its battle formation. Then Duke Xianggong ordered the beginning of the attack during which his army was routed. What's more, the Duke was wounded by an arrow in the leg. The wound worsened steadily until it took his life three days later.

The Book of Han Fei Zi

言 猶 在 耳
yán yóu zài ěr

講過的話還在耳邊；比喻記憶猶新。

春秋時，晉國國君襄公死了。太子夷皋年紀幼小，大臣趙盾等人認爲正在秦國做官的公子雍可以立爲國君，於是便派人去秦國接公子雍。

但是，夷皋的母親堅持要立夷皋。她抱着夷皋來到趙盾家裏，向趙盾說：“襄公在世時，把這個兒子托付給你時說，這孩子如果成材，他便感激你；如果不成材，就是在陰曹地府，他也會怨恨你。現在襄公雖然死去，可是他說的話還好像在耳邊，你怎麼就忘記了呢？”趙盾和其他大夫聽後都無言以對，只好改變了主意，立夷皋爲國君。

出自《左傳》

98

Words Still Ringing in One's Ears

Said of something which is still fresh in one's memory.

KING Xianggong, ruler of Jin of the Spring and Autumn Period, had passed away. The Crown Prince, Yi Gao, being too young to be the new king, court minister Zhao Dun and some others planned to install on the throne Prince Yong, who was now serving as an official in the state of Qin. So they sent someone to ask the Prince to come back.

Yi Gao's mother, however, insisted on having him placed on the throne. She came to Zhao Dun's residence, carrying the Crown Prince in her arms. "Before his death, King Xianggong entrusted Yi Gao to your care. His Majesty said that he would be more than grateful to you if the child could grow up to be a man of ability, and that he would nurse a grudge against you in the nether world if the Crown Prince could not be of any use to the country. Though the king has passed away, his words are still ringing in our ears. How can you possibly forget them?"

Zhao Dun and his colleagues were speechless. They could not but change their idea and put Yi Gao on the throne.

Zuo Qiuming's Chronicles

志 在 四 方
zhì zài sì fāng

一個人有了遠大的志向，就天涯海角都能去。

戰國時，子高遊歷到趙國，和鄒文、季節交上了朋友。子高要離開趙國到魯國去，所有的老朋友都來送行。其中鄒文和季節，竟送了三天。臨別的時候，鄒文和季節兩人都流了淚，捨不得讓他離開。但是，子高只是向他倆揮揮手，作個揖，就匆匆起走了。

子高的隨從不理解他為什麼這樣。子高說："起初我以為鄒文和季節都是大丈夫。現在才知道，他們都不過是意志薄弱、沒有決斷的庸俗之輩！人生在世，應有四方之志，豈能像山鹿那樣，天天聚集在一起才感到心滿意足呢！"

出自《孔叢子》*

*《孔叢子》 假托秦末儒生孔鮒編，疑係三國時魏人僞作。

Having Far-Reaching Aspirations
A Man's Reach Should Exceed His Grasp

When one has a great purpose, he will be ready to go anywhere, even the remotest corners of the earth.

WHEN Zi Gao of the Warring States Period was touring the state of Zhao, he made the acquaintance of Zou Wen and Ji Jie. On the day he was to leave for the state of Lu, many friends came to bid him farewell. Zou Wen and Ji Jie were so reluctant to part with Zi Gao that they travelled with him for three days before they said good-bye to their friend, tears welling up in their eyes. But Zi Gao left determinedly after waving to them and making a gesture of thanks with both hands clasped before his chest.

Zi Gao's attendants asked their master why he had acted like that. "At first, I thought Zou Wen and Ji Jie were all men with lofty ideals. But now I can say that they are both of them mediocre, weak-willed persons. One should have high aspirations, ready to go wherever he is needed. How can one afford to be like a mountain deer that feels content only when it stays with the other animals of the herd?"

*Collected Confucian Statements**

*Said to be compiled by Kong Fu, a Confucian scholar of the late Qin Dynasty (221-207 B.C.). But some claim that it is the work of a Wei scholar of the Three Kingdoms Period (220-280).

抛 磚 引 玉

pāo zhuān yǐn yù

抛出磚去，引回玉來；比喻先發表粗淺的意見或文章，目的在於引出別人的高見或佳作。

唐朝有位詩人叫趙嘏，詩才很高。有一次，他到蘇州去，當地詩人常建一向仰慕趙嘏的詩才，爲了得到趙嘏的詩句，便在靈岩寺的牆壁上先寫了兩句詩。趙嘏到靈岩寺遊覽，看到了那兩句詩，在後面續了兩句，成爲一首完整的詩。因爲趙嘏所寫的詩句比常建的好，所以人們把常建的這種作法叫做"抛磚引玉"。

出自《歷代詩話》*

* 《歷代詩話》 清（1644—1911）吳景旭作。

Casting a Brick to Attract a Piece of Jade

Said of some superficial remarks or a simple article presented by way of introduction so that others may come up with valuable opinions and writings.

ZHAO Gu was a highly accomplished poet of the Tang Dynasty. Once, while he was touring the beautiful city of Suzhou, a local poet, Chang Jian, who admired his talent, wrote two lines on a wall of the city's Divine Rock Monastery in order to induce Zhao Gu to write better sentences. When Zhao Gu visited the monastery and found what Chang Jian wrote, he completed the poem by adding another two lines.

People came to refer Chang Jian's act as "casting a brick to attract a piece of jade" since Zhao Gu was more talented.

Poems of Different Dynasties Reviewed*

*By Wu Jingxu of the Qing Dynasty (1644-1911).

杞人憂天

qǐ rén yōu tiān

杞國人憂慮天會塌下來；比喻不必要的憂心。

　　古時候，杞國有一個人，担心天塌下來，地陷下去，愁得睡不好覺，吃不下飯。他的朋友見他這樣憂慮，就對他解釋說："天不過是些聚集起來的氣體罷了，你整天都是在天的中間活動和休息，爲什麼還担心天塌下來呢？"杞人問："天要真的是氣體，太陽、月亮和星星不會掉下來嗎？"朋友說："太陽、月亮和星星是大氣當中會發光的東西，即使掉下來，也打不着人。"杞人聽了朋友的解釋，覺得有點道理，接着又問："地如果陷下去又怎麼辦呢？"朋友說："地不過是些堆集起來的土石塊罷了，你整天都在地上走來走去，爲什還要担心它會陷下去呢？"杞人聽說地也不會陷，這才放下心來。

出自《列子》

The Man of Qi Feared That the Sky Might Fall

Don't Cross the Bridge Till You Get to It
Borrow Trouble

Said of uncalled-for worry.

THERE lived in the ancient state of Qi a man who feared that the sky might fall and the earth might cave in some day or other. He was so worried that he could not eat or sleep.

　　"The sky is but a mass of different kinds of gases," a friend of this man said to him, trying to dispel his anxiety. "You work and rest all day long in these gases. Why should you worry about the fall of the sky?" The man of Qi asked,

"So the sky is a mass of gases. But would the sun, the moon and the stars fall?" To this question, his friend replied, "The sun, the moon and the stars are illuminating bodies in the atmosphere. Even though they might fall, that wouldn't do any harm to human beings."

Though somewhat convinced, the Man of Qi asked again, "What if the earth should sink in?" His friend said, "The earth is but a mass of heaped soil and rocks. You move about on it every day. Why should you worry about its caving in?"

Having come to realize that the earth would not cave in either, the man of Qi was able to set his mind at rest.

The Book of Lie Zi

困獸猶鬥
kùn shòu yóu dòu

被圍困的野獸還要作最後的搏鬥；比喻陷於絕境的失敗者因不甘心失敗而竭力掙扎。

春秋時，晉楚兩國發生了戰爭，晉國被打敗了。晉軍統帥荀林父自己請求判處死罪，晉景公準備批准。這時，一位叫士貞子的大臣勸阻說：“這是不合適的。三十多年前城濮之戰中，晉軍曾經大敗楚軍，大家都很高興，但晉文公却很憂愁。臣子們問他爲什麼？晉文公說：‘楚國雖敗，但主帥子玉還活着，他會來報復的！一隻野獸被圍困住了還要掙扎，何況子玉是一國之相，豈能甘心失敗！’直到後來楚王殺了子玉，晉文公才放了心。荀林父是晉國的支柱，如果殺了他，這正是楚國所希望的，雖然他打了敗仗，但無損於他對國家的忠誠。”晉景公認爲士貞子的話很有道理，就寬宥了荀林父。

出自《左傳》

Even a Cornered Beast Struggles
Even a Worm Will Turn

Said of a loser who, though at bay, does not resign himself to defeat and puts up a desperate fight.

THE state of Jin was defeated in a war with the state of Chu during the Spring and Autumn Period. Xun Linfu, commander-in-chief of the Jin army, requested capital punishment of himself for failure in his duty. Duke Jinggong, Jin's ruler, was ready to approve the death sentence on the defeated general. A court minister named Shi Zhenzi, however, remonstrated his sovereign, saying, "That won't do, Your Grace. During the Battle of Chengpu more than three decades ago, our army won a significant victory over the Chu army. Everybody was overjoyed at this, except Duke Wengong, who looked much worried, instead. Asked why, he said, 'Though Chu lost the battle, its commander-in-chief, Zi Yu, is still alive and he would certainly take revenge. Even a cornered beast will struggle, not to mention Zi Yu, who is now Chu's Prime Minister. He would never be reconciled to defeat.' Duke Wengong began to feel relieved only when the ruler of Chu had Zi Yu executed on some charge. Now, Xun

Linfu is a pillar of our state. Should Your Grace have him executed, that would exactly suit the wishes of Chu. Although Xun Linfu did not win, he remains loyal to our country."

Seeing the truth of Shi Zhenzi's argument, Duke Jinggong had Xun Linfu pardoned.

Zuo Qiuming's Chronicles

囫圇吞棗
hú lún tun zǎo

把整個棗兒吞下肚去；比喻在學習上不求甚解，含糊了事。

有個醫生告訴人們說："梨對於人的牙齒有好處，但對脾却有害；棗子呢？正好相反，對脾有益，却對牙齒有害。"有個自作聰明的人聽了這話，便對醫生說："我倒有個妙法，可以避免這些缺點！"醫生說："你說說看，有什麼辦法？"那人就說："吃梨子的時候，我只是嚼，却不咽下去，這還會傷害脾麼！吃棗子呢，我不嚼就，一口吞下去，這還會弄得壞牙齒麼！"旁人笑道："你這樣囫圇吞棗，胃口受得了嗎？"

出自《湛淵靜語》*

*《湛淵靜語》　元朝人白珽著。

Swallowing a Date Without Chewing
Swallowing Hook, Line and Sinker

Said of a person who reads without much thinking or learns something without really understanding it.

A doctor used to tell his patients: "Pears are good to the teeth but harmful to the spleen. Dates are just the opposite: they benefit the spleen but do harm to the teeth."

Thinking himself clever, one of the patients said, "I've a clever idea." The doctor asked, "Would you please tell us that clever idea of yours?" "Well," answered the patient, "when I eat a pear, I'll only chew and not swallow it. So it can't harm my spleen. When I eat a date, I'll swallow it whole without chewing so that my teeth won't suffer."

"But what about your stomach?" another patient cut in. "Wouldn't that be too much for it?"

Discourses from the Zhanyuan Study*

*By Bai Ting of the Yuan Dynasty (1271-1368).

助 桀 爲 虐
zhù jié wéi nüè

幫助夏桀作虐；比喻幫助惡人做壞事。

劉邦起兵反秦，當攻破咸陽，打入秦宮時，見宮裏富麗堂皇，美女珍寶，不計其數，心中頓起羨慕之意，想全部留下自己享用。
樊噲勸阻他，他還不高興。張良便說：「只因秦王貪暴，不得人心，
您才得到了今天的勝利。我們既然為天下除了暴君，不應該沿襲他
原來那套奢靡的宮廷生活方式，而應該提倡儉樸的風氣。現在您到
秦宮，就想像秦王一樣享樂，豈不等於幫助古代的暴君桀做壞事
一樣嗎？樊噲的話是忠言，願您聽從他的勸告。」劉邦聽了恍然大
悟，便把宮殿所有的財寶都封閉起來，自己帶領隊伍退駐到咸陽郊
外去了。

出自《史記》

Aiding King Jie in His Despotism
Holding a Candle to the Devil

*Referring to an act that helps a wicked person in his evil
doing, in the same way as one would aid King Jie of the Xia
Dynasty in his tyrannical rule.*

REVOLTING against the Qin Dynasty, Liu Bang led his army
in an attack on its capital Xianyang. When he took the city
and stormed into the Qin palace, he found the buildings were
georgeously decorated and stocked with numberless
treasures. There were, in addition, large numbers of beautiful
court ladies. These attracted Liu Bang, who thought of
helping himself to them. He was displeased with Fan Kuai
when the latter advised him to refrain from doing so.

"It's exactly because the Qin emperor was tyrannical and
unpopular that you've achieved the victory of today," Zhang
Liang said to Liu Bang. "Now that we've got rid of a tyrant
for the common people, we cannot afford to follow the
luxurious, decadent life style of his, but should promote a
thrifty and simple way of life. Wouldn't you be like a person
aiding the ancient King Jie in his despotism if, the moment
you step into the Qin palace, you want to enjoy yourself as
the Qin emperor did? Fan Kuai is right in what he said.

Would you please act on his advice."

Realizing his mistake, Liu Bang had all the treasures sealed and led his men to camp outside Xianyang city.

Records of the Historian

伯樂識馬
bó lè shí mǎ

比喻善於識別和發現真正的人才。

　　有一匹千里馬老了，牠的主人讓牠拖着沉重的鹽車去攀登巍峨的太行山。老馬在崎嶇的山路上艱難地行進。牠勞累得尾巴下垂了，蹄子磨破了，滿身都是汗水。在一座陡峭的山坡前，牠靠着車轅倒了下來，再也走不動了。

　　這時，相馬專家伯樂正乘車迎面而來，他一眼就認出這曾是一匹日行千里的良馬。他惋惜牠現在落得這個下場，於是便跳下車來，撲在馬身上傷心地哭了。他脫下自己的袍子，蓋在老馬身上。老馬也低下頭來，依偎着伯樂。然後，牠仰起頭來放聲嘶鳴，好像遇到了知己。

出自 《戰國策》

Bo Le, the Horse Judger
A Talent Scout

One who can discover talented people and known their worth is now likened to Bo Le of ancient times, who was famous for his ability in judging horses.

A horse that could formerly run 1,000 *li* a day was now old. One day, its owner made it haul a cartload of salt up the lofty Taihang   Mountains. Plodding along the winding mountain paths, it was so exhausted that its tail dangled, its

108

hooves were worn, and its body was soaked with perspiration all over. When it came to a steep slope, it could trudge no more and halted beside the shaft of the cart.

Just then, Bo Le, a renowned horse judger, came in a carriage. He could see at the first glance that the worn-out horse had been a fine steed that could cover as much as 1,000 *li* a day. Feeling sorry for its having come to such a sad end, he alighted and threw himself upon the animal, sobbing. He took off his robe and covered the horse with it. The beast knowingly lowered its head and snuggled up in Bo Le's arms. After a moment, it raised its head and whinnied as if to express its joy at meeting one who knew its real worth.

Anecdotes of the Warring States

近水樓台先得月

jìn shuǐ lóu tái xiān dé yuè

靠近水的樓房最先得到月亮；比喻由於地位或私人關係密切而優先得到利益或便利。

北宋時的政治家和文學家范仲淹任杭州知府的時候，在他身邊工作的許多官員都因他的推薦而得到提拔。唯獨一個叫蘇麟的人，因為在杭州所屬外縣任職，沒有得到這種便利。後來他寫了一首詩送給范仲淹，其中有兩句是：近水樓台先得月，向陽花木易為春。范仲淹讀後心中會意，便徵詢了他的意見和希望，滿足了他的要求。

出自《清夜錄》＊

＊《清夜錄》 記載宋朝雜事，作者宋朝人俞文豹。

A Waterfront Pavilion Gets Moonlight First

Said of a person who is the first to enjoy some benefits because he is in a favourable position or has some influential connections.

WHEN Fan Zhongyan, a Northern Song statesman and scholar, was prefect of Hangzhou, many officials under him were promoted on his recommendation. An exception was Su Lin, who served in an outlying county. So he wrote and sent a poem to Fan Zhongyan. It contained these lines:

"A waterfront pavilion is the first to get the moonlight
And a sun-facing plant is within easier access of springtime."

The scholar prefect, who could read between the lines, asked Su Lin what position he had in mind and' then complied with his request.

Notes Taken on Quiet Nights*

*Written by Yu Wenbao, this is a book recording episodes from the Song Dynasty (960-1279).

空中樓閣
kōng zhōng lóu gé

在空中建造樓房；比喻脫離實際的幻想。

從前，有個愚蠢的富人，他到朋友家去，看到朋友住的三層樓房，寬敞明亮，非常羨慕。他回到家中把匠人找來，問道："你能造他家那樣的樓房嗎？"匠人回答說："那房屋就是我造的。"富人便說："那你現在就替我造一座那樣的樓房。"於是，匠人開始打地基、疊磚墻。富人見了問匠人說："你想造個什麼樣的房子呀？"匠人說："造三層樓房呀！"富人說："我不要下面兩層，光要上面第三層的房子。"匠人說："不疊下面的，怎能蓋上面

110

的！" 不管匠人怎麼解釋，那富人仍堅持己見，只讓他建造第三層樓房。

出自《百喻經》

A Castle in the Air

Said of illusions or visionary prospects.

THERE was a stupid rich man who went to visit a friend one day. He admired the friend's three-storey building which was spacious and bright. Back at home, he found a mason and asked if he could build such a house. "It's me who built that house," replied the mason: "Now I'd have you build for me another one which is exactly like that," the rich man said.

The builder dug the foundation and then began to lay bricks. Seeing what he was doing, the rich man asked, "What kind of house are you building for me?" "A three-storey one," answered the mason. "But I want only the third storey without the first and second," the rich man said. "How can I put up the third storey without first building the lower two?" retorted the craftsman.

No matter how the mason argued and explained, the rich man insisted on having him build only the top storey.

Sutra of One Hundred Parables

盲人摸象

máng rén mō xiàng

雙目失明的人摸象;比喻把部份當作全體。

從前,有個國王命令他的大臣牽來一頭象。四個瞎子知道了,都想知道象是什麼樣子的。可是他們誰也看不見,只好用手摸。有個瞎子摸到象的牙齒,就說:"象的樣子像個又粗又長的蘿蔔。"另一個瞎子摸到了象的耳朵,就說:"象的樣子像個簸箕。"第三個瞎子摸到了象的腿,就說:"象的樣子像個柱子。"第四個瞎子摸到了象的尾巴,就說:"你們都錯了,象就像一根繩子。"他們爭吵了半天,象到底是什麼樣子,誰也說不清楚。

出自《涅槃經》 *

*《涅槃經》 佛教經典之一。

The Blind Men Feeling an Elephant

Said of persons who take the part for the whole.

ONCE upon a time, a king had one of his ministers bring him an elephant. Four blind men who learned the news wanted to know what an elephant was like. Since none of them could see, they had to feel the animal with their hands. The first blind man touched a tusk and said, "An elephant is like a long, thick carrot." Having touched one of the elephant's ears, the second blind man exclaimed, "An elephant resembles a dust pan." The third blind man who felt one of the animal's legs blurted out, "An elephant is similar to a column." After touching the elephant's tail, the fourth blind man shouted, "An elephant is no different from a rope."

They argued and argued, but none of them could tell for sure what an elephant was really like.

*A classical work on the Buddhist faith.

夜 郎 自 大
yè láng zì dà

夜郎國王自認爲他的國土大；比喻驕傲狂妄。

　　西漢時，中國西南部有個叫夜郎的小國家。它的面積大約相當
於漢朝的一個縣。夜郎國王孤陋寡聞，自以爲他的國家比西漢帝國
還要大。當漢朝派使者去訪問夜郎的時候，國王竟向漢朝使臣說：
"漢與夜郎，哪一個的國土大？"

出自《漢書》

The Ridiculously Boastful King of Yelang

A Humble-Bee in a Cow-Turd Thinks Himself a King

The king of the Yelang Kingdom thought that his country was bigger than others. This legend is often quoted in reference to a person who is blinded by presumptuous self-conceit.

THERE was, during the Western Han period, a small kingdom, Yelang, in southwest China. Though it was only the size of a Han county, parochial ignorance made its king assume that his kingdom was more extensive than the whole of the Han empire. So when a Han envoy came to visit Yelang, its king asked him, "Which is the bigger, the Han or Yelang?"

History of the Han Dynasty

刻 舟 求 劍
kè zhōu qiú jiàn

在船上刻了記號去尋找丟失的劍；比喻拘泥固執，不知變化。

有個搭船過江的人，一不小心，將所帶的一柄劍，從船邊落到江裏去了。那人馬上在劍落下的地方，劃了個記號。別人問他："喂，你在船上刻記號做什麼啊！"那人回答說："我的劍是從這個地方落下去的，等會兒船靠岸了，我就從這個有記號的地方下水去把劍找回來。"

等船靠了岸，他果然從刻有記號的地方跳下水去，找了半天，也沒有找到他丟的那柄劍。

出自《呂氏春秋》

114

Marking the Boat to Locate a Lost Sword

Said of a stickler who does not act according to changed circumstances.

A man was ferrying across a river. When, by accident, his sword dropped into the water, he immediately carved a notch on the side of the moving boat to mark the place where his weapon was lost.

"What's the use of making a notch there?" asked a fellow passenger. The man replied, "That's where my sword dropped into the river. I'll jump into the water from the same place to find my sword when the boat moors."

And that was just what he did when the boat got to the other side of the river. However the tried, he could not locate his sword.

The Discoures of Lü Buwei

幸災樂禍

xìng zāi lè huò

在別人遇到災禍時感到高興。

春秋時，晉國發生旱災，派人到鄰邦秦國購買糧食，秦穆公得知後立即把大批糧食運往晉國。第二年，秦國鬧災荒，秦國使者到晉國去買糧食，晉國國君却不賣給。一個叫慶鄭的官員勸晉君說："受了人家的恩惠不報答，見人家有了災難却感到高興，都是不對的。"晉君不聽。秦穆公知道後大怒，親自率領軍隊攻打晉國，晉軍大敗，晉君作了俘虜。

出自《左傳》

Rejoicing in Others' Misfortunes

Said of a person who feels glad when other people meet with disasters or are in difficulties.

ONE year during the Spring and Autumn Period, the state of Jin was suffering from drought. It sent people to the neighbouring state of Qin to purchase grain. Qin's ruler, Duke Mugong gladly supplied huge quantities of grain to the drought-stricken Jin.

The next year, Qin met with the same disaster and dispatched an envoy to Jin to negotiate grain purchases. Jin's sovereign, however, refused the request. For this, one of his officials, Qing Zheng, remonstrated him, saying, "It's wrong not to repay the kindness of others, or to take pleasure in their calamities." But the Jin ruler turned a deaf ear to Qing Zheng's words.

Duke Mugong of Qin was angry to learn of Jin's attitude. He mounted an attack on Jin, personally taking command of his army. Jin was defeated and its ungrateful ruler was taken prisoner.

Zuo Qiuming's Chronicles

116

東 施 效 顰
dōng shī xiaò pín

東施仿效別人皺眉頭；比喻胡亂模仿，效果很壞。

西施是中國古代著名的美人。有一次，她生了心痛病，因此，常把雙手捂着胸口，緊緊地皺着眉頭。可是鄰居們說她這樣顯得更美麗了。

同村有個長得很醜的女子，叫東施，她很羨慕西施的美麗，什麼都要模仿她。於是，她也學着西施的樣子，一見到鄰居，就故意捂着胸口，皺起眉頭。鄰居們見了她這副怪模樣，覺得她比原來更醜，便都避開了她。

出自 《莊子》

Dong Shi Knitting Her Brows in Imitation of Xi Shi
A Jackdaw in Peacock's Feathers

Said of a person who blindly copies others with ludicrous effects.

XI Shi was a famous beauty in ancient China. Once, suffering from heart-burn, she had to knit her eyebrows and cover her chest with both hands. The neighbours, however, commented that she looked even more beautiful that way.

Among Xi Shi's fellow villagers was an ugly girl named Dong Shi. Admiring Xi Shi's beauty, she imitated her in everything. Seeing a neighbour coming her way, she would also frown and put her hands to her chest. All her neighbours tried to avoid her because, by foolishly copying Xi Shi, she looked even more ugly.

The Book of Zhuang Zi

117

東食西宿
dōng shí xī sù

在東家吃飯，在西家住宿；比喻貪得無厭。

古時候，齊國有個姑娘，到了該出嫁的年齡。住在她家附近的兩戶人家，同時送來了聘禮求婚。東邊人家的兒子長得又矮又醜，可是家中富有；西邊人家的兒子一表人材，可是家境貧寒。姑娘的父母一時決定不下來，便把女兒喚來，叫她自己拿主意。父親見女兒不好意思，便說："妳不好意思說出口，就用手勢表示吧！喜歡東家的兒子就舉左手，喜歡西家的就舉右手。"姑娘想了半天，把兩隻手都舉了起來。父母驚訝地問："這是什麼意思？"姑娘忸忸怩怩地說："我想在東家吃飯，在西家住宿。"

出自《藝文類聚》*

* 《藝文類聚》 類書，唐歐陽詢（557－641）編，分歲時、政治、經濟等四十八部類。

Eating in the East Family and Sleeping in the West

Wanting the Best of Both Worlds

Used to describe a greedy person who goes wherever there is profit to gain.

A girl in the ancient state of Qi had reached marriageable age. Betrothal gifts came from two neighbouring families both of which made an offer of marriage. The suitor living to the east was short and ugly but his parents were very rich; the suitor living to the west was handsome but his family was very poor.

Unable to decide which family their daughter was to go, the girl's parents asked her to choose on her own. "If you're too shy to tell us by words," said the parents when they saw her bashfulness, "you can indicate by raising one of your hands. Put up your left hand if you like the boy of the east family, and put up your right hand if you like the boy of the west family."

After weighing the matter up for quite a while, she raised both of her hands. Non-plussed, her parents asked what she meant. The girl answered blushingly, "I would like to eat in the east family and sleep in the west."

*Yiwen Encyclopaedia**

*Compiled by Ouyang Xun (557-641) of the Tang Dynasty, this work deals with forty-eight subjects including annual festivals, politics and economy.

兩 敗 俱 傷

liǎng bài jù shāng

雙方都受到損傷，誰也沒有得到好處。

119

戰國中期，齊、秦兩大強國出現對峙局面。兩個都想採取軍事行動來完成霸業。當齊宣王要攻打魏國時，齊國大臣淳于髡用犬兔追逐的故事來勸阻齊王。他說："有一條獵犬追逐一隻狡兔。牠繞着山腰追了三圈，跨過山崗追了五次，都未追着。結果，前面逃跑的兔子疲乏不堪，後面追的犬也困倦極了，最後各自都死在山腳下。這時，一個農夫走來看見了，不費一點力氣就把牠們都拾去了。如果齊、魏兩國長久攻打不休，必然會國困民窮，強大的秦國就會乘機獲利。"齊王聽後，立即打消了進攻魏國的念頭。

出自《戰國策》

Both Sides Suffer

Fight Like Kilkenny Cats

Said of a struggle which benefits neither of the two sides.

IN the middle part of the Warring States Period, Qi and Qin confronted each other as two powerful states. Both wanted to take military actions to achieve hegemony of its own. When King Xuangwang of Qi planned to attack another state, Wei, his minister Chunyu Kun remonstrated him by telling him the story of a hound chasing a hare:

"A clever hound was chasing a cunning hare. Though the dog had circled around the hillside three times and run over the ridge five times, it failed to catch the hare. Both were utterly exhausted and finally they collapsed, never to rise again. A farmer came their way and, without the least effort, gained a pair of animals.

"If Qi and Wei are involved in a protracted struggle against each other, both states and their people would suffer. This would only benefit the powerful state of Qin."

The story made the king of Qi give up his plan to attack Wei.

Anecdotes of the Warring States

取而代之
qǔ ér dài zhī

把別人趕走，自己來代替。

　　秦朝時，項羽少年時既不願讀書，也不願練武。有一次，他叔父項梁責備他，項羽說：「讀書認字只能記住姓名；學習劍術只能抵得住個把人，我要學會能抵擋萬人的本領。」於是，項梁就教他學習兵法。後來，項梁因殺人，被官吏追捕，就帶項羽一同出逃。

　　一次，秦始皇巡遊會稽時，車馬儀仗浩浩蕩蕩，大路兩旁站滿了看熱鬧的人羣，項梁和項羽也在其中。項羽看到秦始皇出巡的盛況，不禁說：「那個皇帝位子可以奪過來，由我們代替他做啊！」項梁急忙用手掩住他的嘴，說：「別胡說，這會惹禍滅族的！」但項梁心裏却非常讚賞他，認爲他將來必定是個不平凡的人。

　　之後，項羽成爲秦末起義軍的領袖。他統率的起義軍，首先攻進秦都城，推翻了秦朝。

出自《史記》

Taking Another Person's Place
Step into Another Person's Shoes

IN his childhood, Xiang Yu of the Qin Dynasty was not interested in learning book knowledge or the martial arts. When his uncle, Xiang Liang, chided him for his laziness, he argued, "Book reading can only enable me to learn the names of some persons, and learning swordsmanship can only enable me to resist one or two attackers. What I want to learn is the skill of foiling the attack by ten thousand enemies."

Thus Xiang Liang began to teach his nephew the art of war. Later, the uncle was wanted by the authorities for having killed somebody. But he managed to escape, bringing Xiang Yu with him.

Then one day, the First Emperor of the Qin Dynasty came to Guiji on an imperial tour. His pompous entourage drew large crowds of people, including Xiang Liang and his nephew. The grand occasion made Xiang Yu comment subconsciously: "Yes, we can take the emperor's place." His uncle hurried to stop him, saying in a low voice, "No nonsense. That might cause the extermination of our whole clan." Inwardly, however, the old man appreciated Xiang Yu's ambition, concluding that his nephew would become a man of extraordinary accomplishments.

In due course, Xiang Yu became one of the leaders of the insurgent armed forces of peasants who rose against the Qin Dynasty during its last years. His was the first contingent of the peasant rebels that stormed and occupied the Qin capital, contributing enormously to the overthrow of the regime.

Records of the Historian

杯弓蛇影
bēi gōng shé yǐng

把映在酒杯裏的弓影當做是一條蛇；比喻由疑心引起恐懼，把虛幻誤作真實。

晉朝有個叫樂廣的人。有一次，他約一位好朋友來家中喝酒，可是這位朋友好像有什麼心事，酒喝得很少，不一會，便告辭了。

這個朋友回到家裏，頓時生起病來，請醫服藥，也不見效。樂廣聽到這個消息，立刻去探望，問他病是怎麼得的。病人吞吞吐吐地說："那天在你家喝酒的時候，我彷彿看見酒杯裏有條小蛇在游動，我喝了那酒，心中很不自在，回家來就病倒了。"

樂廣聽了，很是奇怪。他回到家中，察看了原來喝酒的地方，發現墻上掛着一把漆着花紋的弓。原來酒杯裏並沒有什麼小蛇，而是弓的影子映落在裏面。他又把那位朋友請來，並當場作了試驗。那位朋友恍然大悟，病也就好了。

出自《晉書》*

*《晉書》 唐房玄齡（579—648）等撰，記述晉朝（265—420）史事的
紀傳體著作。

Mistaking the Bow's Shadow in the Cup for a Snake

Taking Every Bush for a Bugbear

Said of unfounded suspicion and imaginary fears.

ONE day, Yue Guang of the Jin Dynasty invited a friend to drink with him. While drinking, however, the man looked somewhat jittery. He said good-bye after having had only a few drops. Back at home, he fell ill and, despite all manner of drugs, felt no better.

As soon as he had heard of his friend's illness, Yue Guang went to see him and asked how he had contracted it.

"I thought I saw a snake swimming in my cup the other day we drank together," the man said falteringly. "I felt quite uneasy drinking that wine, and I fell ill when I returned home."

Yue Guang was puzzled. When he went back, he examined the place where they drank that day, and saw a patterned bow hanging on the wall nearby. It dawned upon him that the swimming snake was nothing but the reflection of the bow in the cup.

Yue Guang again asked his friend to come over. They repeated what they had done the other day. Now the man understood everything and, then and there, his illness was gone for good.

History of the Jin Dynasty*

*Written by Fang Xuanling (579-648) and others of the Tang Dynasty, this history book consists mostly of biographies.

123

邯鄲學步
hán dān xué bù

　　向邯鄲人學習走路；比喻盲目模仿別人，反而喪失了自己原來的特點。

　　戰國時，燕國有個少年，他聽說趙國首都邯鄲的人，走路姿態非常優美，就不辭辛苦地跋山涉水前往學習。他跟在邯鄲人後面模仿他們走路，學了很久，不但沒有學會別人走路的樣子，反而把自己原來的走法也忘記了，因而他竟不得不爬着返回燕國。

出自《莊子》

Imitating the Handan People in Walking

The Crow Loses Its Own Gait When It
Attempts to Walk Like a Swan

Used to describe a person who, in slavishly imitating others, loses his own originality.

A young man lived in the state of Yan during the Warring States Period. Hearing that people in Handan, capital of the state of Zhao, walked most gracefully, he crossed mountains and rivers to get there to learn their gait. He walked behind the Handan people, acting the ape. Days had elapsed but, instead of being successful, he even forgot how he had walked before. Consequently, on his journey back to Yan, he could only crawl all the way.

The Book of Zhuang Zi

奇貨可居

qí huò kě jū

珍奇貨物可以囤積起來；比喻挾持某種技藝或壟斷某種東西，向別人討高價。

戰國末期，衞國的大商人呂不韋去趙國做生意，遇見被作爲人質扣押的秦國公子子楚。他認爲從子楚身上可以做一筆政治性的投機生意，便同他父親商量。他問他父親道："種田的利息大約有多少倍？"他父親說："十倍。""販賣珠寶的利息呢？""百倍。""擁立一個國王的利息呢？"他父親驚叫道："啊呀！那就多得難以計算了！"呂不韋笑道："那麼子楚這種珍奇的貨物囤積起來，可以賺取大利啊！"於是，他對子楚百般籠絡，並拿出六百兩黃金賄賂趙國看守子楚的官吏，放子楚逃回秦國。子楚回國後不久就登上了王位，他感謝呂不韋的恩情，任命呂爲相國，封給他許多土地。

出自《史記》

A Rare Commodity Worth Hoarding

Said of a precious product which can be monopolized or held back in anticipation of fabulous profits.

TOWARDS the close of the Warring States Period, a big merchant, Lü Buwei, of the state of Wei, went to do business in the state of Zhao. While there he came across a man of extraordinary calibre, Prince Zi Chu of Qin, who was held as a hostage by the Zhao government.

Lü Buwei calculated that he could gain some political capital by holding Prince Zi Chu as a stock-in-trade. He told his idea to his father and asked, "What's the profit of farming?" The old man replied, "The return could be ten times what you put in." Lü Buwei asked again, "And the profit of trading in jewellery?" His father answered, "A hundred times your capital." "And· the profit of installing a king on the throne?" This third question took the elder Lü by surprise. "Oh," he exclaimed, "the profit of that could never be over-estimated." Lü the junior said, chuckling, "So we can make a fabulous profit out of hoarding such a rare commodity as Prince Zi Chu."

Consequently, Lü Buwei tried all he could to woo the prince of Qin. He gave 600 ounces of gold to the Zhao guards who then let Prince Zi Chu escape.

Soon afterwards, Zi Chu ascended the throne. To express his gratitude for Lü Buwei's valuable help, he appointed him Prime Minister in addition to a generous reward of land.

Records of the Historian

孤 注 一 擲

gū zhù yī zhī

把所有的錢，都放在一次賭注上；比喻在危急時刻，盡所有力量，作最後一次冒險。

宋眞宗時，北方的契丹發兵入侵，當時朝中很多大臣主張遷都避敵。宰相寇准竭力反對，主張堅決抵抗，並請眞宗皇帝親自領兵出征。宋眞宗採納了寇准的主張出兵澶州（今河南濮陽一帶），終於獲得了勝利。契丹求和，雙方簽訂了和約。宋眞宗對於寇准，從此就更加信任了。但是，另一宰相王欽若，嫉妒寇准的功勞，在皇帝面前說了寇准許多壞話。有一次，他對皇帝說："陛下！您知道賭博嗎？賭博的人輸到最後，往往拿出全部剩下的錢，下一筆賭注，以決勝負。這次陛下出征，就是寇准不顧您的安危，把您當做最後的一筆賭注啊！"

出自《宋史》*

* 《宋史》　元朝脫脫等人撰，記載宋朝史事，紀傳體。

Staking Everything in a Single Throw
Putting All One's Eggs in One Basket

Used in reference to a last, desperate effort when the situation is most critical.

DURING the reign of Emperor Zhenzong of the Song Dynasty, the northern tribe of Qidan (Khitan) made armed intrusions into the Song empire. Many court ministers proposed moving the capital to another place so as to avoid battle. Only Prime Minister Kou Zhun was strongly opposed to the proposal; he advocated resistance and requested the Emperor personally to lead a punitive expedition against the Qidan intruders. The Emperor agreed and led an army to Chanzhou (present-day Puyang, Henan Province) where it defeated the aggressors. Qidan sued for peace and a peace treaty was signed between the two sides.

After this, Emperor Zhenzong placed ever greater trust in Kou Zhun. But Kou's counterpart, Wang Qinruo, who was jealous of Kou's contribution to the country, made many malicious remarks against him in the presence of the Emperor. "Don't you know gambling, Your Majesty?" Wang said to the Emperor one day. "Towards the end of a gambling session, the loser will stake all he has on a last cast of the dice. And that is what Kou Zhun did in the expedition against the Qidan. He gave no consideration to Your Majesty's safety at all, because he wanted to bet his bottom coin on it."

History of the Song Dynasty*

*Written by Tuotuo (1314-55) and others of the Yuan Dynasty, this work records the events of the Song Dynasty mainly through biographies.

歧 路 亡 羊

qí lù wáng yáng

在岔道上丟失了羊；比喻沒有正確的方向，就找不到眞理。

有一天，楊子的鄰居家跑掉了一隻羊。鄰居發動了所有的親屬去尋找，又去請楊子家的僕人幫忙找羊。楊子知道了這件事，嘆口氣說："咦！只跑掉了一隻羊，爲什麼要這麼多人去找呢？"鄰居回答說："岔道太多，所以追的人就該多一些。"

等了一會，找羊的人回來了。楊子問他的鄰居："你家的羊找到了嗎？"鄰居搖搖頭說："沒找到。"楊子又問："怎麼沒找到呢？"鄰居回答說："岔道太多，每條岔道上又有岔道，不知道牠到底跑往哪一條路上去了。找羊的人沒有辦法，只得回來了！"

出自《列子》

A Sheep Going Astray on a Forked Road

Said of the impossibility of finding the truth if one goes in the wrong direction.

A neighbour of Yang Zi's lost a sheep. The owner asked all his relatives as well as Yang Zi's servant to help find the animal.

"Why should you trouble so many persons for the sake of a single sheep?" Yang Zi asked his neighbour. The latter replied, "The road where it got lost has too many branches. So more persons are needed."

Before long, his relatives and Yang Zi's servant returned. "Have they found your sheep?" Yang Zi asked the neighbour. The answer was "No." "Why?" Yang Zi was puzzled. His neighbour said, "The road has numerous branches and sub-branches. Nobody knows which direction the sheep has gone. They had to give up their effort and come back."

The Book of Lie Zi

味如鷄肋

wèi rú jī lèi

味道和吃鷄肋一樣；比喻對某些事情不感興趣，但又不得不做。

三國時，曹操帶兵攻打漢中，久久不能取勝。一天，他出了個叫"鷄肋"的口令。一位叫楊修的侍從官非常聰明，聽到這個口令後，馬上收拾行李。別人問他爲什麼？楊修說："鷄的肋骨吃起來沒有味道，扔掉又可惜，魏王是用牠來比喻漢中，因此我知道他要退兵了。"果然曹操很快就下令撤離了漢中。

出自《三國誌》

As Tasteless as Chicken Ribs

Said of something which is uninteresting and yet has to be kept or done.

DURING the Three Kingdoms Period, Cao Cao of Wei launched an attack on Hanzhong. Annoyed by lack of progress despite prolonged effort, one day he ordered that "Chicken Rib" be used as the password for his army. Thereupon, one of his aides, the clever Yang Xiu, began to pack his things. Asked why he was ready to leave, Yang Xiu said, "Chicken ribs are tasteless and yet it is a waste to throw them away. Using 'Chicken Ribs' as the password, His Majesty has likened Hanzhong to such a tasteless thing. So I know he is going to order a withdrawal."

Exactly as had been expected, Cao Cao soon ordered his troops to withdraw from Hanzhong.

History of the Three Kingdoms

130

明察秋毫

míng chá qiū haó

連鳥獸秋天新長的細毛都看得清楚；比喻目光敏銳，能深入觀察問題。

戰國時的齊宣王想稱霸，做衆諸侯的領袖，因此，向孟子請教。

孟子說："我們孔子的門徒，不講霸道，只講王道——用道德的力量來統一天下。"

齊宣王問道："像我這樣的人，能不能用王道統一天下呢？"

孟子說："能！我聽說，有一次你看見一個人牽着一頭牛去宰殺，你看到牠那恐懼的樣子，感到不忍。憑你這種好心，就可以行王道，施仁政，統一天下。問題不在於您能不能，而在於你幹不幹罷了！比方有人說他能舉重三千斤，但實際上卻舉不起一根羽毛。比方他又說，他能看清秋天鳥獸的毫毛那樣細微的東西，但實際上卻看不見滿車的木柴。你相信這種說法嗎？"

齊宣王說："那當然不相信！"

孟子緊接着說："如今您的好心能用來對待動物，却不能用來愛護老百姓，那麼您的好心也同樣是難叫人相信的。看來，一根羽毛之所以舉不起，是那個人根本不肯舉的緣故；一車木柴之所以看不見，是那個人根本沒有看的緣故。顯然，這是幹不幹的問題，而不是能不能的問題。您問，您能不能行王道，統一天下，問題也是如此。"

出自《孟子》

Sharp-Sighted Enough to See an Animal's Autumn Down

See Through a Millstone

Said of a person who is capable of discerning the minute detail in everything and of penetrating deeply into a problem.

DURING the Warring States Period, King Xuanwang of Qi wanted to achieve hegemony over all the other ducal states. He sought the advice of Mencius on the matter.

"We disciples of Master Confucius," said Mencius,', "do not stand for hegemony. We stand for the Kingly Way, for unifying the country by virtue of morality."

"Can a person like me unify the whole country by the Kingly Way?" asked the Qi ruler.

"Yes," replied Mencius. "I've heard that one day, when Your Majesty saw a farmer leading an ox to the slaughterhouse, you felt sorry for it. Since you're so compassionate, you can follow the Kingly Way, carry out a policy of benevolence and finally unify the country. The heart of the matter is not whether you can unify the country, but whether you will try. Suppose a person says he can lift three thousand catties [1,500 kilogrammes], but in reality he can't lift a single feather. Suppose he says he can see something as fine as the autumn down of an animal, but in reality he can't see even a cartload of firewood. Can Your Majesty believe such a person?"

"Of course not," answered King Xuanwang.

"Now," went on Mencius, "Your Majesty can show pity for an animal, but you can't be equally compassionate to the common people. So Your Majesty's kindness is also unbeliev- able. It seems to me that the above-mentioned person can't lift a feather merely because he doesn't want to. Likewise, he can't see a cartload of firewood merely because he doesn't want to, either. Obviously, the matter is not whether one can do something, but whether he really wants to. The same reasoning applies to the question whether Your Majesty can

unify the country through the Kingly Way."
The Book of Mencius

爭 先 恐 後
zhēng xiān kǒng hòu

爭着向前，唯恐落後；比喻熱烈緊張的競爭場面。

　　春秋時，晉國有個著名的駕車能手叫王良。大夫趙襄子請他去，向他學習駕車技術。學了不久，趙襄子就要跟王良比賽趕車。比賽的時候，趙襄子換了三次馬，三次都未賽過王良。趙襄子很不高興，埋怨王良未把全部駕車技術敎給他。王良回答說："我的技術全敎給您了，只是您沒有很好地運用。駕車首先要把馬套得合適，使牠駕起來輕快；其次，駕車的人要一心一意注意馬的行動，這樣才能跑得快。可是，在比賽過程中，當您落在我後邊時，就一心想如何能趕上我；當您跑在我前面時，又恐怕被我趕上。您的注意力老放在我身上，哪還有心思去趕好車呢？這就是您落後的原因。"

出自《韓非子》

Striving to Be the First and Fearing to Lag Behind

Said of a contest in which one vies with another to win the first place.

DURING the Spring and Autumn Period, there lived in the state of Jin a man named Wang Liang, who was a famous driver. A senior official called Zhao Xiangzi asked to learn charioteering from him. Before he had learned much, Zhao Xiangzi challenged Wang Liang to a contest of driving skill.

133

But he failed to overtake Wang Liang even though he changed horses three times. So he complained that Wang Liang had not taught him all he knew.

"I've taught Your Excellency all I can. It's only that you don't know how to use what you've learned. In driving, one must, first and foremost, have the horses harnessed properly so that they will be able to run ahead unimpeded. Secondly, one must pay full attention to the performance of one's horses so that they may be made to run at top speed. I noted, however, that when Your Excellency fell behind me in our contest, all your thought was on how to overtake me; and that when you got ahead of me, you were afraid of my overtaking you. How could you concentrate on making your horses perform as best as they could when you always focused your attention on me? This was the reason why you could not win."

The Book of Han Fei Zi

刮目相看
guā mù xiāng kàn

擦亮眼睛去看；比喻用新的眼光，看待一個人，改變舊的看法。

三國時，吳國著名大將呂蒙，幼年時家境貧困，沒有讀過書。吳國國君孫權曾勸呂蒙要好好學習。可是呂蒙說：“軍隊裏事情太多，沒有時間讀書。”孫權說：“過去許多著名的軍事家，都是在戎馬忙亂之中刻苦讀書的。你為什麼不能抓緊時間堅持自學呢？”

呂蒙從此發奮讀書，進步很快。都督魯肅，平素對呂蒙有些輕視，後來，經人勸說後，才勉強去拜訪呂蒙。呂蒙熱情招待他，並問魯肅此次去新駐地對防守有何打算？魯肅滿不在乎。隨口答應道：“尚未考慮，到時候看着辦吧。”呂蒙批評了魯肅對待職務不嚴肅的態度，同時獻計五條，當場提筆寫出。魯肅頓時改變態度，撫摸着他的背，親切地說：“我一直認為你能武不能文，現在學識如此淵博，你已經不是以前的阿蒙了！”呂蒙笑道：“人們三天不見，便要用新的眼光看待他，何況隔了這麼久呢！”

出自《三國誌》

Rubbing One's Eyes Before Looking at Somebody

Said of the necessity of regarding somebody in a new light instead of sticking to an old view.

LU Meng, a famous general of Wu during the Three Kingdoms Period, came of a poor family and had no chance to go to school in his childhood. Sun Quan, the Wu ruler, told him to do his best and read as many books as possible. But Lü Meng said, "As a commander, I'm too busy to learn." Sun Quan rejoined, "Many famed strategists of the past led an equally busy and unsettled life. But they made the best use of their time and studied diligently on their own. Why can't you do the same?"

Convinced, Lü Meng began to study hard, and he made quick progress. One day, Lu Su, a military governor of Wu who had thought little of Lü Meng, was passing the latter's headquarters on his way to somewhere else. But he called on

Lü Meng at the suggestion of his colleagues.

Lü Meng warmly received Lu Su and asked him what defence plan he had for the region newly placed under his jurisdiction. "I haven't considered the matter yet," said Lu Su in a casual manner. "It can be worked out at the last minute." Lü Meng criticized him for lack of a sense of responsibility, and made a five-point proposal which he wrote down on a piece of paper then and there.

This made Lu Su change his attitude. Patting Lü Meng on the back, he said with affection, "I've all along regarded you as merely a military man. But now you've become a man of wide knowledge, no longer the former Lü Meng at all."

Hearing the military governor's comment, Lü Meng said with a smile, "We have to rub our eyes before looking at someone even after an absence of three days, let alone a much longer period."

History of the Three Kingdoms

知其然，不知其所以然
zhī qí rán, bù zhī qí suǒ yǐ rán

知道這樣，但不知道為什麼是這樣；用來形容對事物一知半解的人。

戰國時，鄭國的列子跟關尹子學射箭。有一次，列子射中了靶，就跑去問關尹子："我學得差不多了吧！"關尹子反問道："你知道你為什麼射中嗎？"列子回答說："不知道。"關尹子說："不知道為什麼射中，怎麼能說學會了呢？"於是，列子又一連學習了三年，又向關尹子請敎。關尹子說："現在你知道為什麼射中了嗎？"列子回答："知道了。"關尹子說："射中了並且知道為什麼射中，這才算學好了。"

出自《列子》

136

Knowing the Hows but Not the Whys

Said of a person who has only limited or half-baked knowledge of something.

LIE Zi of Zheng of the Warring States Period was learning archery from Guan Yinzi. One day, having hit the bull's-eye, he went to ask his teacher, "Don't you think I've learned what I have to?" Guang Yinzi said, "But do you know why you have been able to hit the bull's-eye?" Lie Zi could only say "No." "Well," rejoined Guan Yinzi, "if you don't know why, how can you say that you've mastered the skill?"

So Lie Zi continued to learn for another three years. After that, he again asked for comments by his teacher, who put to him this question, "Do you know now why you can hit the bull's-eye?" Lie Zi answered, "Yes, I do." "Only when you can hit the bull's-eye and know the reason why," said Guan Yinzi, "can it be said that you have really learned the skill."

The Book of Lie Zi

物 以 類 聚
wù yǐ lèi jù

同類的動物總是聚集在一起;比喻氣味相投的人在一起。

戰國時,淳于髡在同一天裏,接連推薦了七個賢士給齊宣王。齊宣王覺得很奇怪,問他說:"我聽說,人才是難得的!走遍千里能選拔到一個賢士,就算是相當不易了;現在,你一天就推薦七個賢士給我,不是太多了嗎?"淳于髡說:"不對。你看同類的鳥,總是聚集在一起的;同類的野獸,也總是一道行走的。比如說,我們要尋找柴胡和桔梗這類藥草,如果到洼地上去尋找,哪怕尋一輩子,也得不到一株;如果到山裏去尋找,那就可以用車子來載運了。天下的事物,都是同類的相聚在一起的,我們人也是這樣。我淳于

137

髡總算是賢士吧，你要我挑選賢士，就好像到河裏去汲水，用火石去打火那樣容易。"

出自《戰國策》

Like Attracts Like

Birds of a Feather Flock Together

Said of people who fall into the same group because they are of a mind.

CHUNYU Kun of Qi of the Warring States Period recommended seven virtuous scholars to King Xuanwang in a single day. The King, who was surprised by what Chunyu did, said to him, "As people say, it is hard to recruit virtuous scholars. You would be reckoned lucky if you could find one such person after travelling a thousand *li*. Now you've recommended to me seven of them in one and the same day. Don't you think it is extraordinary?"

"Not at all," replied Chunyu. "As Your Majesty knows, birds of a feather flock together, and beasts of the same paws roam together. Also, if you try to find the medicinal herbs thorowax and balloonflower roots in a swamp, you would be looking for them all your life in vain. But if you go into the mountains, you can gather them by the cartload. Things of a kind come together, so do people of a mind. As for myself, who can be counted as a virtuous scholar, it is as easy for me to find virtuous scholars as it is to get water from a river or to get fire by striking a flint."

Anecdotes of the Warring States

金玉其外，敗絮其中
jīn yù qí wài, bài xù qí zhōng

外面如金似玉，裏面是爛棉花；比喻徒有其表。

　　明朝時候，有個賣水果的人，很會保存柑子。他保存的柑子，冬夏不爛。柑子的皮像玉一樣潤滑，顏色像金子一般黃亮，可是裏面却像破棉絮一樣。有個顧客質問他爲何欺騙人，賣水果的人笑了笑說：“世上欺騙人的人多得很，難道只有我一個嗎？那些腰裏佩着兵符，坐在虎皮椅子上耀武揚威的人，難道眞有帶兵打仗的本領嗎？那些頭戴烏紗帽，腰圍玉帶的人，難道眞有治理國家的本事嗎？現在，老百姓困苦已極，他們不去救濟，下面官吏胡作非爲，他們不去禁止。他們整天不幹事，耗費着百姓種的糧食。他們哪一個不是金玉其外，敗絮其中呢？您這位先生爲什麼看不到這些，却只看到我這樣一個賣水果的人呢？”買柑子的人聽了這番話就不再作聲了。

*《誠意伯文集》 明劉基（1311－1375）作。

Gold and Jade on the Outside but Rotten Cotton on the Inside

All That Glitters Is Not Gold

Said of something superficially attractive but actually worthless.

THERE was, during the Ming Dynasty, a fruit seller. His oranges were so well kept that they could last throughout the year. But although outwardly as smooth as jade and as shiny as gold, inwardly they were like rotten cotton.

When a customer asked him why he tried to deceive people, the pedlar replied with a smile, "Am I the only swindler in this world? No. There are many many others. Take, for instance, those cocky generals armed with tallies and sitting in chairs covered with tiger skin. Are they really capable of directing battles? And those officials wearing black gauze caps and jade belts — they really capable of running the country? They do nothing to help the common people who are now suffering. They do nothing to check the evil doings of their subordinates. They do nothing useful at all, but only eat the grain produced by the common people. Aren't they all as shiny as gold and jade without but like rotten cotton within? Why do you fix your eyes only on a fruit seller like me, instead of those I've just mentioned?"

This argument left the customer speechless.

Collected Works of the Earl of Loyalty *

*By Liu Ji (1311-75) of the Ming Dynasty.

140

兔 死 狗 烹
tù sǐ gǒu pēng

兔子死了，獵狗被烹來吃了；比喻為人效勞賣力，事後却被其殺害。

春秋時，楚國的文種和范蠡是非常要好的朋友，後來兩人都到越國去做官。公元前 494 年，越國被吳國戰敗，越王被俘。之後，越王在文種和范蠡的輔佐之下，勵精圖治，經過十年的艱苦奮鬥，使越轉弱為強，終於滅掉了吳國。越王復國後，范蠡便自行引退，跑到齊國去經商。文種自以為有功，不肯走。後來，范蠡寫了一封信給文種，勸他捨棄功名利祿，以免招災惹禍。信上說："飛鳥打光了，弓箭就被收藏起來；兔子打光了，獵狗就被殺了煮來吃。越王此人，只可同他共患難，不能同他共安樂。現在他用不着我們了，你為什麼還不快走呢？"文種沒有聽從范蠡的勸告，結果被越王殺害了。

出自《史記》

The Hounds Are Cooked When the Hares Have Been Bagged
Kicking Down the Ladder

Said of the slaying of servants who have outlived their usefulness.

WEN Zhong and Fan Li of the state of Chu during the Spring and Autumn Period were bosom friends. Both became officials in the state of Yue. In the year 494 B.C., Yue was defeated in a battle with the state of Wu and its king was taken prisoner. Later, aided by Wen Zhong and Fan Li, the Yue ruler worked hard for a whole decade. His kingdom became stronger and stronger until it conquered Wu.

After Yue's new success, Fan Li retired of his own accord and went to Qi where he became a trader. But Wen Zhong stayed behind, thinking that he had done meritorious service for Yue. Shortly after his departure from Yue, Fan Li wrote Wen Zhong a letter, advising him to give up his official position and high salary in order to avert misfortunes. He said, "When the birds have been shot down, the bow will be tucked away together with the arrows. When all the hares have been killed, the hounds will be cooked for food. The ruler of Yue is a man whose difficulties, not joys, one can share. We've now outlived our usefulness. So why don't you leave the state of Yue?"

Wen Zhong, who did not heed his friend's advice, later died at the hands of the Yue sovereign.

Records of the Historian

狐假虎威
hú jiǎ hǔ wēi

狐狸依仗老虎的威勢；比喻依附着別人的勢力欺壓人。

老虎在森林中捉住了一隻狐狸，便要吃牠。狡猾的狐狸對老虎說："我是天帝派到森林裏來做獸王的，你可不能吃我。"老虎看狐狸是這麼個小傢伙，會當獸王，着實有些不信。

狐狸說："你如果不相信，就跟我到林子裏去走一遭，看野獸見了我怕不怕。"老虎同意了。狐狸走在前面，老虎緊緊地跟着，一路走去。

森林中的野獸，看見老虎來了，都嚇得拼命地逃跑。狐狸便對老虎說："你看，沒有誰不怕我。"老虎說"你的威風真不小，牠們看見你，真的一下子都跑掉了。"其實，野獸怕的是老虎，哪裏是狐狸呢！

出自《戰國策》

The Fox Borrowing the Tiger's Might

An Ass in a Lion's Skin

Said of a person who bullies others by virtue of powerful connections.

THE tiger caught a fox in the forests and was about to devour it when the crafty fox said, "You can't eat me, for I have been appointed King of Beasts by the Heavenly Emperor." Seeing that the fox was such a small animal, the tiger could not very well believe its words.

"If you don't believe me," said the fox, "you can go with me into the forests and see if the animals do not flee from me." Agreeing to this, the tiger followed the fox into the woods. All the beasts ran away in fright at the sight of the tiger. "Now you can see for yourself," boasted the fox, "there's no animal that is not afraid of me." "You're really so mighty," admitted the tiger, "that they all flee for life when they see you coming."

The tiger did not realize that it was he himself, and not the fox, that the animals were afraid of.

Anecdotes of the Warring States

洛陽紙貴

luò yáng zhǐ guì

洛陽的紙價昂貴；比喻作品風行一時。

西晉時，文學家左思為了寫一篇以魏、蜀、吳的國都為內容的《三都賦》，遊歷了許多古城舊都，閱讀了大量資料，經過整整十年時間，終於把"三都賦"寫成了。但他的著作並未引起人們的重視。

左思十分懊喪，於是他去求見當時的名儒皇甫謐，呈上文稿。皇甫謐讀罷，十分讚賞，立即做了題序。左思再去拜見大學者張載和劉逵，請他們為《三都賦》做了註釋。《三都賦》一經名家認可，舉國轟動。富貴人家到處請人抄寫，紙張供應頓時緊張，洛陽的紙價因此也上漲了許多。

出自《晉書》

Paper Becoming Expensive in Luoyang

This describes a piece of writing that has become very popular.

ZUO Si, a writer who lived during the Western Jin Dynasty, wanted to write about the capitals of the kingdoms of Wei, Shu and Wu. He travelled to many cities and capitals, read a great number of reference books and spent ten years to finish the "Prose-Poem on the Three Capitals". But his work did not attract any attention.

Greatly distressed, Zuo Si went to see Huangfu Mi, a widely known scholar of his time, and presented his manuscript to him. After reading it, Huangfu expressed his admiration and wrote a preface to it there and then. Zuo Si then called on Zhang Zai and Liu Kui, two other great scholars, and asked them to write notes for the "Prose-Poem on the Three Capitals". Once recognized by famous names, the work created a great stir in the whole country. Rich families everywhere employed scribes to make copies of it. This resulted in a shortage of paper and pushed up its price in Luoyang.

History of the Jin Dynasty

前 倨 後 恭
qián jū hòu gōng

從前傲慢，現在謙恭；指以財產、地位來看待人的市儈表現。

戰國時，策士遊說之風甚盛，有個叫蘇秦的策士，去秦國遊說，由於秦王不採納他的建議，只得離開秦國回洛陽老家去。蘇秦的旅費已經花完，衣服破破爛爛。家裏的人，見他這樣狼狽地回來，都不理他。父母不跟他講話，妻子只顧織布，看也不看他一眼，他要求嫂子做飯，嫂子不但不給做，還奚落了他一頓。蘇秦很難過，於是發奮讀書。一年之後，蘇秦又去各國遊說，這次他改變了先前的主張，勸說各國聯合起來和秦國對抗。他先後說服了燕、趙等六國結成同盟，蘇秦擔任了這六個國家的宰相，聲勢煊赫一時。一次，他因公路過老家洛陽，他的父母趕到城外三十里外的大路口等候。回到家中，妻子躲在旁邊，不敢正眼看他。他嫂子便趴在地下，連連叩頭。蘇秦笑道："嫂子，妳為什麼從前那樣傲慢，現在又這樣謙恭！"他嫂子一邊哆嗦，一邊答道："如今你做了大官，發了大財哩！"

出自《戰國策》

Arrogant at First and Humble Later

Keeping Two Faces under One Hood

This describes the snobbishness of some people who treat a man according to his wealth and position.

AT the time of the Warring States, there was a prevailing practice of men of learning going about selling their ideas to the rulers of the states. One such man was named Su Qin. He went to the state of Qin to offer his advice to its King. The King refused to take him on, and Su had to leave and return to his home in Luoyang. The money he carried with him was gone, and his clothes were in tatters. Seeing the sorry plight he was in, his family gave him the cold shoulder. His parents refused to speak to him. His wife busied herself at the loom and ignored him. He asked his sister-in-law to cook some food for him but she refused with a snigger. Su Qin felt very sad and was determined to study harder. A year later, he went out on another idea-selling trip to the various states. He changed his stand and advised the various states to unite against Qin. Accordingly, he persuaded Yan, Zhao and four other states into forming an alliance, and he himself became the Prime Minister of all these six states. His fame resounded throughout the states. Once when he passed his home town Luoyang on an official journey, his parents waited for him by the roadside thirty *li* away from the city. When he was home, his wife stood at the side and did not dare look at him in the eye. His sister-in-law was prostrate on the floor and kowkowed without stopping. Su Qin smiled and asked her, "Sister-in-law, why were you so arrogant before and are so humble now?" Trembling, she answered, "You've become a high official and a very rich man."

Anecdotes of the Warring States

染於倉則倉，染於黃則黃
rǎn yú cāng zé cāng, rǎn yú huáng zé huáng

把絲丟進黑水裏就染成黑色，丟進黃水裏就染成黃色；比喻環境影響人的品質。

墨子經過一家染坊，看見幾個工人正在把一束束的絲投進染缸裏。墨子嘆息說："絲原來是雪白的，但丟進黑水裏就變成黑色，丟進黃水裏就變成黃色，所以染的時候，不可不小心謹慎啊！這個道理，對爲人處事都同樣有用。倘若一疏忽，就會像把絲染錯了顏色一樣，想要改變它，也很困難了。"

出自《墨子》

Becoming Black in a Black Dye and Becoming Yellow in a Yellow Dye
He Who Lives with Dogs Will Rise with Fleas

This implies that a man's character is influenced by environment.

WHEN Mo Zi was passing a dyeing workshop, he saw a few workers putting skeins of silk into vats of dye. He said with a sigh, "Silk is snow-white. When it is thrown into the black dye, it becomes black, and when it is thrown into the yellow dye, it becomes yellow. One must be very careful when dyeing a thing. The same is true of a man's conduct. The slightest carelessness is like dropping the silk in a wrong vat of dye. It's very difficult to change its colour once it is dyed."

The Book of Mo Zi

147

城下之盟

chéng xià zhī méng

在城下簽訂盟約；表示被迫求和，並接受屈辱條欵。

絞國是春秋時的一個小國，當時強大的楚國是它的近鄰。有一次，楚軍攻打絞國，包圍了絞國的都城。絞軍堅守，楚軍一時攻打不下，就在南門外駐紮下來。後來，楚軍採用了誘騙的辦法，把一些士兵偽裝成火伕，到山上去打柴，以引誘絞軍出城。絞軍發現後，果然出城追捕。楚軍乘機開往北門，截斷了絞軍的歸路，把絞軍打得大敗。絞國被迫在城下和楚國訂立了和約。

出自《左傳》

Treaty Signed at the City Wall

A City That Parleys Is Half Gotten

A treaty signed with the enemy who has reached the city wall means accepting humiliating terms of peace under duress.

THE state of Jiao in the Spring and Autumn Period was a small country, a close neighbour of the powerful state of Chu. The Chu army launched an attack on Jiao and encircled its capital. The Jiao soldiers stubbornly defended their city and the Chu army, unable to take it, set up camp outside its south gate. Later, the Chu army used a ruse, sending some soldiers, disguised as cooks, to gather firewood on the hills, in order to lure the Jiao forces out of the city. When the Jiao soldiers discovered the disguised cooks, they came out of the city to capture them. The Chu army took the opportunity to move to the north gate, cut their route of retreat and utterly defeated them. The state of Jiao was forced to sign a peace treaty with the state of Chu.

Zuo Qiuming's Chronicles

148

按 圖 索 驥

àn tú suǒ jì

依照圖示去尋找千里馬;原意爲墨守成規,現用來比喻根據綫索去尋找所需要的東西。

伯樂是戰國時的養馬能手,他最能識別馬的好壞。他把識別馬的方法寫了一部書叫《相馬經》,書中寫道:"千里馬的額角很豐滿,眼睛很大,四隻蹄子很端正。"

但是,他的兒子並不聰明。他拿着父親寫的《相馬經》去尋找千里馬。他走出門外,看見一隻大癩蛤蟆,連忙帶回來告訴父親說:"我找到一匹千里馬,和你《相馬經》上說的大致相同,只是蹄子不太端正。"伯樂看了又好氣又好笑,對他說:"這種馬太喜歡跳了,不能騎啊!"

出自《藝林學山》*

*《藝林學山》 明胡應麟(1551—1602)撰。

Finding a Fast Horse According to a Picture

Originally meaning following conventions, it now means looking for what one wants according to clues.

BO Le was a famous horse breeder in the Warring States Period. A good judge of horses, he wrote down his methods in the *Canon for Judging Horses*. "A fast steed has a well filled-out forehead, big eyes and four straight hooves," he wrote.

His son, who was not very bright, tried to find a fast horse according to what was described in his father's book. One day he saw a big toad outside the gate of his house. He

149

hurriedly took it home and said to his father, "I've found a good horse. It's roughly the same as you said in the *Canon.* Only its hooves are not quite straight." This made Bo Le both angry and want to laugh. "This 'horse' is too jumpy. One can't ride on its back," he said.

Forests of Arts and Mountains of Learning*

*By Hu Yinglin (1551-1602) of the Ming Dynasty.

指鹿爲馬
zhǐ lù wéi mǎ

把鹿説成馬；比喻故意混淆是非。

秦始皇死後，他的兒子胡亥繼位，歷史上稱爲秦二世。丞相趙高想篡奪帝位，但又怕羣臣不服，於是想測驗一下有多少人順從自己。一天，趙高牽了一頭鹿獻給秦二世，説這是一匹馬。秦二世笑着説："丞相錯了，這是一頭鹿，怎麼説是馬呢？"他接着問左右羣臣到底是鹿還是馬。羣臣都懼怕趙高,有的沉默不答,有的對趙高阿諛奉承硬說是馬,也有的人直說是鹿。事後,趙高把說鹿的人都一一殺害了。

出自《史記》

Calling a Stag a Horse

Talking Black into White

Meaning deliberately confounding right and wrong.

AFTER the First Emperor of the Qin Dynasty passed away, his son Hu Hai succeeded to the throne and became known in history as the Second Emperor of Qin. His Prime Minister Zhao Gao plotted to usurp the throne but was not sure if the other ministers would yield to him. He wanted to test them and see how many of them would succumb to him. One day, he brought a stag and presented it to the Emperor, saying that it was a horse. The Second Emperor laughed and said, "You're wrong. It's a stag. Why do you call it a horse?" He then asked his ministers if it was a stag or a horse. The ministers were fearful of Zhao Gao. Some kept their mouths shut, and some fawned on Zhao Gao and asserted that it was a horse. But there were some who spoke the truth and said that it was a stag. Later, Zhao Gao killed one by one all those who said that it was a stag.

Records of the Historian

英雄無用武之地
yīng xióng wú yòng wǔ zhī dì

英雄沒有施展才能的地方；指有本領沒處使用。

東漢末年，曹操統一了北方以後，乘勝南下，佔領了戰略要地荆州（在今湖北）。劉備被迫逃到了夏口（今漢口）。爲了說服東吳孫權聯合抗曹，劉備派諸葛亮出使東吳。

諸葛亮到了東吳，對孫權說："曹操擁有百萬大軍，威震全國。劉備這樣的英雄却沒有用武之地，逃到了夏口這個小地方。目前，形勢很緊張，或者是投降曹操，或者聯合抗曹，不能再猶疑了。"孫權接受了諸葛亮的意見，決定與劉備聯合起來抵抗曹操。

出自《資治通鑑》

A Hero Having No Place to Display His Prowess

A Square Peg in a Round Hole

This means having no place to use one's talents.

AFTER re-uniting the north at the end of the Eastern Han Dynasty, Cao Cao marched south and occupied the strategic town of Jingzhou (in modern Hubei Province). Liu Bei was forced to flee to Xiakou (today's Hankou). He sent Zhuge Liang to the state of Wu to try to persuade Sun Quan to join force with him against Cao Cao.

When Zhuge Liang reached the state of Wu, he said to Sun Quan, "Cao Cao has a great army a million strong and his might is known far and wide. Even a hero like Liu Bei has no place to display his prowess and had to flee to a small town like Xiakou. The situation now is critical. It's a question of either to surrender to Cao Cao or to unite against him. There's no time to hesitate." Sun Quan accepted Zhuge Liang's advice and decided to form an alliance with Liu Bei against Cao Cao.

History as a Mirror

苛政猛於虎
kē zhèng měng yú hǔ

苛政比老虎還兇猛。

孔子坐着馬車經過泰山腳下，看見路邊有一個婦女，正伏在一座新墳上，哭得非常傷心。孔子停下馬車，叫他的學生子路上前問問情由。子路走到墳前，問道："大嫂，聽你的哭聲，好像有重大的悲傷。"婦人抬起頭，抽泣着說："幾年前，我的公公被老虎咬死了；後來我的丈夫也被老虎咬死了；現在，我的兒子又被老虎咬

153

死了，我怎麼不悲傷呢？”孔子聽到這裏就問道：“這裏既然有老
虎傷人，爲什麼不搬走呢？”婦人回答道：“這兒地方偏僻，沒有
苛政。”孔子嘆了一口氣，對學生們說：“你們記住，苛刻的政治
比吃人的老虎還兇猛啊！”

出自《禮記》*

* 《禮記》 儒家經典，西漢人撰，記載秦漢以前的典章制度和各種禮儀。

A Tyrannical Government Is More Fearful Than Tigers

WHEN Confucius was passing the foot of Mount Taishan in a
horse cart, he saw a woman bending over a new grave, crying
brokenheartedly. He stopped the cart and asked his disciple
Zi Lu to go up and find out what had happened. Zi Lu
walked up to the grave and asked, "Madam, we heard you
cry. Something very sad must have happened." The woman
raised her head and, still sobbing, said, "A few years ago my
father-in-law was killed by a tiger. Later, my husband was
also killed by a tiger. Now it is my son who was killed by a
tiger. How could I not feel sad?" When Confucius heard what
the woman said, he asked, "Since there are tigers here, why
didn't you move to somewhere else?" The woman answered,
"This is an out-of-the-way place. The tyranny of the
government cannot reach us." Confucius sighed and said to
his disciples. "You must remember: A tyrannical government
is worse than man-eating tigers."

*The Book of Rites**

*A Confucian classic compiled in the Western Han Dynasty (206
B.C.-A.D. 24). It records the rites and institutions before the Qin and
Han dynasties.

南 柯 一 夢
nán kē yī mèng

在南柯做的一個夢；比喻一場空歡喜。

　　唐朝有個叫淳于棼的人。有一天。他在住宅南面的大槐樹下飲酒，不覺酩酊大醉，便睡着了。淳于棼夢見自己被槐安國王請去當了駙馬，做了南柯郡太守。他治理南柯二十年，享盡了榮華富貴。妻子生了五男二女，兒子也都做了大官，女兒嫁給豪門貴族。後來，敵人侵犯，他帶兵作戰，打了敗仗，國王猜疑他，便打發他回家。淳于棼驚醒過來，見夕陽斜照，桌子上的酒杯照樣擺在那裏，才知道原來是做了一場夢。他追尋夢境踪跡，原來所謂槐安國，就是他家住宅南面那棵大槐樹下的一個螞蟻窩，南柯郡則是槐樹南枝上另一處較小的蟻穴。

出自《南柯太守傳》*

* 《南柯太守傳》小說，唐人李公佐（約770－約850）撰。

Dream of Southern Branch
A Pipe Dream

This is an allusion to illusory joy.

IN the Tang Dynasty, there was a man named Chunyu Fen. One day while he was drinking under a big scholartree on the southern side of his house, he became drunk and dozed off. He dreamed that he was chosen by the King of the state of Scholartree to marry thyprincess and appointed governor of the prefecture of Southern Branch. He governed Southern Branch for twenty years and enjoyed all the glories and riches of life. His wife borne him five sons and two daughters. All the five sons became high officials and the two daughters married into powerful aristocrat families. Later, there was an enemy invasion. He engaged the enemy at the head of an army, but was defeated. The King began to distrust him and sent him to his home town. When Chunyu Fen woke up from his dream, he saw the cup he had been drinking with was still on the table bathed in the setting sun. Only then did he realize that he had been dreaming. He tried to look for the place where he had been in his dream and found that the so-called state of Scholartree was an ant hole under the scholartree on the southern side of his house, and the prefecture of Southern Branch was a smaller ant hole on the southern branch of the tree.

Biography of the Governor of Southern Branch *

*A story written by Li Gongzuo (c.770-c.850) of the Tang Dynasty.

南 轅 北 轍.
nán yuán běi zhé

車把朝南，車輪痕跡却向北；比喻做事不得法，結果適其反。

魏王準備攻打趙國，大夫季梁正去外地辦事，聽到這個消息，就馬上趕回來見魏王，對魏王說："我這次回來的時候，在太行山下看見一個人駕着馬車向北走，他告訴我說，他要到楚國去。我問他：'楚國在南方，你為什麼向北走？'他說：'我的馬好。'我說：'馬盡管好，但不是到楚國去的路啊！'他說：'我的路費充足。'我說：'路費雖多，但方向不對也不成啊！'他又說：'我的車夫趕車的本領好。'我說：'你這些條件越好，朝北走去，就離楚國越遠了。'"

魏王點頭稱是。季梁接着又說："大王想當各國君王的首領，那就該讓各國君王都信任您。現在大王憑着兵强馬壯，打算借攻打趙國來提高威望，這種錯誤的舉動越多，離開您的目標可就越遠，正像那個要到楚國去而逕直往北走的人一樣，總也到不了目的地。"

出自《戰國策》

South-Pointing Shafts and North-Going Tracks

Looking One Way and Rowing Another

While the carriage shafts point to the south, the tracks of the carriage lead to the north. This describes a contradictory situation resulting from an improper way of doing things and ending in the opposite of what one originally intended.

WHEN the King of Wei intended to attack the state of Zhao, his minister Ji Liang was away from the capital. When he heard of the King's intention, he immediately rushed back to see him. He said to the King of Wei, "On my way back, I saw a man at the foot of the Taihang Mountains riding in a carriage going to the north. He told me he wanted to go to the state of Chu. I said to him, 'The state of Chu is in the south. Why do you go towards the north?' He said, 'I've a good horse.' I said, 'Even if your horse is a good one, you are not on the right road to the state of Chu.' He said, 'I've plenty of money for the journey.' I said, 'Even if you have plenty of money, you're not travelling in the right direction.' He then told me, 'I've a good driver.' I said, 'Although you've all the favourable conditions, the farther you go towards the north, the farther you're away from the state of Chu.' "

The King nodded with approval, and Ji Liang continued, "As Your Majesty wishes to become the king of kings, it's important to win the confidence of the other kings in Your Majesty. Your Majesty now has a strong army and wishes to raise prestige by launching an attack on the state of Zhao. The more mistaken actions of this kind are taken, the further Your Majesty will be away from the objective. It's just like the man who wished to go to the state of Chu, but travelled

157

towards the north. He would never reach his destination."

Anecdotes of the Warring States

風馬牛不相及
fēng mǎ niú bù xiāng jí

走失的牛馬，也不會跑到對方的境內；比喻彼此毫不相干。

齊桓公領兵攻打蔡國。把蔡國打敗後，接着又進攻楚國。當時，
齊國在黃河以北，楚國在長江以南，彼此間毫無利害衝突。因此，
楚成王派人對齊桓公說：「你住北邊，我住南邊，兩國相隔很遠，
即使馬牛走失，也不會跑到對方境內，你為什麼要領兵攻打楚國？」
齊桓公無言以對，之後，接受了楚國的請求，結盟和好，撤回了抵
達楚國邊境的軍隊。

出自《左傳》

Even Straying Horses and Cows Do Not Cross into Each Other's Territories

As Different As Chalk Is from Cheese

This is a metaphor meaning two things having absolutely nothing to do with each other.

DUKE Huangong of Qi led his forces in an attack against the state of Cai. After defeating Cai, he started an attack against the state of Chu. The state of Qi in the north of the Huanghe River and the state of Qi in the south of the Changjiang River had no conflict of interests at all. King Chengwang of Chu, therefore, sent an envoy to the Duke of Qi to say to him, "You live in the north, and I in the south. Our two countries are separated by a great distance. Even our straying horses and cows don't cross into each other's territories. Why do you want to attack Chu?" The Duke was unable to answer. He accepted the King's request, signed a treaty of alliance with Chu and pulled back his army that had reached the Chu border.

Zuo Qiuming's Chronicles

食言而肥

shí yán ér féi

吞食諾言而致肥；比喻說話不算數，不履行諾言。

春秋時，魯國有個大臣叫孟武伯，他一貫說話不算數。有一次，魯哀公舉行宴會，在宴會上，孟武伯見哀公寵幸的臣子郭重也在座，就對郭重說："你為什麼吃得這樣胖呀？"魯哀公聽了很不高興，就借機諷刺孟武伯說："他經常吞吃自己的諾言，哪能不胖呢？"

出自《左傳》

Growing Fat by Eating One's Words

Going Back on One's Words

This is said of someone who goes back on his words.

IN the Spring and Autumn Period, there was a court official named Meng Wubo in the state of Lu. He was known for always going back on his words. Once Duke Aigong of Lu gave a banquet. When Meng saw that the Duke's favourite minister Guo Zhong was also at the banquet, he said to Guo, "What do you eat that has made you grow so fat?" The Duke was annoyed. "He often eats his words. That's why he's grown fat," said the Duke sarcastically.

Zuo Qiuming's Chronicles

負 荆 請 罪
fù jīng qǐng zuì

背着可以打人的荊條，請求對方懲罰；比喻主動向別人認錯、道歉。

戰國時，趙王有兩個忠勇愛國、才能出眾的賢臣：一個是國相藺相如，一個是大將廉頗。

藺相如因出色地完成對秦國的外交工作，深得趙王讚許，被任命爲國相，位居上卿，比廉頗的官銜還高一點。廉頗心裏不服，對人說：“我這個大將，是出生入死，在戰場上拼了多少次性命得來的，不像藺相如光憑一張嘴！如今他居然爬到我的上頭了，我要遇見他，非給他個難看不可。”

藺相如聽到這話，就經常留意，避開廉頗，不和他見面。別人以爲藺相如害怕廉頗，廉頗也頗得意。可是藺相如說：“秦王那樣的威勢，都嚇不了我，我哪裏會怕廉頗將軍？今天，秦王不敢侵犯趙國，就是因爲我和廉頗團結一致。如果我跟他鬧意見，互相攻擊，那正是秦王所歡迎的。我之所以避開廉頗，是以國事爲重，把個人恩怨放在一邊啊！"

這些話傳到了廉頗耳朵裏，廉頗非常感動，也覺得慚愧，於是就袒露着背，背着荊條，親自到藺相如家裏請罪，請藺相如用荊條狠狠地打他。藺相如沒有打他，也沒有責備他。從此，兩人成了非常好的朋友。

出自《史記》

Carrying a Birch and Asking for Punishment
Kissing the Rod

This describes someone who admits his mistake and offers apologies on his own initiative.

THE King of the state of Zhao in the Warring States Period had two loyal, courageous and patriotic ministers, who were men of extraordinary talents. One of them was Lin Xiangru, the Prime Minister, and the other was General Lian Po.

For his outstanding diplomatic work in dealing with the state of Qin, Lin Xiangru won the approval of the King and was made the Prime Minister, an official position slightly higher than that of Lian Po. Lian Po held a grudge against it and said to others, "I'm a general. I won my rank on the battlefield, risking my life in untold dangers. All Lin Xiangru can do it to wag his tongue, and he's holding a position higher than mine. I'm going to shame him when I see him."

When this reached Lin's ear he was very careful and intentionally avoided Lian Po. Others thought he was afraid of Lian Po, and Lian Po himself was overjoyed. But Lin said, "I was not scared even by the overbearing King of the state of Qin. Why should I be afraid of General Lian Po? The state of Qin doesn't dare invade the state of Zhao because Lian Po and I are united as one man. If we allow ourselves to be

161

swayed by personal feelings and attack each other, that would play into the hands of Qin. I avoid Lian Po because I think the affairs of the state is more important. Personal feelings should be put aside."

When this was relayed to Lian Po, he was deeply moved and felt ashamed of himself. He bared his back, shouldered a birch and came to Lin's house to apologize, asking Lin to punish him by beating him with the birch. Lin did not beat or reproach him. The two became close friends.

Records of the Historian

後 來 居 上
hòu lái jū shàng

把後來的放在上面；比喻後來的人超過先前的。

汲黯、公孫弘和張湯都是漢武帝的臣子。當汲黯身居高位時，公孫弘和張湯還是小官。後來，公孫弘和張湯都被提拔了：公孫弘當了丞相，張湯做了御史大夫。原來汲黯手下的屬吏，有的也與他並列了，有的甚至超過了他。汲黯心胸狹窄，很不滿意。一次，他見到漢武帝時說：“您用人好像堆積柴草一樣，把後來的放在上面。”漢武帝聽了，沒有理他。

出自《史記》

A Late Comer Occupies a Better Place

The Best Is Behind

Used in reference to what comes from behind and surpasses what is in front.

Ji An, Gongsun Hong and Zhang Tang all served under Emperor Wudi of the Western Han Dynasty. When Ji An held a high position, the other two were still petty officials. But later Gongsun Hong was promoted to be Prime Minister and Zhang Tang chief censor. Some of Ji An's former subordinates were also given posts of the same level as his or even became his superiors.

Out of jealousy, Ji An said to Emperor Wudi, "Your Majesty appoints officials in the same way as one piles up straw, putting what comes late on top of what is already there."

The Emperor paid no attention to this unreasonable allusion.

Records of the Historian

狡兔三窟

jiǎo tù sān kū

狡猾的兔子有三個窩；比喻藏身的地方多，便於逃避災禍。

齊國宰相孟嘗君派他的門客馮諼到他的封地薛邑去收債。馮諼到薛邑後，不但沒有討債，反而假傳遵照孟嘗君的命令把債契燒毀。

孟嘗君知道後，很不高興。一年後，孟嘗君被齊王免去宰相職務，只得回到薛邑去。當他離薛地還有一百里光景的時候，當地百姓全都扶老攜幼前來歡迎。孟嘗君很受感動，嘆服馮諼是個有遠見的人。馮諼說：“狡猾的兔子要為自己準備下三個藏身的洞，才能免被捕殺。現在你才有一個洞，還不能高枕無憂，我願替你再造兩個洞。”於是，馮諼到了魏國，對魏王說：“孟嘗君很有本領，哪個國家把他請去治理國家，那個國家就一定會富強。”魏王聽了，就派使者帶上禮物來請孟嘗君。一連三次，孟嘗君都不應允。齊王看到魏國這樣重視孟嘗君，就仍請他做了宰相。

之後，馮諼又建議孟嘗君向齊王請求在薛邑建立一座宗廟，把先王祭祀祖宗的器物放在那裏，以標誌薛邑永遠是他的封地。宗廟落成後，馮諼對孟嘗君說：“現在三個洞穴都造好了，你可以安安穩穩地過日子了。”

出自《戰國策》

A Cunning Rabbit Has Three Holes
The Mouse That Hath but One Hole Is Wickly Taken

Meaning having more than one place to hide in time of danger.

PRINCE Meng Chang, Prime Minister of the state of Qi, sent Feng Xuan, one of his followers, to his fief Xueyi to collect debts. When Feng got there, instead of collecting the debts, he burned all the receipts of loans and said to the people there that it was Prince Meng Chang's order to do so. When the Prince learned of this, he was displeased. A year later, the Prince was removed from his post by the King of Qi and had to return to his fief Xueyi. When he was still a hundred *li* from Xueyi, the local people, both young and old, all came out to welcome him. The Prince was deeply moved and realized that Feng Xuan was a far-sighted man. Feng said to him, "A cunning rabbit has three holes to hide itself in order

164

to avoid being captured and killed. Now you have only one hole. It's not time to relax. I'm willing to build two more holes for you." Feng went to the state of Wei and said to its King, "Prince Meng Chang is a man of great ability. Whatever country can enlist his services will certainly become powerful and prosperous." The King of Wei was convinced. He sent an envoy with gifts to Prince Meng Chang inviting him to work for the state of Wei. The envoy came three times, but the Prince still refused to go to Wei. Seeing that the state of Wei thought so highly of Prince Meng Chang, the King of Qi agains asked him to be his Prime Minister.

Later, Feng Xuan advised the Prince to ask the King of Qi to have a royal family temple built in Xueyi and place there the sacrificial vessels used by the former King, which meant that Xueyi would be the Prince's permanent fief. When the temple was completed, Feng said to the Prince, "Now that all the three holes are in place, you may pass your days in peace."

Anecdotes of the Warring States

疾風知勁草
jí fēng zhī jìng cǎo

在大風中才能看出堅韌的草；比喻在嚴重的考驗下，才能看出一個人的堅強意志。

東漢時，劉秀起兵反對王莽，部隊過潁陽時，當時有個叫王霸的人，帶領一羣朋友去見劉秀說："將軍帶領正義之師討伐王莽，我們仰慕您的威名，願意參加您的隊伍。"劉秀高興地收納了他們。王霸跟隨劉秀，立了不少戰功。後來劉秀在戰鬥中不斷失利，在潁陽和王霸一起跟從劉秀的幾十個人，都一個個悄悄地溜走了，只有王霸仍忠心耿耿地為劉秀效勞。有次劉秀無限感慨地對王霸說："過去在潁陽投奔我的人都跑光了，只有你還獨自留在這裏，真是只有在大風中才能顯出堅韌的草來啊！"

出自《後漢書》

A Gale Tells the Hardiness of a Blade of Grass
A Good Seaman Is Known in Bad Weather

This compares to a man of strong will who can stand severe tests.

IN the Eastern Han Dynasty, Liu Xiu raised an army to fight against Wang Mang. When his army passed Yingyang, a local man named Wang Ba came to see him with a group of his friends. He said to Liu Xiu, "You're at the head of a righteous army fighting against Wang Mang. We admire your great name and want to join your army." Liu Xiu was very pleased to take them. Wang Ba followed Liu Xiu and performed many meritorious feats. Later, when Liu Xiu suffered a series of defeats, the several score of people who

166

joined him with Wang Ba slipped away one after another. One day, Liu Xiu sighed with emotion and said to Wang Ba, "All those who joined me in Yingyang have left. Only you are here. It is true that only a gale can tell the hardiness of a blade of grass."

History of the Later Han Dynasty

兼聽則明，偏信則暗
jiān tīng zè mìng, piān xìn zè àn

聽取多方面的意見，就會明智；聽取單方面的意見，就會昏暗。

魏徵是唐太宗時的一位大臣。他頗有學識，並且敢於向皇帝直言勸諫，在朝廷中有很高的威信。有一次，唐太宗問他："人君怎樣才能明智，怎樣就會昏暗？"魏徵回答說："廣泛地聽取各方面的意見，就明智；只愛聽少數人的話，就會昏暗。"並列舉了歷史上一些賢明的君主作例子。魏徵還寫了《諫十思疏》，勸導太宗要經常自省，兢兢業業，關心百姓痛苦。後來魏徵死了。太宗很難過，感慨地說："魏徵好比一面鏡子，能照見我的得失，魏徵一死，我就無法再照了。"

出自《資治通鑑》

Listen to Many Sides and You Will Be Enlightened; Heed Only a Few and You Will Be Benighted

WEI Zheng was a minister during the reign of Emperor Taizong of the Tang Dynasty. He was a learned man, who dared to speak out and point out where the Emperor was wrong. He therefore enjoyed very high prestige at court.

"What makes the ruler of a country wise and what makes him foolish?" Emperor Taizong once asked him. "Listen to many sides and you will be enlightened; heed only a few and you will be benighted," answered Wei Zheng. He named a few enlightened emperors in history as examples. Wei Zheng also wrote "Advice to the Emperor to Think About Ten Things", reminding Taizhong to examine himself, work conscientiously and concern himself with the hardships of the people. Later, when Wei Zheng died, the Emperor was very sad. With emotion, he said, "Wei Zheng was like a mirror. I could see my success and failure in it. Now Wei Zheng is dead, I can no longer see myself in the mirror."

History as a Mirror

班 門 弄 斧
bān mén nòng fǔ

在魯班（古代著名巧匠）門前揮舞斧頭；比喻在大行家面前賣弄本領。

明朝時，有個叫梅之渙的文人，到采石（在今安徽當塗縣境）去憑弔唐代大詩人李白之墓，見墓前被遊人題滿了詩句。他感到這些遊人在大詩人墓上這樣亂題歪詩，實在太不自量了。於是，他做了一首詩，詩句是："采石江邊一堆土，李白之名高千古，來來往往一首詩，魯班門前弄大斧。"用來譏諷這些遊人。

Wielding the Adze Before Ban's Door
Teaching One's Grandmother How to Suck Eggs

Wielding the adze at the master carpenter Lu Ban's front door alludes to displaying one's inferior skill in front of a great master.

IN the Ming Dynasty, a man of letters named Mei Zhihuan travelled to Caishi (in today's Dangtu County, Anhui Province) to pay homage to Li Bai, the great poet of the Tang Dynasty, at his tomb. Mei saw the tomb was littered with doggerels scribbled by visitors. Indignant at the presumptuousness, he wrote a poem himself to ridicule the would-be poets. His poem reads:

"A pile of earth by the river at Caishi is Li Bai's tomb.
His name will resound for a thousand years as a great poet.
Passers-by like to write a doggerel to his memory.
Are they not flaunting their skill with the adze before Lu Ban's door?"

草木皆兵
cǎo mù jiē bīng

把草木看成士兵；形容緊張恐怖，人心惶惶。

東晉時，前秦佔領了中國的北部地區，和偏安東南的晉朝，形成南北對峙的局面。

前秦王符堅，當時氣勢甚盛，曾親自率領八十萬大軍，大舉南侵，企圖統治全中國。東晉派大將謝石、謝玄等領兵八萬前去抵抗，雙方兵力相差如此懸殊，晉朝的很多官員，都很害怕。那時符堅已攻破壽陽（今安徽北部的壽縣），晉軍避開正面攻勢，襲擊洛澗地區（今安徽淮南東南）並渡過了澗水，打敗了秦軍左翼部隊，首先挫敗了秦軍的銳氣。

晉軍各路軍隊，乘勝前進。這時，秦王符堅不像起初那樣驕傲了。他和他的弟弟符融登上壽陽城樓，但見晉軍佈陣嚴整，十分威武，遙望城西北的八公山上，以為山上的草木，都是晉兵。他對符融說："敵人很強大啊！誰說晉軍不行呢？"

晉軍到了淝水，要求符堅略向後撤，以便渡河在河東岸決戰。符堅想利用晉軍渡河之機發動襲擊，因此同意了晉軍的要求。誰知撤退命令一經傳出，秦軍大亂，都爭相逃命，晉軍尾隨攻擊，秦軍大敗，死亡的人有十之七、八。

這就是歷史上有名的戰役"淝水之戰"。

出自《晉書》

Every Bush and Tree Looks Like an Enemy
Taking Every Bush for a Bugbear

This describes a state of extreme nervousness.

IN the Eastern Jin time, the whole of the northern part of China was seized by the Former Qin Dynasty and the Jin was pushed to the southeast. The two dynasties stood face to face, one in the north and the other in the south.

Fu Jian, the King of the Former Qin was very arrogant. He led an army of 800,000 and marched against the south in an attempt to put the whole of China under his rule. The Eastern Jin generals Xie Shi, Xie Xuan and others resisted him with an army of 80,000. As there was a great disparity of strength between the two armies, many court officials of the

170

Jin were worried. Fu Jian had by then taken Shouyang
(today's Shouxian in northern Anhui Province). The Jin army
avoided a frontal encounter, launched an attack on the
Luojian area (to the southeast of today's Huainan, Anhui)
and crossed the Jianshui River. It defeated the Qin army on
the left flank and initially deflated its arrogance.

The different units of the Jin army advanced further after
their victory. Fu Jian was now not as proud as he was at first.
He and his brother Fu Rong mounted a tower on the city
wall of Shouyang and saw that the Jin army was positioned
in a mighty array. When he looked afar towards Mount
Bagong, he thought every bush and tree on the mountain was
an enemy. He said to his brother Fu Rong, "The enemy is
very powerful. Who said the Jin army is no good?"

When the Jin army reached the Feishui River, they
demanded that Fu Jian withdraw a short distance so that the
Jin army could cross the river and fight a decisive battle on
the eastern bank of the river. Fu Jian intended to launch a
surprise attack while the Jin army was crossing the river, and
therefore agreed to the Jin army's request. However, when
the order to withdraw was given, the Qin army plunged into a
great confusion, all the soldiers trying to run away to save
their dear lives. The Jin army attacked from behind. The Qin
army suffered a debacle losing seven or eight out of every
ten. This was the famous Battle of the Feishui River in
history.

History of the Jin Dynasty

起 死 回 生
qǐ sǐ huí shēng

把死了的人重新救活；形容醫術高明。

　　春秋時代，有一位著名醫生，名扁鵲。有一次，他路過虢國，
聽說太子突然患病死去。扁鵲聽了很懷疑，便和弟子一同向王宮走
去。向一位臣子問清了太子的病情後，扁鵲說："我是個醫生，我

171

能把太子救活過來。"臣子不信，扁鵲說："你以為我是胡說嗎？你進去看看，太子的下半截身子還是溫暖的哩！"

號君聽到後，立即親自出來迎接扁鵲。扁鵲勸國王不要難過。他給太子診斷以後說："這是尸厥症，現在還可以治。"說着，扁鵲叫弟子備針，他給太子的頭、手、脚等處扎了幾針。一會兒，太子慢慢甦醒過來。後來，太子又連續服了扁鵲開的藥，二十多天後，就恢復了健康。

這消息一傳開，人們都誇扁鵲，說他能夠把死人治活。可是扁鵲說："我並不能醫治死人，這是由於他沒有真正死去，所以我才能使他活過來。"

出自《史記》

Bringing the Dead Back to Life

Snatching from the Jaws of Death

This is said of a doctor of extraordinary skill.

THERE was a famous doctor named Bian Que in the Spring and Autumn Period. One day when he was passing through the state of Guo, he heard that the Prince had suddenly died from illness. He was doubtful about the circumstance of the death. So he and his disciple together went to the palace. After asking about the symptoms of the Prince's illness from a court official, Bian Que said, "I'm a doctor. I think I can bring the Prince back to life." The court official would not believe him. Bian Que said, "Do you think I'm talking nonsense? You can go in and see. The lower half of the Prince's body is still warm."

When the King of Guo heard him, he immediately came out to welcome him. Bian Que told the King not to grieve. After having examined the Prince, he said, "He's gone into a coma. It's not too late for treatment yet." He asked his disciple to get his needles ready, and he applied them at several places on the Prince's head, hands and feet. Presently,

172

the Prince gradually recovered consciousness. After taking the medicine prescribed by Bian Que for more than twenty days, he was able to return completely to health.

The news soon spread far and wide. People praised Bian Que, saying that he was able to bring the dead back to life. But Bian Que said, "I cannot bring the dead back to life. I was able to revive him because he did not actually die in the first place."

Records of the Historian

桔化爲枳
jú huà wéi zhǐ

桔樹變成枳樹；比喻環境能影響人的品質。

有一次，晏子代表齊國出使楚國，楚王設宴招待他。在飲酒的時候，有兩個兵士捆着一名犯人走進大廳，跪在楚王面前，楚王問道："你們綁的是什麼人？"兵士答道："是齊國人，一個盜竊犯。"楚王轉過頭來看着晏子說："哦！是你們齊國人，齊國人都是慣於偷東西的吧！"晏子知道這是楚王有意諷譏他，站起來回答說："我聽說桔樹生在江南，就結出桔子，如果移到江北，就長成枳樹。它和桔樹的葉子很相似，但果實的味道大不相同。這是什麼原因呢？因爲江南和江北的水土不一樣，老百姓生長在齊國，從來不會偷東西，到了楚國却會偷。請問，這不是楚國的水土使人變得善於偷竊了嗎？"

出自《晏子春秋》*

* 《晏子春秋》 戰國時人搜集關於晏子的言行編輯而成。

173

Sweet Orange Turns into Trifoliate Orange

Meaning environment may change a man's character.

WHEN Yan Zi came to the state of Chu as an envoy from the state of Qi, he was received by the King of Chu at a banquet. While they were drinking, two soldiers brought a tied-up criminal to the King in the hall. "Who's the man you've tied up?" asked the King of Chu. "He's a thief from the state of Qi," replied the soldiers. The King turned to Yan Zi and said, "Why, he's your countryman. Men in the state of Qi must all be fond of stealing!" Seeing that the King of Chu was being sarcastic, Yan Zi stood to his feet and said, "I heard that when oranges are planted south of the river, they bear sweet oranges. When they are planted north of the river, they turn into trifoliate orange trees. Although their leaves are similar, their fruit is quite different. Why is that so? Because water and soil on either side of the river are different. People in the state of Qi never steal. But when they come to the state of Chu, they learn to steal. May I ask, is this not the water and soil of the state of Chu that have turned people into thieves?"

Anecdotes of Yan Zi*

*Recorded and compiled by writers of the Warring States Period (475-221 B.C.).

唇亡齒寒
chún wáng chǐ hán

嘴唇沒了，牙齒就會感到寒冷；比喻利害關係十分密切。

晉國舉兵攻打虢國，但晉軍要開往虢國必須通過虞國的國境。於是，晉國的國君獻公用美玉和駿馬，做爲禮物，送給虞國，要求借路。

虞王身邊的一位臣子宮子奇勸虞王說：“不要答應他們！虞國和虢國好像嘴唇和牙齒一樣，互相關聯着。嘴唇沒有了，牙齒豈能自保？如果借路去攻打虢國，虢國滅亡了，我們虞國也會跟着被滅掉。”

虞王不聽，接受了晉國的禮物，同意晉軍通過。晉軍攻取了虢國之後，回過來又把虞國也滅掉了。虞公被俘，美玉和駿馬，仍然回到了晉獻公的手裏。

出自《左傳》

When the Lips Are Gone, the Teeth Are Exposed

This idiom describes closely related interests.

THE state of Jin amassed an army, intending to attack the state of Guo. But to reach Guo, the Jin army had to pass through the state of Yu. Duke Xiangong, the ruler of Jin, delivered gifts of beautiful jades and fast horses to Yu requesting the passage of his army.

Gong Ziqi, a minister close to the King of Yu, advised the King, "We mustn't give them the permission. The states of Yu and Guo are closely related as the lips and teeth. When the lips are gone, the teeth cannot survive. If we give passage to the Jin army, the state of Guo will be subjugated, and Yu will fall after Guo."

The King of Yu did not listen to his advice. He took the gifts from Jin and permitted the Jin army to pass through. After overrunning the state of Guo, the Jin army destroyed the state of Yu too. The King of Yu was captured, and the gifts of jades and horses were taken back by Duke Xiangong of Jin.

Zuo Qiuming's Chronicles

破釜沉舟
pò fǔ chén zhōu

把鍋打碎，把船鑿沉；形容誓死不退的決戰精神。

秦朝末年，各地紛紛反秦。秦將章邯率領的軍隊在大敗楚軍之後，又北上進攻趙國。楚王派宋義、項羽率軍前去救援。宋義畏懼秦軍，在漳河邊上停留了四十多天，不敢前進。項羽殺了宋義，立即命令軍隊渡過漳河。渡河之後，項羽又下令鑿沉船隻，打碎飯鍋，把宿營地燒毀，每人只帶三天的口糧，表示不打勝仗，決不生還。楚軍一到前綫，立即切斷了秦軍的運糧後路。之後，與秦軍在鉅鹿城下經過九次激烈戰鬥，終於把强大的秦軍殲滅了。從此，項羽名聲大振，成爲各地抗秦軍隊的領袖。

出自《史記》

Breaking the Cauldrons and Sinking the Boats

Burning One's Boats

This describes the determination to fight a decisive battle and never to retreat.

AT the end of the Qin Dynasty, the people rose in revolt everywhere. After defeating the Chu army, the Qin general Zhang Han and his army marched north to attack the state of Zhao. The King of Chu dispatched Song Yi and Xiang Yu with an army to go to its rescue. Song Yi was afraid of the Qin army. He stayed by the Zhanghe River for more than forty days and did not dare to advance. Xiang Yu killed Song Yi and ordered the army to cross the river immediately. After crossing the river, he ordered that all the boats be sunk, all the cauldrens smashed and the camp site burned. Each soldier was to carry only three days' ration, showing the determination never to return alive without winning victory. When the Chu army reached the battle front, it cut off the Qin army's route of supply. Later, it engaged the Qin army in nine ferocious battles at the city of Julu and destroyed the powerful Qin army. After that Xiang Yu rose greatly in prestige and became a leader of the armies fighting against Qin.

Records of the Historian

破鏡重圓
pò jìng chóng yuán

破裂的鏡子，又重新合在一起；比喻夫妻分離後，又重新團聚。

南北朝末年，北周丞相楊堅，殺了北周皇帝，建立了隋朝；接着，又舉兵南下，進攻南陳。南陳有個官吏，叫徐德言，他的妻子

177

樂昌公主是南陳皇帝的妹妹。他眼看國家快要滅亡了，怕在戰亂中跟妻子離散後，難以相會。他取過一面鏡子，一剖兩半，一半交給樂昌公主，一半自己留下。他們互相約定，在離散後的第一個元宵節，在隋朝都城街上出售破鏡，藉以尋訪對方。

南陳被滅亡以後，樂昌公主被俘，送往都城，被迫在皇帝的叔父楊素的府中服役。徐德言懷念妻子，不辭長途跋涉，來都城尋訪。到了約定日期，果然看見有一個老人，出賣半面破鏡，經過驗証，和自己的那一半，完全相合。問了老人，知道樂昌公主已是楊素的侍女，料想無法再見，就在鏡子上題了一首詩：“鏡與人俱去，鏡歸人未歸，無復嫦娥影，空留明月輝。”樂昌公主見了這首詩，萬分悲痛。楊素知道了這件事，也很同情他們，就把徐德言找來，讓他把妻子領回去，重新團聚。

出自《本事詩》 *

* 《本事詩》 唐孟棨作。

A Broken Mirror Rejoined

This alludes to the reunion of husband and wife after an enforced separation.

AT the end of the Southern and Northern Dynasties, Yang Jian, Prime Minister of the Northern Zhou Dynasty, killed the Emperor of Northern Zhou and founded the Sui Dynasty. He then sent his army south to attack the Southern Chen Dynasty. There was an official at the Southern Chen court named Xu Deyan. His wife Princess Lechang was the Southern Chen Emperor's younger sister. Seeing that his country was about to perish, he feared that he and his wife might become separated in the turmoil and never meet again. He found a mirror, broke it into two, handed one half to the princess and kept the other half himself. They agreed that on the first Lantern Festival after their separation, they would try to sell the broken mirror in the street of the capital of the

Sui Dynasty to seek out each other.

When the Southern Chen fell, Princess Lechang was taken prisoner and carried to the Sui capital, where she was forced to work as a servant maid in the house of Yang Su, the Emperor's uncle. Xu Deyan missed his wife and took a long and hard journey to the capital to look for her. On the appointed day, he saw an old man trying to sell a broken mirror. After examining it, he found that the broken half of a mirror matched exactly his own half. He questioned the old man and was told that the Princess was now serving as a maid in the house of Yang Su. He concluded that there was no way for him and his wife to see each other again. So he wrote a poem on the other half of the mirror, which reads:

"Both the mirror and my love are gone.

Now the mirror is here, but not my love.

Nowhere shall I see her,

Though the moon still shines overhead."

When Princess Lechang saw the poem, she was overcome by sorrow. Later, Yang Su learned this and was sympathetic with them. He managed to find Xu and allowed his wife to leave and reunite with him.

*Narrative Poems**

*By Meng Qi of the Tang Dynasty (618-907).

179

退避三舍
tuì bì sān shè

退到三舍（九十里）以外的地方；比喻對人忍讓，不敢與爭。

春秋時，晉國公子重耳，逃奔到楚國避難。楚王設宴招待，並問他道："公子如果回到晉國做了國君，怎樣報答我呢？"重耳回答說："玉帛珍寶，你們有的是，我們用的都是你們剩下的東西，還用什麼來報答您呢？"楚王說："雖然如此，總也可以說說用什麼報答吧。"重耳說："要是托你的福回到了晉國，將來如果晉楚兩國發生戰爭，我一定叫晉軍退三舍路程，以報答您對我的盛情。"

重耳回國後做了國君，稱爲晉文公。後來，楚國侵犯宋國，晉國出兵救援。當晉楚兩軍交戰的時候，重耳爲實踐自己的諾言，果然命令晉軍向後退了九十里。

出自《左傳》

Withdrawing Three *She*
Keeping One's Distance

To withdraw three she (a she *is thirty* li) *means to exercise forbearance and avoid entering into rivalry.*

PRINCE Chong Er of the state of Jin in the Spring and Autumn Period once took refuge in the state of Chu. At a banquet given in his honour, the King of Chu asked him, "How would you repay me when Your Highness goes back to Jin and becomes the ruler there?" Chong Er said, "You have plenty of silk and satin, jade and jewels. What we have there are leftovers from those of yours. I really don't know what I shall repay you." But the King insisted upon an answer. "Even if that is so, you still can think of something to pay me back," said he. Chong Er then said, "If I can re-establish myself in Jin with your blessing, I shall repay your kindness by ordering my army to withdraw three *she* in case there is a conflict between our two states."

After the Prince returned to the state of Jin, he indeed became the ruler of his country and became known as Duke Wengong of Jin. Years later, when the state of Chu invaded the state of Song, the state of Jin dispatched an army to Song's rescue. As the armies of Jin and Chu confronted each other on the battlefield, Chong Er indeed ordered the Jin army to withdraw ninety *li* as he had promised.

Zuo Qiuming's Chronicles

郢 書 燕 說
yǐng shū yàn shuō

燕人解說郢人的書信；比喻望文生義，胡亂解釋。

有一個人，住在楚國的郢都。有一天晚上，他給在燕國做相國的朋友寫信，蠟燭不亮，於是他對拿蠟燭的人說："舉燭！"這時，他不注意，把"舉燭"兩字也寫到信上去了。

他的朋友接到這封信，猜不透"舉燭"兩字是什麼意思。後來，他自言自語地說："啊！我明白了，'舉燭'是崇尚光明的意思，也就是要我規勸國王選拔和重用正直的人。"於是，他把這意見告訴了國王。國王採納了他的建議，把國家治理得很好。國家是治理好了，但和這封信原來寫的意思却毫不相干。

出自《韓非子》

Yan's Interpretation of a Ying Letter

Meaning a misinterpretation of the original without really understanding it.

A man living in Ying in the state of Chu wrote a letter one evening to his friend who was the Prime Minister of the state of Yan. As the candle was not bright enough, he said to his attendant, "Raise the candle." Saying so he absent-mindedly included the words "Raise the candle" in the letter.

When his friend received the letter, he could not make out what he meant by "Raise the candle". Later, the Prime Minister said to himself, "Ah, I understand. 'Raise the candle' means love of brightness. He was telling me to advise the King to select and put in office those who are honest and upright. He then told what he thought to the King. The King accepted his advice and the state become very well governed. But this really had nothing to do with what was meant in the letter.

The Book of Han Fei Zi

胸 有 成 竹
xiōng yǒu chéng zhú

胸中有竹子的形象；比喻在處理事情之先，心裏已有了主意。

宋朝有個畫家叫文與可，善於畫竹子。他在自己的住房周圍，栽了許多竹子，一年四季，常去觀察竹子的不同姿態與變化。因而對竹子的形象非常熟悉，所以他畫出的竹子生動逼眞。《宋史·文同傳》里說："當時人們紛紛請他畫竹，送去的絹，堆了一大堆，他有時厭煩地把它們扔在地上。"

當時，文與可的一位很要好的朋友晁補之寫了一首詩讚揚他的繪竹藝術，其中有兩句："與可畫竹時，胸中有成竹。"

Having the Picture of Bamboo in One's Mind

Meaning to be mentally prepared to cope with a situation according to a preconceived plan.

THE Song Dynasty painter Wen Yuke was good at painting pictures of bamboo. He planted many bamboos around his house and observed closely the changes in their appearance in all the four seasons of the year. He was therefore very familiar with the image of bamboo. The pictures of bamboo he painted looked both lively and real. "The Biography of Wen Tong [Yuke]" in the *History of the Song Dynasty* says that many people came to ask him to paint pictures of bamboo. He was sometimes so annoyed by the big pile of silk they had brought with them that he threw all of it to the floor.

Wen Yuke had a very good friend named Chao Buzhi. In praise of Wen's paintings of bamboo, Chao wrote in a poem:
"When Yuke paints bamboo,
He has the pictures of bamboo in his mind."

鬼 由 心 生
guǐ yóu xīn shēng

鬼是心裏想出來的；比喻胆小多疑。

從前有個人，叫涓蜀梁，他生性愚蠢，胆子又小。有一次，他在一個明亮的月夜走路，偶而低一下頭，看到自己的影子，以爲是一個魔鬼趴在地上；再一抬頭，看見自己額前頭髮，又以爲是一個妖怪站在前面。他嚇得掉頭就跑，一路上累得精疲力竭，剛剛跑到家裏，就斷了氣。

出自《荀子》*

*《荀子》 戰國時儒家學派荀況（約公元前313－前238年）著。

Ghosts Are Conceived in the Mind
The Devil Rides on a Fiddlestick

JUAN Shuliang was a stupid and timid man. Once when he was walking on a bright moonlit night, he incidentally lowered his head and saw his own shadow. He thought it was a ghost prostrating on the ground. He raised his head and saw a lock of his own hair. He thought it was a ghost standing in front of him. Scared out of his wits, he turned round and started to run until he was utterly exhausted. As soon as he reached home, he died.

*The Book of Xun Zi**

*By Xun Kuang (c. 313-238 B.C.), a Confucian scholar of the Warring States Period.

徒勞無功
tú láo wú gōng

白費力氣，沒有成效。

春秋時，有一次孔子準備從魯國到衞國去。他的學生顏回問一個叫師金的人："我的老師到處遊說，勸人家接受他的主張，可是到處碰壁。這次去衞國，你估計情況怎樣？"

師金搖搖頭說："還是不行。"

顏回問是什麼原因，師金回答說："我給你打個比方吧！船是水上最好的交通工具，車是陸上最好的交通工具，但是如果把船放在陸地上使用，那就不行。古今差別很大，你的老師想把過去的東西搬到現在來實行，就好比把船推到陸地上行走一樣，只能是徒勞無功。"

出自《莊子》

A Futile Attempt
Plowing the Sands and Sowing the Waves

IT happened in the Spring and Autumn time. Once when Confucius planned to travel from the state of Lu to the state of Wei. His disciple Yan Hui asked a man named Shi Jin, "My teacher goes everywhere trying to sell his ideas. He tried to pursue others to take his stand. But wherever he went he met with refusal. What do you think of his trip to the state of Wei?"

Shi Jin shook his head and said, "He won't succeed."

Yan Hui asked why. Shi Jin answered, "Let's draw an analogy. Boats are the best means of transport on water, and carriages are the best means of transport on land. A boat cannot be used on land. There's a great difference between today and the old days. Your teacher's intention to practise what are things of the past is like trying to propel a boat on land. It's a futile attempt."

The Book of Zhuang Zi

185

紙 上 談 兵
zhǐ shàng tán bīng

根據兵書談論軍事；比喻空發議論，不解決實際問題。

戰國時，趙國名將趙奢的兒子趙括，在年輕的時候，就讀過不少兵書，常常在人們面前談論作戰用兵的事情，即使父親趙奢也難不住他。很多人認爲他很有才能，但是他父親却認爲他夸夸其談，不能承担重任。

一次，秦國進攻趙國。趙國大將廉頗採用了築壁壘堅守的方法。後來，趙王聽信了秦國散佈的流言，以爲廉頗年老懦弱，不能抵擋敵軍，就改派趙括代替廉頗。趙括到了前綫，死搬兵書上的敎條，完全改變了廉頗持久抗戰的計劃。秦將白起聽到這個消息，非常高興，便用計先截斷了趙軍的運糧後路，然後把趙軍團團包圍。趙軍糧絕，趙括企圖突圍，被秦軍一箭射死，四十多萬趙軍一下子盡被殲滅。

出自《史記》

Fighting a War on Paper
Talking Hot Air

Meaning making useless comments without solving any problem.

DURING the Warring States Period, Zhao Kuo, the son of the famous general Zhao She of the state of Zhao, had read many books of military strategy even when he was still very young. He liked to talk about war and the deployment of soldiers. Even his father could not baffle him. Many people thought he was a man of talent. But his father knew that he could only talk glibly and was not fit for shouldering a task of any importance.

When the state of Qin invaded Zhao, the Zhao general Lian Po adopted a strategy of building strong walls of defence. Swayed by the rumours spread by the state of Qin, the King of Zhao thought Lian Po was too old, lacked courage and was unable to resist the enemy. He replaced Lian Po with Zhao Kuo. When Zhao Kuo came to the battle front, he slavishly followed what was written in the books of strategy and changed Lian Po's plan of fighting a protracted war. When Bai Qi, the Qin general, heard the news, he was very pleased. He played a ruse and cut off the Zhao army's supply route and encircled the Zhao forces. With his supply of provisions cut off, Zhao Kuo tried to break out of the encirclement and was killed by an arrow. The 400,000-strong army of the state of Zhao was destroyed in one battle.

Records of the Historian

涸 轍 之 鮒

hé zhé zhī fù

一條橫臥在乾涸車轍裏的鯽魚；比喻處在困難中，急待救濟。

187

莊周家裏很窮，有一天，他到監河侯那裏借糧食。監河侯說：
"我快要收租子了，等我收到租子後，借給你三百兩銀子，好嗎？"
莊周聽了非常氣憤，便說："昨天我到這兒來，路上聽到叫喊聲，
發現在乾涸的車轍裏躺着一條鯽魚。我問牠：'鯽魚呀！你爲什麼
跑到這兒來？'鯽魚答道：'我從東海來，快乾死了，請你給我一小
桶水，救救我的命。'我說：'我正要去南方，讓我把大江的水給
你引來吧。'鯽魚氣憤地說：'我只要求一小桶水，等你把大江的
水引來，我早就乾死了。你還不如趁早到賣乾魚的攤子上去找我
呢！'"

出自《莊子》

The Carp in the Dry Rut
At the End of One's Tether

This alludes to someone who is in a difficult position and needs immediate help.

ZHUANG Zhou was very poor. He went to Lord Keeper of the River one day to borrow some grain. The Lord said to him, "I shall soon go out to collect rents. After I've collected the rents, I'll lend you three hundred taels of silver. How about that?" Zhuang Zhou was indignant. "When I was on my way here yesterday," he said, "I heard a cry. I found a carp lying in a dry rut on the road. 'Carp,' I asked. 'What's brought you here?' The carp said, 'I came from the East Sea. I'm dying from lack of water. Please get me a small bucket of water and save my life.' I said, 'I'm going to the south. I'll divert the water in the great river here by digging a canal.' The carp was indignant. 'I need only a small bucket of water. I'll be thoroughly dried up when you've diverted the water from the great river. You'll have to go to a stall selling dried fish and find me there.' "

The Book of Zhuang Zi

188

梁上君子

liáng shàng jūn zǐ

屋樑上的先生；常用來指竊賊。

東漢時，有一個叫陳寔的人，為人正直、厚道，深受人們的愛戴。一天夜裏，有個人到陳寔家去偷東西，躲在屋樑上。陳寔假裝沒看見。他把子孫從睡夢中喊醒，對他們說："一個人應該隨時檢點自己。幹壞事的人，他的惡性並不是生下來就有的，只是長期習慣於那樣幹，最後才墮落到這個地步。梁上的那位先生就是這樣的人。"那個竊賊自知被發現，便從屋樑上跳下來向陳寔請罪。陳寔說："看你的相貌，不像個作惡的人，想來你是由於貧困才來幹這種事的吧？"說罷，就拿出兩匹絹送給他，讓他回去了。

出自《後漢書》

The Gentleman on the Beam
Light-Fingered Gentleman

This is a synonym for a thief.

CHEN Shi of the Eastern Han Dynasty was an honest and kind-hearted man, well loved by the people. One night, he found a thief had slipped into his house and was hiding on a beam of the house. He pretended that he had not seen him. He waked up his sons and grandsons from their sleep and said to them, "One must think carefully what one is doing. Those who do bad things are not necessarily born bad. It is long years of habit that make them stoop so low. The gentleman on the beam is such a person." Seeing that he had been discovered, the thief jumped down from the beam and asked to be punished. "Judging by your looks, you don't strike one as a bad person. It is probably poverty that makes you do this," said Chen. He then produced two bolts of silk, gave them to him and let him go.

History of the Later Han Dynasty

望洋興嘆
wàng yáng xīng tàn

望着海水嘆息；比喻自知能力不如別人。

秋天，大河、小河裏的水都漲起來，流入黃河，黃河的河面突然寬闊起來。人們站在岸邊，看不清對岸的牛馬。這時，黃河之神河伯很是得意，以爲天下最壯觀的景色都被他佔有了。河伯順着河道往東走去，一直走到了渤海，他向前一看，一片汪洋，無邊無際。

這時，河伯才改變了他那驕傲的神態，望着大海感嘆地說："原先我以爲誰都比不上我，今天，我才知道海比我更大，如果我不到這裏來看看，就要惹那些有見識的人譏笑了。"

出自《莊子》

Lamenting One's Inadequacy Before a Vast Ocean

This describes something that is in sight but beyond reach, or someone who knows that he is not as good as others.

WHEN the large and small rivers flooded in autumn, they all flew into the Huanghe River. The Huanghe then suddenly broadened and people on the opposite bank could not see clearly the oxen and horses on the other side of the river. It was the time when Hebo, the god of the Huanghe, felt most proud of himself. He thought that all the most magnificent scenes in the world belonged to him. He followed the course of the river to the east until he reached the Bohai Sea. He found in front of him a boundless expanse of water.

It was only then that Hebo stopped feeling so proud. He looked at the sea and said with a sign, "I thought no one could compare with me. I didn't know until today that the sea is larger than I am. Luckily I've brought myself here. Otherwise, I should become a laughing stock to the knowledgeable people."

The Book of Zhuang Zi

望 梅 止 渴
wàng méi zhǐ kě

望梅止渴；比喻拿空想來自慰。

三國時，有一次曹操率領兵馬長途跋涉去打仗。在行軍途中，碰上炎熱天氣，士兵們一個個口乾舌燥，很想喝水，但又找不到水。這時，曹操心生一計，指着前方對士兵們說："前面有大片的梅樹林，樹上結滿梅子，又甜又酸，可以解渴。"士兵們一聽，想起梅子的酸味，嘴裏都流出了口水，也就不感到渴了。

*《世說新語》 南北朝時宋人劉義慶著，記載晉朝士大夫的言談、軼事。

Quenching the Thirst by Looking at Plums

A Barmecide Feast

Meaning console oneself by imagination.

ONCE at the time of the Three Kingdoms, Cao Cao was leading his army on a long-distance march to the battlefront. The weather was scorching hot, and the soldiers were parched with a burning thirst. They wanted water but could not find any. Cao Cao struck upon a clever idea. Pointing his finger forward, he said to the soldiers, "There's a large grove of plum trees ahead, fully laden with plums. They are sweet and sour and may quench your thirst." His words reminded the soldiers of the sour taste of the plums, and their mouths began to water, which made them feel less thirsty.

*New Social Anecdotes**

*By Liu Yiqing of the Song Dynasty of the Southern and Northern Dynasties. It records the sayings and anecdotes of the Jin Dynasty scholars.

192

推己及人
tuī jǐ jí rén

用自己對事物的考慮與安排去爲別人設想；指要體諒別人。

　　春秋時，有一年冬天，齊國一連下了三天的大雪。齊景公披着狐皮袍子坐在廳堂裏欣賞雪景。這時大夫晏嬰走了進來，站在景公身邊。景公對他說：“今年天氣眞怪，一連下三天大雪，却一點不覺得冷。”晏嬰看着景公的衣着，故意問道：“天氣是眞的不冷嗎？”景公沒有理解他的意思，晏子便直率地說：“我聽說古代的賢君自己吃飽了，總要想想是否還有人餓着，自己穿暖了，還要想想是否有人凍着。現在天氣這樣冷，大王却沒有爲別人着想，這樣，怎麼能得到別人的愛戴呢！”景公聽了晏嬰這席話，立即下令拿出衣服和食物分給那些受飢寒的人。

出自《晏子春秋》

Putting Oneself in the Position of Another
Putting Oneself in Another's Shoes

Meaning to imagine oneself in another man's position and understand him.

ONE winter during the Spring and Autumn Period, it snowed continuously for three days in the state of Qi. Duke Jinggong of Qi was sitting in a hall in his fox-fur robe admiring the snow scene when the court official Yan Ying walked in and stood beside him. The Duke said to him, "The weather is strange this year. It's snowed for three days and I don't feel cold at all." Yan Ying looked at the Duke's robe and asked purposely "Is it really not cold?" The Duke did not understand him, so Yan Ying said plainly, "I heard that in the old days when virtuous rulers had food to eat, they always thought if there were people who were hungry, and when they had warm clothing themselves, they always thought if there were people who were still cold. The weather is so cold today, and Your Grace hasn't put yourself in the position of others. How can Your Grace expect to win the love of the people?" After the Duke heard what Yan Ying had said, he immediately ordered that clothing and food be distributed to those who were suffering from hunger and cold.

Anecdotes of Yan Zi

掛羊頭賣狗肉
gùa yáng tóu mài gǒu ròu

掛着羊頭賣的却是狗肉；比喻以好的名義做招牌，實際上兜售低劣的貨色。

齊景公是個昏庸無能的國君。他喜歡宮廷裏的婦女穿男人的衣飾，因而齊國的一些婦女照樣模仿起來，風行一時，齊景公發現後派官吏去禁止，結果無效。一天，丞相晏嬰來見景公，景公對他說："我派官吏去禁止婦女扮男裝，但禁不了，這是什麽原因？"晏嬰回答說："你在宮裏提倡男裝，而在宮外却禁止這種打扮，這正如懸掛牛頭做招牌，實際上賣的是馬肉。如果你在宮裏也禁止，那麽宮外的婦女就不敢再男裝打扮了。"景公覺得有理，就照辦了。果然未出一個月，這個風氣就煞住了。

後來，人們把"掛牛頭賣馬肉"變爲"掛羊頭賣狗肉"這一成語。

出自《晏子春秋》

194

Hanging Up a Sheep's Head and Selling Dogmeat

Crying Up Wine and Sell Vinegar

Meaning trying to sell goods inferior to what they purport to be.

DUKE Jinggong of Qi was a stupid and incompetent ruler. He had a propensity to have the women in his court wear men's clothing. Other women in the state of Qi began to imitate the court ladies and it soon became a vogue. When the Duke found this out, he sent some officials to put a ban on it, but to no avail. One day, Prime Minister Yan Ying had an audience with the Duke. The Duke said to him, "I sent some officials to prohibit women from wearing men's clothing. But they couldn't stop it, why?" Yan Ying answered, "You encourage women to wear men's clothing at court, but prohibit other women doing the same. This is just like hanging up an ox head as a sign and actually selling horsemeat. If you ban it in the court too, the other women wouldn't dare dress themselves as men." The Duke thought what Yan Ying said was right and acted on it. Indeed, in less than a month, the practice was stopped.

Later, people changed "hanging up an ox head and selling horsemeat" into "hanging up a sheep's head and selling dogmeat" and began to use it as an idiom.

Anecdotes of Yan Zi

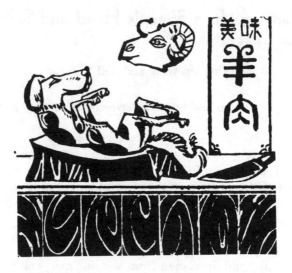

掩 耳 盜 鈴
yǎn ér dào líng

把耳朵捂住去偷鈴鐺；比喻自己欺騙自己。

有一個人，看見人家大門上掛着一隻門鈴，便想把它偷來。他知道：如果他去摘那門鈴，只要手一碰到它，就會响起來。可是他忽然想出法子來了。他認爲：鈴响所以會闖出禍來，只因爲耳朵能聽見，假如把耳朵掩起來，不是就聽不見鈴聲了嗎？於是他便先把自己的耳朵掩起來，然後去偷那隻門鈴。可是，他仍然給人發覺了，因爲別人並沒有掩着耳朵。

出自《呂氏春秋》

Plugging One's Ears to Steal a Bell

The Cat Shuts Its Eyes When Stealing Cream

Meaning to deceive oneself.

A man who saw a bell hanging at the front door of a house wanted to steal it. He knew that if he tried to unfasten the bell, it would ring as soon as his hand touched it. But he hit upon an idea. He presumed that the ringing of the bell might bring disaster upon him because his ears could hear it. If he plugged his ears, he would not hear the bell. So he plugged his ears and went to steal the bell. He was discovered because others had not plugged their ears.

The Discourses of Lü Buwei

捨 本 逐 末
shě běn zhú mò

丟掉根本，追求枝節；比喻做事情輕重倒置，主次不分。

齊襄王派使臣帶着書信去問候趙太后，趙太后接過信，還未打開，就向使臣問道："你們國家今年的收成怎樣？百姓都安居樂業嗎？齊王好嗎？"齊襄王的使臣聽了，很不高興，說道："我奉齊王的派遣來問候王后，王后也應該先向齊王問好。現在你却先問年成豐歉和百姓的生活，這不是有意輕視國王嗎？"

趙太后向他解釋道："你想想看，要是沒有好的年成，哪裏還有百姓？要是沒有百姓，哪裏還有君王？過去人們一貫拋開根本的東西，而去詢問一些枝節，這難道是正常的嗎！"

出自《戰國策》

Going After the Trifles and Neglecting the Essential

Meaning reversing the order of importance and priority.

KING Xiangwang of the state of Qi sent an envoy with a letter to offer greetings to the Queen Mother of Zhao. The Queen Mother took the letter. But before opening it she asked the envoy, "How is the harvest in your country this year? Are the people living and working in peace and happiness? How is the King?" On hearing her questions, the envoy appeared displeased. "I have been sent by the King to offer greetings to the Queen Mother," said he. "Your Majesty should have asked after the King first. And yet Your Majesty first asked about the harvest and the livelihood of the people. Is this not deliberately slighting the King?"

The Queen Mother explained to him: "Think. If there is no good harvest, where will the people be? If there are no people, where will the King be? Going after the trifles and neglecting the essential. That was what happened in the past. Was that normal?"

Anecdotes of the Warring States

專 心 致 志
zhuān xīn zhì zhì

精神集中，一心一意地鑽研。

　　古時候，有個叫秋的下棋名手。他的本領是全國獨一無二的。有兩個學生跟他學棋，其中的一個，總是集中精神，一心一意地跟他學。另外的那一個，雖然也同樣坐在那裏聽講，眼睛看着棋子，可是他對獵鳥更有興趣，他老是記掛着天空飛翔的鴻雁，想怎樣拿了箭去射牠們。結果，一個學生很快便學好了，另一個始終沒有學好。這是什麼原因呢？是不是一個學生更聰明呢？當然不是，只是其中的一個不專心地學習罷了。

出自《孟子》

Concentrating One's Attention

QIU was a famous chess player. Nobody in the whole country could beat him on the chessboard. Two students came to learn chess from him. One of them always concentrated his attention to learn from him with all his mind. The other also sat there and listened to him, and his eyes were also on the chess pieces. But he was more interested in bird-shooting. His mind was always on the wild geese flying in the sky and on how to shoot them with bow and arrow. One student learned it very quickly, while the other did not learn as well as the first student. Why? Was one student more clever than the other? Of course not. It was only because one of them did not concentrate his attention.

The Book of Mencius

屠 龍 之 技
tú lóng zhī jí

宰龍的技術；比喻毫無實用價值。

有個叫朱泙漫的人，他變賣了家產，到很遠的地方去拜一個叫支離益的人做老師，跟他學習殺龍的本領。他在那裏花了三年功夫，才學成歸來。人們問他究竟學了些什麼，他一面興奮地回答，一面把殺龍的技術指手劃腳地表演給大家看。有人問道：「什麼地方有龍呢？」朱泙漫目瞪口呆了半天，沒有話可答。原來他辛辛苦苦地學來的那套本領，沒有絲毫用處。

出自《莊子》

The Art of Killing Dragons
As Much Use as a Headache

Meaning something that has no practical value at all.

ZHU Pingman sold all his property and took a journey to a very far-away place, where he found his teacher in a man named Zhi Liyi, from whom he learned the art of killing dragons. He spent three years there before he mastered the art. When he returned home, people asked him what he had learned. He gesticulated excitedly as he described to them the skill of killing dragons that he had learned. Somebody asked him, "Where can you find a dragon?" He was dumbfounded and unable to answer. The skill he had worked very hard to learn had actually no practical value at all.

The Book of Zhuang Zi

將欲取之，必先與之
jiāng yù qǔ zhī, bì xiān yǔ zhī

要想從對方得到東西，必須先給對方東西。

晉國有個叫智伯的貴族，向另一個叫魏宣子的貴族索取土地，被魏宣子拒絕了。魏宣子的朋友任章對魏宣子說："您爲什麼不把土地割讓給他呢？"魏宣子說："智伯仗着權勢強要我的土地，我不能給。"

任章說："智伯貪得無厭，你把土地給了他，一定會助長他的貪婪，他會進一步向別的貴族勒索土地。這樣，貴族們就會聯合起來，共同對付他，智伯滅亡的日子就爲期不遠了。古書上說：'要打敗別人，必先暫且幫助他，想要得到別人的東西，必須暫且先給人家一些東西。'你要想戰勝智伯，就得先割讓土地給他。"魏宣子採納了任章的建議，把一些土地割給智伯。智伯得了土地，果然又繼續向其他的貴族索取。之後，貴族們聯合起來，共同擊敗了智伯，瓜分了他的土地。魏宣子不但收回了原來割讓出去的土地，而且分得了更多的土地。

出自《韓非子》

To Give in Order to Take

MARQUIS Zhi Bo was a noble of the state of Jin. He demanded land from another noble named Wei Xuan Zi and was refused by Wei. Ren Zhang, a friend of Wei Xuan Zi, said to Wei, "Why didn't you give him land?" Wei said, "Marquis Zhi Bo uses his power and influence to extort land from me. I won't give him."

Ren Zhang said, "The Marquis is insatiably greedy. If you give him land, his greed will grow. He'll blackmail other nobles for more land. The nobles will then unite to oppose him. The Marquis' days are numbered. It's said in the ancient

books, 'In order to defeat someone, you must help him first.
In order to take, you must give.' If you want to defeat the
Marquis, you must cede land to him." Wei Xuan Zi followed
Ren Zhang's suggestion and ceded some land to Zhi Bo.
Having gained new land, the Marquis indeed tried to extort
more land from the other nobles. The other nobles joined
forces, defeated him and divided his land among them. Wei
Xuan Zi not only recovered all the land he had ceded, but
gained more.

The Book of Han Fei Zi

貪 小 失 大
tān xiǎo shī dà

貪圖小的失去大的；比喻貪圖小利而造成重大損失。

秦惠王想出兵攻打蜀國，苦於蜀國地處西南，山多路險，交通
阻塞。秦王打聽到蜀王是個貪利的人，就派了幾個技藝出衆的石匠
雕琢了五頭栩栩如生的石牛，並將許多黃金掛在石牛尾巴下，假說
是神牛屙的金屎。消息傳到蜀國後，蜀王便派使者到秦國去參觀，
表示願購買這五頭神奇的石牛。秦王得知後說，他願將石牛無償地
送給蜀王，但希望蜀王修築一條溝通秦蜀兩國的大道，以便將石牛
運去。蜀王信以爲眞，下令徵召民夫，開山塡谷，修路築橋。準備
迎接金牛。當道路修通後，秦國乘蜀國沒有防備，一舉滅了蜀國。

出自《新論》*

* 《新論》 東漢桓譚（公元前？—56年）著。

Coveting Small Gains and Incurring Great Losses

Penny Wise, Pound Foolish

KING Huiwang of the state of Qin intended to attack the state of Shu, but was discouraged by the mountains that barred his way to that state in the southwest. When he learned that the King of Shu was a greedy man, he ordered a few stonemasons of outstanding skill to carve five life-like stone oxen and hanged a great many lumps of gold at the end of their tails. He then invented a rumour that they were divine oxen that dropped gold. When the rumour reached the state of Shu, its King sent his envoys to the state of Qin to have a look and express his intention to purchase them. The King of Qin said that he was willing to give the stone oxen to the King of Shu as gifts, but hoped that the King of Shu would build a road leading from Qin to Shu so that he could have the stone oxen shipped there. Unsuspectingly, the King of Shu drafted labourers to hew off mountains and level valleys, build a road and put up bridges in preparation to receive the divine oxen. When the road was completed, the King of Qin launched a surprise attack and wiped out the state of Shu in one stroke.

New Views *

*By Huan Tan of the Eastern Han Dynasty. (? B.C.-A.D. 56)

欲 速 不 達
yù sù bù dá

想要快反而達不到目的。

孔子的學生子夏，到魯國一個縣城去做縣官。臨走時，去向孔子請教怎樣辦理政事。孔子知道子夏有目光短淺，只看眼前利益和性子急躁的毛病，就對他說：“做事要循序漸進，不要只圖快，不要只顧眼前利益。如果性急貪快，反而達不到目的；如果只顧眼前小利，往往辦不成大事。”

出自《論語》

The More Haste, the Less Speed

ZI Xia, a disciple of Confucius, was going to his post as a county magistrate in the state of Lu. Before his departure, he came to Confucius and asked him how the affairs of the government should be run. Confucius knew that the trouble with Zi Xia was that he tended to focus his attention only on the immediate interests and was impetuous. He therefore said to him, "Whatever you do, do it step by step instead of pursuing mere speed. Don't focus your attention only on the immediate interests. The more haste, the less speed. Attention to minor and immediate interests prevent one from accomplishing great things."

Confucian Analects

得 心 應 手
dé xīn yìng shǒu

心裏怎麼想，手就怎麼做；比喻做事情很順利。

齊國的國君桓公在堂上讀書，堂下有個叫輪扁的工匠正在砍木頭製車輪。輪扁忽然放下工具走上堂來問桓公道：“請問國君看的是什麼書？”

桓公答道：“我看的是聖人的書。”輪扁又問：“聖人還活着嗎？”桓公說：“早死掉了。”輪扁說：“這樣說來，國王所讀的書，不過是古人的糟粕罷了。”桓公聽後很生氣，說：“你這個做

204

工匠的怎敢胡亂議論！你有什麼根據，講出來，可放過你。講不出來，決不饒你的性命。"

輪扁從容地答道："就拿我做車輪的工作來說，我拿斧頭砍削車輪，不快不慢，心裏怎麼想，手就怎麼做，做出來的車輪既牢固又靈活。這樣熟練的技巧只能從長期工作中得來，我不能單純用口授的方法傳給我的兒子，我的兒子也不能不經過實踐而把它繼承下來。由此可見，聖人既然已經死去，他們留下來的書，也都成了過去的東西，難道國王所讀的，還不是古人的糟粕嗎？"

出自《莊子》

The Hands Do What the Mind Thinks
As Clay in the Hands of a Potter

WHEN Duke Huangong, the ruler of the state of Qi, was reading in the hall, a wheelwright was making a wooden carriage wheel outside the hall. The wheelwright put down his tool and came into the hall. "May I ask what book is Your Majesty reading?" he asked the Duke.

"I'm reading the books of the sages," said Duke Huangong. "Are the sages still living?" the wheelwright asked again. "They died a long time ago," the Duke said. "That means Your Majesty is reading the trash of the ancients," said the wheelwright. Duke Huangong was very angry. He said, "How dare you, an artisan, come here and talk nonsense. Tell me what made you say so, and I may let you go. Otherwise, you'll die for it."

Unhurriedly, the wheelwright answered, "Take my work of making a carriage wheel. I cut the wood with an axe, neither too fast, nor too slow. What the mind thinks what the hands do. When the wheel is finished, it is sturdy and turns smoothly. This skill can only be learned through long years of practice. I can't teach my son the skill by words of the mouth only. Nor can my son learn it without practice. This shows that since the sages were dead, what they left behind

in the books are things of the past. What is Your Majesty
reading, if not the trash of the ancients?"

The Book of Zhuang Zi

得 意 洋 洋
dé yì yáng yáng

高興自滿的樣子。

春秋時,晏嬰做齊國宰相的時候,有一天,坐着馬車出門去。馬
車正好從馬夫的家門前經過。馬夫的妻子從門縫裏看見她的丈夫,
很得意地坐在車子的大傘下,揮着鞭子。

馬夫回到家裏,他的妻子就要和他離婚。馬夫摸不着頭腦,就
問:"你到底爲什麼要跟我離婚呢?"她說:"晏子做了齊國的宰
相,在各國都有名望。今天我看見他,低頭坐在車子上,他的態度
是那麼地謙虛。但是你呢,你只是他的馬夫,却得意洋洋,神氣活
現,自以爲了不起,所以我不願再跟你一同生活了。"

從此之後,馬夫就改變了態度,變得很謙虛。晏子看見他的態
度和以前大不相同,就問他是什麼緣故。他把事情的經過告訴了晏
子,晏子覺得他能夠這樣快地改變態度,是很好的,後來就推薦他
做了官吏。

出自《晏子春秋》

Smug and Conceited
Having One's Nose in the Air

YAN Zi, Prime Minister of the state of Qi during the Spring
and Autumn Period, went out one day in his carriage driven
by his coachman. His carriage happened to pass his coachman's house. From the door that was ajar the coachman's

wife saw her husband sitting under the great carriage awning twirling his whip and looking immensely smug and conceited.

When the coachman returned home, his wife said that she wanted to divorce him. The coachman, who could not make head or tail of it, asked, "Why do you want to divorce me?" His wife said, "Yan Zi is the Prime Minister of the state of Qi and enjoys a high prestige in all the states. When I saw him today, he looked so modest, sitting in the carriage with his head lowered. But you, his coachman, looked so immensely smug and conceited and arrogant as if you were really somebody. I don't want to live with a man like you."

After that, the coachman changed his attitude and became a very modest person. When Yan Zi saw the great difference, he asked his coachman why he had changed. The coachman told him what had happened. Yan Zi thought it was very good that he could change his attitude quickly and, later, recommended him to be an official.

Anecdotes of Yan Zi

得過且過
dé guò qiě guò

只要勉強過得去，就過一天算一天；比喻做事敷衍塞責。

傳說，五台山上有一種鳥叫寒號鳥，有四隻脚，兩扇肉翅。每當盛夏季節，牠的身上長滿了五彩絢爛的羽毛，因此自鳴得意地叫："鳳凰不如我，鳳凰不如我！"等到深冬，牠的羽毛全脫落了，像剛出殼的幼鳥一樣，在寒風中瑟索發抖。牠無可奈何地叫道："得過且過，得過且過！"天氣轉暖，寒號鳥又繼續跳着叫着，忘却了冬天的威脅。

出自《南村輟耕錄》*

* 《南村輟耕錄》 元末明初時人陶宗儀著，記元朝典章制度。

207

Muddling Along
Letting Things Drift

ACCORDING to legend, there was a bird named Hanhao in the Wutai Mountains. It had four legs and two fleshy wings. Every summer, it was covered with colourful feathers. It was very pleased with itself and cried, "The phoenix is not as beautiful as I am! The phoenix is not as beautiful as I am!" When winter came, all its feathers came off and it looked like a newly batched bird. Shivering in the cold wind, it cried helplessly, "Muddling along! Muddling along!" When the weather turned warm again, Hanhao again began to jump about and sing, forgetting all about the threat of winter.

Notes Taken During Intervals of Ploughing in South Village*

*A record of the institutions of the Yuan Dynasty by Tao Zongyi who lived at the end of the Yuan Dynasty (1271-1368) and the beginning of the Ming Dynasty (1368-1644).

徙宅忘妻
xī zhái wàng qī

搬家而遺忘了妻子；比喻善忘的糊塗人。

有一次，魯國國君哀公問孔子道："聽說有人搬家而遺忘了妻子，沒有讓她遷移，您說真有這樣的人嗎？"孔子說："怎麼沒有？這不算稀奇，還有連自己都遺忘的呢？"哀公更加懷疑。孔子說："譬如古代的夏桀、商紂這樣的暴君，他們荒淫無度，窮奢極慾，不理國事，不顧民生。那些讒臣酷吏，還拍馬奉承，慫恿鼓動他們做更多的壞事；忠誠正直的人，反被拋在一邊，連進言諫議的機會都沒有。結果，國家亡了，暴君們自己的命也終於保不住。他們不僅遺忘了國家，遺忘了人民，連自己也遺忘了。"

出自《孔子家語》*

*《孔子家語》 原本已失，今本係三國時人纂輯。

Moving House and Forgetting to Take the Wife

As Stupid as a Donkey

This is said of a foolish and forgetful man.

DUKE Aigong, ruler of the state of Lu, asked Confucius, "I heard that when a man moved house he forgot to take his wife with him and left her behind. Is there really such a man?" Confucius said, "Why not? That was not the strangest thing that happened. There were people who forgot about themselves." But the Duke became more doubtful. Confucius then continued, "Take such tyrannical rulers as King Jie of Xia and King Zhou of Shang in the ancient times. They lived a debauched life of luxury and extravagance and ignored the affairs of the state and livelihood of the people. A pack of treacherous and heartless court officials, moreover, fawned on them and instigated them to do more evils. The honest and upright people were pushed aside and did not even have an opportunity to offer their advice. The result was that their countries perished and the tyrannical rulers lost their own lives. They forgot not only their countries and people, but also themselves."

*Anecdotes of Confucius**

*The original book was lost. The available edition was compiled in the Three Kingdoms period (220-280).

殺鷄焉用牛刀

shā jī yān yòng niú dāo

殺鷄何必用宰牛的刀；比喩辦小事情何必費大力氣。

　　孔子的學生子游在魯國武城縣做縣官。有一次，孔子來到武城，聽見彈琴唱歌的聲音，他微笑一下對子游說："治理武城這個小地方，還用得着禮樂嗎？比如殺鷄，何必用宰牛的大刀！"

　　子游回答道："以前我聽老師講過，百姓學了禮樂就會相親相愛。我照你的話去做，你爲什麼又取笑我？"孔子聽了，對跟隨他去的學生們說："子游說得對，我剛才說的那些話不過是開個玩笑罷了。"

出自《論語》

Why Use an Ox-Cleaver to Kill a Chicken?
Using a Steam-Hammer to Crack Nuts

Meaning to perform a minor feat with unnecessarily great effort.

CONFUCIUS' disciple Zi You became the magistrate of Wucheng County in the state of Lu. When Confucius came to Wucheng, he heard music and singing. He smiled and asked Zi You, "Do you need rites and music to rule over a small place like Wucheng? Why use an ox-cleaver to kill a chicken?"

　　Zi You answered, "I heard you, my teacher, say in the past that when the people know rites and music they will live in peace and friendship. I've been following your instructions. Why do you ridicule me?" Confucius then turned to his students who had come with him and said, "Zi You is right. I was joking when I said what I said."

Confucian Analects

210

割肉自啖

gē ròu zì dàn

割下身上的肉自己吃；比喻表面上看來勇敢，實際上愚蠢。

　　齊國有兩個有名的勇士，一個住在東城，一個住在西城。有一天，他們倆在路上相遇，都非常高興，相約到酒館裏去喝酒。兩個人喝了幾杯，一個說："讓我去買幾斤肉來下酒，好嗎？"另一個說："眞是多此一舉，你我身上有的是肉，幹嗎還要花錢去買呢？"於是兩個人大笑了一陣，各自拔出刀來，把身上的肉一塊一塊地割下來。結果，這兩位勇士因流血過多，都死了。

出自《呂氏春秋》

Eating One's Own Flesh

This describes someone who displays foolish bravado.

THERE were two brave warriors in the state of Qi, one living in the eastern part of the city, the other in the western part. One day they met in the street. As they were very happy, they went together to an inn to drink. After each having downed a few cups, one of them said, "How about a few catties of meat to go with the wine?" The other said, "That's not necessary. We both have a lot of meat on ourselves. Why spend money on it?" And, laughing uproariously, each of them drew a knife and cut off pieces of flesh from his body. Both warriors died from losing too much blood.

The Discourses of Lu Buwei

曾參殺人

zēng shēn shā rén

曾參殺人，比喻流言可怕。

有一次，曾參別了老母，離開家鄉到山東的費邑去。費邑有個和曾參同姓同名的人，殺死了人。有人聽到這消息，也不把它弄個清楚，就去告訴曾參的母親說："聽說，你們的曾參在費國殺死人了！"那時，曾參的母親正在織布，聽了這消息，頭也不抬的回答說："我的兒子，決不會殺人的！"說着，仍然很安心地坐着織布。過了一會，又有人來報告說："曾參殺了人了！"曾參的母親仍是沒有理睬，穩穩當當的坐着織布。過了不久，又跑來一個人，同樣的說："曾參殺了人了！"

曾參的母親，聽了第三個人的報告，害怕了，立刻扔下手中的梭子，急急忙忙地離開布機，跳牆逃跑了。

出自 《戰國策》

Zeng Shen Killed a Man

This shows how fearful a rumour is.

ZENG Shen said goodbye to his old mother, left home and went to Feiyi in Shandong. A man with the same name as Zeng Shen's killed a man in Feiyi. When someone heard this, without finding out which Zeng Shen it was, he told Zeng Shen's mother, "People say your Zeng Shen's killed a man in Feiyi." Zeng Shen's mother was weaving cloth. On hearing the news, she did not even raise her head. "My son will never kill a man," said she. Later, another man came to make the same report, "Zeng Shen's killed a man." Still Zeng Shen's mother did not bother with it. Then, a third man ran into her house and said the same thing, "Zeng Shen's killed a man."

Upon hearing the third man's report, Zeng Shen's mother became frightened. She immediately put down the shuttle in her hand and hurriedly climbed over the wall and ran away.

Anecdotes of the Warring States

項莊舞劍，意在沛公
xiàng zhuāng wǔ jiàn, yì zài pèi gōng

項莊舞劍的目的在於殺沛公劉邦；比喻說話或行爲的眞實意圖在於攻擊某人某事。

項羽的謀士范增勸項羽趁劉邦勢力尚未强大，把劉邦消滅掉。劉邦聽說項羽準備攻打他，便親自到鴻門拜見項羽。項羽設宴招待他。飲酒之間，范增多次向項羽暗示，要他趁此機會把劉邦殺掉。項羽却默默不語，故意不睬范增。范增十分着急。便出去把項羽的弟弟項莊叫來，對他說：“大王心太慈善，不忍下手。你快進去假裝敬酒，之後就給客人舞劍助興，趁機會把劉邦殺死。

項莊敬完酒，向項羽說：“大王和劉邦一同飲酒，沒有什麼娛樂，讓我來舞劍助興吧！”劉邦的謀士張良見情勢危急，出去找到衞士樊噲。樊噲問張良：“現在情況怎麼樣？”張良說：“甚急！現在項莊正在宴會上舞劍，他的用意是要殺死沛公啊！”於是樊噲進去和項莊一起舞劍。之後，劉邦在樊噲保護下安全脫險。

出自《史記》

When Xiang Zhuang Played the Sword His Intention Was to Kill the Revered Pei

The Revered Pei was Liu Bang. The idiom alludes to words or acts with a hidden motive.

XIANG Yu's adviser Fan Zeng urged Xiang Yu to kill Liu

Bang before he became too powerful. When Liu Bang heard that Xiang Yu intended to attack him, he came in person to Hongmen to see Xiang Yu. Xiang Yu received him at a banquet. While they were drinking, Fan Zeng several times hinted to Xiang Yu that he should take this opportunity to finish off Liu Bang. But Xiang Yu·did not say a word and refused to take notice of Fan. Fan Zeng grew very impatient. He came out, sent for Xiang Zhuang, Xiang Yu's brother and told him, "The Duke is too kindhearted. He couldn't bear to do it. You go in at once and pretend to come to offer wine. Then, you can play the sword to entertain the guests and find a chance to kill Liu Bang."

After offering wine to them, Xiang Zhuang said to Xiang Yu, "There's no entertainment while the Duke and Liu Bang are drinking. Let me play the sword to cheer you up." Liu Bang's adviser Zhang Liang saw that the situation was critical. He brought the guard Fan Kuai in. "How are things?" Fan Kuai asked Zhang Liang. "Very critical. Xiang Zhuang is now playing the sword at the banquet. But his intention is to kill the Revered Pei." Fan Kuai then went into the banquet hall and played his sword together with Xiang Zhuang. Later, it was under Fan Kuai's protection that Liu Bang made his escape to safety.

Records of the Historian

越 俎 代 庖
yuè zū dài páo

掌管祭祀的人放下祭器去代替厨師做飯；比喻超越自己的職務
範圍，去包辦別人的事情。

中國古代有一位受人愛戴的帝王叫堯。堯年老時，要把天下讓
給賢能的許由。許由堅決不接受，並且說："您已經把天下治理得
很好了，爲什麼還要我來代替您呢！小鳥在林中築巢，只需佔一根
樹枝，鼴鼠在河邊飲水，最多喝滿一肚子。像我這樣的人，要這麼
大的天下有什麼用處呢！厨師雖然沒有把飯菜做好，但是掌管祭祀
的人也決不能放下祭器去代替厨師的工作啊！"

出自《莊子》

Laying Down the Sacrificial Vessels to Do the Cook's Work
To Be a Back Seat Driver

Meaning overstepping one's functions and meddling in other people's business.

YAO was a king in ancient China who enjoyed the love and
esteem of the people. When he grew old, he wanted to pass
his crown to a capable man named Xu You, who firmly
refused and said: "You've been governing the country very
successfully. Why do you want me to replace you? When a
bird builds a nest, it takes only one branch of a tree. When a
mole drinks at a river, it drinks only one bellyful. What is the
use of a man like me to a great country like ours? The cook
may fail to prepare a good meal. But the master of
ceremonies should by no means lay down the sacrificial
vessels and do the cook's work."

The Book of Zhuang Zi

215

煮豆燃萁
zhǔ dòu rán qí

用豆秸煮豆；比喻內部不和，自相殘殺。

　　魏文帝曹丕，常想謀害他的弟弟曹植。有一次，兄弟們在一起吃豌豆。曹丕想出一個壞主意，限曹植在走七步路的短時間內，做出一首詩來；如果不能完成，就要重重地處罰。曹植一面踱步，一面想，正踱到第七步時，馬上做出一首詩來了："煮豆燃豆萁（音其），豆在釜中泣，本是同根生，相煎何太急！"魏文帝聽了這首詩，自覺慚愧，只好把自己的惡計打消了。

出自《世說新語》

Burning Peastalks to Cook Peas

This alludes to internal strife, fratricide.

216

CAO Pi, Emperor Wendi of Wei, had always been plotting against his brother Cao Zhi's life. Once when the two brothers were eating peas together, Cao Pi suddenly hit upon a scheme. He ordered Cao Zhi to take seven steps forward and compose a poem within the time he took these seven steps. If he could not do it, he would be severely punished. As Cao Zhi began to step forward, his mind worked busily, and he completed the poem on his seventh step, which read:

"Peastalks are burned to cook peas.

The peas in the cauldron cry:

'We both came from the same root.

Why must one be so cruel to the other?'

When Emperor Wendi heard the poem, he felt ashamed of himself and had to drop his scheme.

New Social Anecdotes

揠苗助長
yà miáo zhú zhǎng

把苗拔高幫助他們生長；比喻做事違反常規，急於求成，反而把事情弄糟了。

從前，有個宋國人，日夜盼望田裏的稻子快些長起來。有一天，他想出了一個妙計：下到田裏把每棵稻子，都從土裏向上拔高了一些。他忙碌了一天，累得筋疲力盡，回到家裏，告訴家裏人說："我今天好累啊！不過，田裏的稻子，倒是都長高了。"

他的兒子聽了，非常奇怪，連忙跑到田裏去看。只見滿田的稻子都枯萎了。

出自《孟子》

Helping Young Shoots to Grow by Pulling Them Upward

A Watched Pot Never Boils

This alludes to doing something against nature for the sake of quick results, which often spoils it.

A Man in the state of Song was anxious day and night that his rice shoots were not growing fast enough. He hit upon an idea one day. He came to his plot and pulled up every one of the young shoots so that they all looked higher. When he returned home, he said to his family, "I'm tired out today. But the rice in the field has grown higher."

Puzzled by his words, his son ran to the field and saw that all the young rice shoots had withered.

The Book of Mencius

朝 三 暮 四
zhāo sān mù sì

早晨三個，晚上四個；原指玩弄欺騙手法，現用來比喻反覆無常。

宋國有個玩猴子的，養了一大羣猴子。日子長久了，他懂得了猴子的性情，猴子也懂得了主人的話。因此，他更愛猴子了，寧願省下家裏每天吃的糧食，去餵養猴子。

後來，家裏吃的口糧不夠了，他想把餵猴子的口糧減少些。但怕猴子不聽話，就故意對猴子說："我每天早上給你們三顆栗子，晚上給四顆，夠吃了嗎？"猴子們都嫌給得太少了，呲牙咧嘴地表示不滿。

隔了一會，主人又騙猴子們說："早上給三顆，晚上給四顆，你們既然嫌少，那麼，改爲早上給四顆，晚上給三顆，這樣，總該滿意了吧！"猴子們聽了這番話，表示十分滿意，便伏在地上搖頭擺尾了。

出自《列子》

Three in the Morning, Four in the Evening
Chop and Change

This originally referred to playing tricks; it now means to be inconsistent.

A monkey-trainer in the state of Song kept a large group of monkeys. As time went on, he began to know the temperament of the monkeys, and the monkeys began to understand their master's words. For this reason, he became more fond of his monkeys. He would rather stint his family's food to feed the monkeys.

219

Later, when there was hardly enough food in the family, he wanted to reduce the monkeys' feed. As he was afraid that the monkeys might not like it, he deliberately said to the monkeys, "I'll give you three chestnuts in the morning and four in the evening. Would that be enough?" The monkeys disliked it because there were too few. They all bared their teeth to express their discontent.

After a short time, the trainer said to the monkeys, "Since you think three in the morning and four in the evening are not enough, I will give you four in the morning and three in the evening. Now you must be satisfied." At his words, the monkeys all prostrated on the ground and wagged their tails to show their perfect satisfaction.

The Book of Lie Zi

華 而 不 實
huá ér bù shí

只開花不結果；比喻虛有其表而毫無實際的人和事物。

晉國大夫陽處父出使到衞國去，路過一個叫寧邑的地方。住在一家客店裏。店主人看見陽處父相貌堂堂，舉止不凡，悄悄對他妻子說："我早就想投奔一個品德高尚的人，可是多少年來，隨時留意，却沒有找到一個合意的。今天我看陽處父這個人不錯，我決心跟他去了。"

店主得到陽處父的同意，離別妻子，跟着他走了。一路上陽處父就和店主東拉西扯地談起來，還沒有走出寧邑多遠，店主就改變主意，不跟陽處父去了。

店主的妻子見丈夫折回，就問他爲什麼這麼快就回來了。店主回答道："我看了他的外表覺得不錯，誰知他的言論却非常令人討厭，我怕跟了他去，沒有得到益處，倒先遭受禍害，所以我打消了原來的主意。"

出自《國語》*

*《國語》。歷史書籍，記載西周末到春秋時的歷史，相傳爲左丘明作。

Flowering Without Bearing Fruit

Having All One's Goods in the Window

Said of a person who is superficially clever, or of a thing that is flashy without substance.

ON his way back from his mission to the state of Wei, Yang Chufu, an official of the state of Jin, passed a place named Ningyi. He stayed at an inn. Seeing that Yang was a man of noble and dignified bearing, the innkeeper whispered to his wife, "I've since long ago wanted to cast my lot with a man of noble character. Although I've looked for many years, I haven't found anyone to my liking. I think Yang Chufu is not bad. I've decided to follow him."

After obtaining Yang Chufu's consent, the innkeeper bade farewell to his wife and went off with Yang. On their way, Yang and the innkeeper talked about this and that and every kind of thing. Before they had gone very far from Ningyi, the innkeeper changed his mind and said that he would not go with Yang.

When the innkeeper's wife saw that her husband had come back, she asked why he had returned so quickly. The innkeeper said, "When I saw his appearance I thought he was very good. But when I heard him talk, I was very annoyed by his opinion of things. I was afraid that if I went with him I might suffer instead of benefiting from him. That's why I changed my mind."

*Anecdotes of the States**

*A book of history recording the events from Western Zhou to the Spring and Autumn Period and attributed to Zuo Qiuming.

欺 以 其 方
qī yǐ qí fāng

用合乎情理的辦法來欺騙別人。

有人送給鄭國大臣子產一條活魚。子產就叫管魚池的人把魚放到池塘裏去。那人把魚煮來吃了，回來告訴子產說："我把魚放到池塘裏去了。剛放下時，牠呆呆地不動，一會兒，就得意洋洋地游起來，很快就不知去向了。"子產高興地說："魚兒找到合適的地方了。"管魚塘的人出來和別人說："誰說子產聰明？我把魚吃了，他還說：'找到合適的地方了。'"

出自《孟子》

Knowing the Right Way to Cheat
Playing a Clever Trick

SOMEBODY gave Minister Zi Chan of the state of Zheng a live fish. Zi Chan told the fish pond keeper to put it in the pond. The keeper cooked the fish and ate it. Then he came back and told Zi Chan, "I've put the fish in the pond. It stayed still at first. In a short time, it began to swim happily and soon disappeared." "The fish has found a good place to live," said Zi Chan, very pleased. When the fish pond keeper came out of Zi Chan's house, he said to others, "Who says Zi Chan is clever? I ate the fish and he said, 'The fish has found a good place to live.' "

The Book of Mencius

發 憤 忘 食
fā fèn wàng shí

形容勤奮好學或工作幹勁大。

孔子周遊列國，從蔡國來到楚國葉縣。葉縣的縣官葉公接待了他，因爲葉公對孔子的爲人不了解，便向孔子的學生子路探問。子路一時回答不上來。回來後子路對孔子講了。孔子說："你爲什麼不這樣回答：他的爲人啊！專心讀書連吃飯都常常忘了；他達觀快樂，什麼憂慮都沒有；他根本不曉得衰老之年逐漸來臨。"

出自《論語》

Working So Hard as to Forget One's Meals

ON his tour of the various states, Confucius arrived at Yexian in the state of Chu from the state of Cai. Lord Yegong, the magistrate of Yexian, received him. As he did not know Confucius, he asked Confucius' disciple Zi Lu what kind of a person Confucius was. Zi Lu was unable to tell him. Later, he told Confucius what had happened. Confucius said, "Why didn't you tell him that Confucius is such a person that when he immerses himself in his books he forgets his meals, that he is such an optimistic person that he never worries about anything, and that he doesn't know that old age is gradually approaching."

Confucian Analects

開 卷 有 益
kāi juàn yǒu yī

只要翻開書本，就會得到益處。

宋朝初年，宋太宗指派學者們編寫了一部規模宏大的百科全書《太平御覽》。全書共一千卷，分五十五門，採用書籍達一千六百多種，內容極爲豐富。宋太宗對這部書很感興趣，自己規定，每天都要看二、三卷。

有人說："宋太宗每日事情繁多，還要閱讀這部書，實在太辛苦了。宋太宗聽了却說："我體會到了讀書的趣味，只要翻開書本，就有益處，我一點也不覺得勞累。"

出自《澠水燕談錄》 *

* 《澠水燕談錄》 宋王闢之作。

Reading Is Always Profitable
A Book That Is Shut Is but a Block

EARLY in the Song Dynasty, Emperor Taizong appointed a group of scholars to compile a stupendous encyclopaedia — the *Imperial Library of the Taiping Reign*. It is a collection of 1,000 volumes classified under fifty-five subjects. More than 1,800 existing works were included in it. He set a rule for himself to read two or three volumes a day.

Some people said that since the Emperor had to deal with so many things every day, it was really too tiring for him to read the books. When Emperor Taizong heard the comment, he said, "I'm interested in reading, and I find reading is always profitable. I don't feel tired at all."

*Leisurely Talks at Shengshui**

*By Wang Pizhi of the Song Dynasty (960-1279).

畫 蛇 添 足
huà shé tiān zú

畫蛇添上足；比餘增添多餘的東西。

楚國有一家人，祭過了祖宗之後，便將一壺祭祀時用過的酒，留給辦事人員喝。辦事人員很多，僅僅一壺酒，到底給誰喝呢？有人提議：每人在地上畫一條蛇，誰畫得快畫得好，就把這壺酒給他。大家都認爲這辦法很好。

有一個人很快就把蛇畫好了。這壺酒就歸他所得。這時，他回頭看看別人，都沒有畫好，就得意洋洋地說：「你們畫得好慢呀！等我再畫上幾隻蛇脚吧！」正在他畫蛇脚的時候，另一個人已經把蛇畫好了。那人把酒壺奪了過去說：「蛇是沒有脚的，你怎麼畫上了脚？」說罷，就喝起酒來。

出自 《戰國策》

Drawing a Snake and Adding Legs
Gilding the Lily

Meaning adding something superfluous.

225

A family in the state of Chu gave a pot of wine used in the ancestor memorial ceremony to the family stewards. As there was only one pot of wine for many stewards, the stewards could not decide who was to drink it. Someone suggested that each of them draw a snake on the ground, and the one who finished first with a good picture of a snake would have the wine. They all agreed, saying it was a good method.

The man who finished first took the wine. When he turned and saw that the others had not finished, he said complacently, "You've all been so slow. I'm adding some legs to my snake." As he was adding legs to his snake, another man finished his. This man took the wine from him and said, "A snake has no legs. Why should you add legs?" As he said so, he began to drink the wine.

Anecdotes of the Warring States

畫龍點睛
huà lóng diǎn jīng

　　畫完龍再點眼睛；比喻説話或做文章在關鍵性的地方加上一兩句話，使內容更加精辟有力。

226

傳說，南北朝時，大畫家張僧繇有一天到一座寺廟裏去玩。他一時高興在墻壁上畫了四條龍，但都沒有畫上眼睛。人們見了覺得奇怪，問他爲什麼不畫眼睛。他回答說，如果畫了眼睛，龍就要飛上天去。人們不相信他的話，要求他把眼睛畫上去。於是他就在其中兩條龍上畫了眼睛。果然，頓時天空烏雲滾滾，雷電交加，那兩條龍脫離墻壁，飛上天去了。沒有畫上眼睛的那兩條龍，仍舊留在墻壁上。

出自《歷代名畫記》*

* 《歷代名畫記》 唐張彥遠著。

Adding Eyes to a Painted Dragon
Adding the Finishing Touches

Meaning adding a word or two to clinch the point.

LEGEND has it that one day when Zhang Sengyou, a great painter of the Southern and Northern Dynasties, spent his leisure in a temple, a momentary joyful food prompted him to paint four dragons on a wall. People were puzzled when they saw that he had not painted the eyes, and asked him why. He told them that if he had painted the eyes, the dragons would fly into the skies. People would not believe him and urged him to add the eyes. He then painted the eyes of two of the dragons. Sure enough, the sky suddenly was blackened by dark clouds and filled with thunder and lightning. The two dragons freed themselves from the wall and flew to the sky. The two without eyes still remained on the wall.

*Famous Paintings in History**

*By Zhang Yanyuan of the Tang Dynasty (618-907).

量體裁衣
liàng tǐ cái yī

量體裁衣;比喻按照實際情況辦事情。

宋朝末年,北京城裏有位裁縫很有名氣。他裁的衣服,長短肥瘦,無不合體。有一次,御史大夫請他去裁製一件進宮廷穿的朝服。裁縫量好了尺寸,又問:"請教老爺,您當官多少年了?"御史聽了很奇怪,反問他:"你問這些幹什麼?"裁縫回答說:"年青相公初任高職,意氣盛,走路的時候挺胸凸肚,裁衣就要後短前長;做官幾年以後,意氣微平,衣服應當一般長短;當官年久而將遷退,則內心悒郁不振,走路時低頭彎腰,做的衣服應當前短後長。所以,我如果不問明您做官的年資,怎麼能裁出稱心合體的衣服來呢?"

出自《履園叢話》*

* 《履園叢話》 清錢泳著。

228

Making the Clothes Fit the Body

Meaning to proceed from actual conditions.

A tailor of considerable fame lived in the city of Beijing at the end of the Song Dynasty. The clothes he tailored all fitted perfectly. An imperial censor asked him to make a court robe. "How many years has Your Excellency been in your official position?" asked the tailor. Perplexed by the tailor's question, the imperial censor questioned in reply, "Why do you ask?" The tailor explained, "When a young scholar took his first high official post, he is very confident and walks with his chest and stomach out. His clothes should be made longer at the front and shorter at the back. When someone has been an official for some years, he becomes less overbearing, and his clothes should be made even in length at the front and back. When someone has been an official for many years and is near his time of retirement, he becomes downcast in his spirit and walks with his head lowered and his back bent. His clothes should be made short at the front and longer at the back. How am I to make your clothes fit you if I don't ask you how many years you've been in your official position?"

Talks at Luyuan Garden*

*By Qian Yong of the Qing Dynasty (1644-1911).

買 櫝 還 珠
mǎi dú huán zhū

買下盒子，退還了珍珠；比喻取捨不當。

楚國有個珠寶商人，到鄭國去賣珍珠。他用名貴的木材，雕了一個盒子。又用各種方法，把盒子裝飾得很美觀，還用高貴的香料

229

來薰盒子，使它散發出濃烈的香味，然後把珍珠裝在裏面。有個鄭國人看到這個裝珍珠的盒子那麼精美，就出高價買了，但把珍珠還給了那個珠寶商人。

這個鄭國人，只知盒子好看，却不曉得珍珠的價值實在要比盒子的價值高許多倍。

出自《韓非子》

Buying the Box and Returning the Pearls

Grasping the Shadow and Letting Go the Substance

Meaning taking the wrong thing.

A jeweller of the state of Chu came to the state of Zheng to sell his pearls. He made a box of high-quality wood, decorated it beautifully and treated it with high-quality perfume until it gave off a rich, pleasant fragrance. He then placed the pearls in the box. When a man in the state of Zheng saw that the box was so beautiful, he paid a high price for it, took the box, but returned the pearls to the jeweller.

The man of the state of Zheng knew that the box was beautiful, but he did not know that the pearls were many times more valuable than the box.

The Book of Han Fei Zi

滅 此 朝 食
mìe cǐ zhāo shí

消滅了敵人再吃早飯；形容先要完成緊急的事。

春秋時，齊頃公領兵攻打魯國和衞國。晉國應魯、衞兩國的請求，派大將郤（音系）克帶兵前去援救。齊頃公自恃兵力衆多，不把晉軍放在眼裏，渴望一舉全殲晉軍。交戰的那一天，齊頃公早晨起來，部下請他用飯，他驕傲地說："我們先消滅了敵人，然後再回來吃早飯。"他不等拉戰車的馬披上護身甲就登上戰車，衝殺出去。晉軍奮力迎擊，晉將卻克親自擂鼓助戰，結果把齊軍打得大敗。齊頃公的戰車被打壞了，好不容易才得以脫險。

出自《左傳》

Wiping Out the Enemy Before Having Breakfast

First Things First

This means that what is important must be accomplished first.

DUKE Qinggong of the state of Qi during the Spring and Autumn Period launched an attack against the states of Lu and Wei. At the request of Lu and Wei, the state of Jin sent its general Xi Ke with an army to their rescue. Backed by a great army Duke Qinggong held the Jin army in contempt and was anxious to wipe it out in one battle. On the day of the battle, the Duke rose early in the morning. When his subordinates asked him to have his breakfast, he said arrogantly, "We'll wipe out the enemy first and then come back for breakfast." He mounted the chariot and rushed out before the protective armour was placed on the horses. The battle was extremely fierce, and the Jin general Xi Ke himself beat the battle drum to encourage the Jin soldiers who fought heroically. The Qi army was badly defeated at the end, and Duke Qinggong's chariot was damaged. It was with much difficulty that he managed to escape with his life.

Zuo Qiuming's Chronicles

運斤成風

yùn jīn chéng fēng

揮動斧頭帶來一股風；比喻技術熟練。

　　從前，楚國有個人在鼻尖上塗了一點刷牆的白粉，薄得像蒼蠅翅膀一樣。他請他的老朋友匠石給他斫掉。匠石揮動鋒利的大斧，對準他朋友的鼻子劈將過去，匠石動作異常迅速，只聽得揮動斧頭時一股風聲，楚人鼻子上的白粉被砍掉了，而鼻子則一點沒有傷着。

　　宋元君聽到這件事後，差人把匠石召來，要他表演一番。匠石說：「我倒會使用斧頭，可惜我那位願被削砍的朋友已死去很久了啊！」

出自《莊子》

Swinging the Axe and Creating a Gust of Wind

This is used to describe remarkable skill.

A man in the state of Chu dabbed the tip of his nose with whitewash as thin as a fly's wing and asked his old artisan friend Jiang Shi to remove it with his axe. Jiang Shi swung his axe and brought it suddenly down on his friend's nose. His movement was so swift that one could hear the wind carried by the axe. The whitewash was removed and his friend's nose was unhurt.

When Duke Yuanjuan of the state of Song heard of this, he asked the artisan to demonstrate it for him. Jiang Shi told him, "I know how to use the axe. But it is a pity that my friend who was willing to risk his nose died long ago."

The Book of Zhuang Zi

塞 翁 失 馬
sài wēng shī mǎ

住在邊境的一位老人丟失了馬；比喻雖然受到了暫時的損失，卻因此得到了好處。

北方邊境上，住着一個老頭。有一天，他家的一匹馬丟失了，鄰居都來安慰他。可是老頭並不着急，他說："這說不定是件好事。"過了幾個月，那匹馬自己回來了，還帶回來一匹駿馬。鄰居都來向他祝賀。老頭並不高興，他說："這說不定是件禍事。"有一天，老頭的兒子騎着那匹駿馬外出，因駿馬跑得太快，摔下馬來折斷了大腿骨，正中了老頭的預言。

出自《淮南子》*

* 《淮南子》 漢劉安（公元·前179－前122年）撰，內中記載很多寓言。

The Old Man at the Frontier Lost His Horse

A Blessing in Disguise

This idiom implies that a temporary loss may turn out to be a gain.

AN old man living on the northern frontier lost a horse. His neighbours all came to console him. But the old man was not worried at all. "It may turn out to be a good thing," he said. A few months later, the horse came back by itself and brought another fast horse with it. The old man's neighbours came again to congratulate him. But he was not overjoyed at all. "This may turn out to be a disaster," said he. One day, the old man's son went out riding on the fast horse. The horse ran too fast, and his son fell down and broke his leg.

233

The old man's prediction proved to be right.

The Book of Huai Nan Zi*

*Compiled by Liu An (179-122 B.C.) early in the Han Dynasty, the book contains many fables.

痴人說夢
chī rén shuō mèng

傻子述說自己做過的夢；比喻說荒誕不經的話。

　　從前，有一個富家子弟，生性癡呆。一天早上，他從床上爬起來，懵懵懂懂，到處張望。忽然，一把拉住進來拿東西的女僕，問道："昨天夜裏，妳夢見我沒有？"女僕莫明其妙，回答道："沒有。"他聽後非常生氣地說："我明明在夢中看見妳，妳爲什麼當面撒謊？"之後，他跑到他母親那裏，扯着她的衣襟大喊大叫說："這個女僕真該打，我明明夢見了她，她却說沒有，存心欺騙主人，真是豈有此理！"

234

出自《餘墨偶談》*

*《余墨偶談》 清孫濮撰。

A Fool Telling About His Dream

Meaning talking nonsense.

ONCE a rich family had a stupid son. One morning when he got out of his bed, he was not yet fully awake and cast his stares here and there. Suddenly he seized hold of a woman servant who had come into the room for something. He asked her, "Did you see me in your dream?" The woman servant could not make head or tail of it and said, "No, I didn't." He was very angry. "I saw you in my dream. Why do you tell an outrageous lie?" he said. He then ran to his mother and, pulling at the hem of her coat, cried, "The woman servant must be beaten. I definitely saw her in my dream, and yet she said she didn't see me. She is deliberately cheating her master. This is outright preposterous!"

Random Talks Recorded in Residual Ink *

*By Sun Yun of the Qing Dynasty (1644-1911).

逼上梁山
bī shàng liáng shān

逼得上了梁山；比喻被迫無奈而幹某些事。

　　北宋末年，晁蓋和他的同伙佔據了梁山一帶的水泊，與官兵作對。當時有個武藝高超的人叫林冲，在高俅手下任禁軍教頭。高俅的兒子高衙內在廟會上看上了林冲的妻子，想霸佔她，但被林冲教訓了一頓。高衙內懷恨在心，便在高俅面前告了林冲的狀。之後，

235

高俅把林冲騙入商議軍機大事的廳堂，以林冲想謀刺高俅的罪名把他發配到滄州去。在前往滄州途中，高俅偷偷地指使兩個押送林冲的解差設法把他害死，但林冲被他的結拜兄弟魯智深搭救了。林冲到滄州後，被分配去管理草料場。高俅又派官差來燒草料場，想把林冲燒死。林冲忍無可忍，殺了官差。這時，他已無處棲身，就投奔了梁山。

出自《水滸傳》*

*《水滸傳》 長篇小說，明施耐庵著。

Driven to Join the Liangshan Rebels
Going to the Greenwood

Meaning to be forced to do something.

AT the end of the Northern Song Dynasty, Chao Gai and his followers occupied the marshy land around Mount Liangshan and set themselves against the government soldiers. Lin Chong, a man of unusual military skill, was then serving as an instructor in the Imperial Guards commanded by Gao Qiu. Young Master Gao, Gao Qiu's son, took a fancy to Lin Chong's wife when he saw her at a temple fair. He wanted to take her for himself but was chastised by Lin Chong. Out of malice, he complained against Lin with his father, who trapped Lin in the Military Council Hall. Accused of intending to murder Gao Qiu, Lin was exiled to Cangzhou. While Lin was on his way to Cangzhou, Gao Qiu secretly ordered the two escorts to murder him, but Lin Chong was saved by his sworn brother Lu Zhishen. In Cangzhou, Lin was assigned to look after the fodder depot. Gao Qiu again sent his officers to set fire to the fodder depot in another attempt to take Lin's life. At the end of his forebearance, Lin killed the officers. Realizing that by now he had nowhere else to go, he joined the rebels on Mount Liangshan.

*A novel by Shi Nai'an of the Ming Dynasty (1368-1644).

葉 公 好 龍

yè gōng hào lóng

葉公愛好龍；比喻對某事物只是表面上愛好，而並非出於眞心，實際上是畏懼它。

　　葉公是個出名的喜歡龍的人，他住的房子裏，墙上畫着龍，柱子上雕着龍，他穿的衣服上綉着龍，帽子上鑲着龍。

　　天上的眞龍，聽說葉公這般喜歡龍，就飛到葉公家裏。那眞龍把頭伸進南窗，把尾巴繞到北窗。葉公看到了，嚇得渾身發抖，急忙躲了起來。原來葉公所喜歡的是那些畫在墙上、雕在柱子上的假龍，而不是眞的龍。

出自《新序》

Lord Yegong's Love of Dragons

This implies professed love of what one really fears.

LORD Yegong was known for his love of dragons. He had dragons painted on the walls and carved on the pillars of his house. His robes were embroidered with dragons and his hat was decorated with dragons.

　　When a real dragon in the sky heard of Lord Yegong's love of dragons, it flew to his house. The dragon put its head into the southern window of the house and its tail into the northern window. When Lord Yegong saw the dragon, he trembled with fear and hurriedly hid himself. What Lord

237

Yegong loved were fake dragons painted on the walls and carved on the pillars, not the real dragons.

New Discourses

萬事俱備，只欠東風
wàn shì jù bèi, zhǐ qiàn dōng fēng

一切都齊備，只差東風了。"東風"在這裏比喻重要條件或時機。

魏王曹操率領二十萬大軍，企圖在長江南岸的赤壁消滅劉備和孫權，統一全國。當時劉備只有兩萬兵力，但在謀士諸葛亮的策劃下，聯合孫權，採用火攻方法，打敗了曹操，這就是中國歷史上著名的"赤壁之戰"。

在他們準備用火燒曹軍戰船時，正是冬天，只有西北風，而根據他們當時所處的位置，一定要有東南風才能發揮火攻的威力。爲此，孫權的大將周瑜急出病來了。諸葛亮猜到周瑜的心事，去探病時寫了十六個字給他，即："欲破曹公，宜用火攻，萬事俱備，只

238

欠東風。"周瑜甚爲佩服諸葛亮，就向他請敎，諸葛亮說他能借東風。一天，東南風起時，他們順風放火，頓時曹軍戰船火焰瀰漫，一直燒到岸上的軍營，曹軍大敗。

出自《三國演義》*

*《三國演義》　長篇歷史小說，明初羅貫中（約公元1330—1400）撰。

Everything Is Ready Except the East Wind

"East wind" here refers to an important condition or opportunity.

CAO Cao of Wei led an army 200,000 strong and intended to destroy Liu Bei of Shu and Sun Quan of Wu at Chibi on the southern bank of the Changjiang River and unite the whole country. Liu Bei then had only an army of 20,000. But, following the scheme formulated by his adviser Zhuge Liang, he united with Sun Quan and used fire in the battle and put Cao Cao to rout. This was the famous Battle of Chibi in Chinese history.

The plan to use fire in the battle required southeast wind to blow the flames onto Cao Cao's war vessels. But it was winter and a northwest wind was blowing. Zhou Yu, the commanding general of Wu, became so worried that he took to his bed. Zhuge Liang guessed what was on Zhou Yu's mind. He came to see Zhou Yu at his sickbed and wrote down sixteen characters, meaning "To destroy Cao Cao, the best weapon is fire. Everything is ready except the east wind." Zhou Yu was deeply impressed by Zhuge Liang's resourcefulness and asked him what was to be done. Zhuge Liang said he could make the wind blow from the east. On the day when a southeast wind began to blow, they started their attack with fire, and in no time Cao Cao's war vessels were engulfed in flames. The fire spread to Cao Cao's army camp on the bank. Cao Cao suffered a disasterous defeat.

Tales of the Three Kingdoms *

愚 公 移 山
yú gōng yí shān

愚公老人搬山；比喻有毅力，不怕困難。

北山愚公快九十歲了。他家的大門面對着太行山和王屋山，出門做事眞不方便。有一天，愚公召集全家大小，對他們說：“我們大家出力搬走這兩座大山，開出一條大路來，你們贊成嗎？”大家都很贊成，只有他的妻子有些疑慮。她說：“就憑我們這點人，恐怕連一堆小土堆也平不了，別說這麼又高又大的兩座山！再說，挖出來的那些石頭、泥塊往那裏送呢？”大家都說：“挖出來的石頭、泥塊，把它搬到渤海灘上去。”

第二天，愚公就帶領全家人，動手挖山了。

有一個叫智叟的老頭兒，人很精明。他看見愚公他們這樣辛辛苦苦地挖山，覺得好笑，便去勸告愚公說：“你這個人爲什麼這麼傻！你這麼大歲數了，用盡你們氣力，也拔不了山上的幾根草，怎麼搬得了那麼大的山呢？”

愚公深深地嘆了口氣，回答說：“我看你眞是糊塗透頂了。不錯，我是老了，活不多久了。可是我死了，還有兒子，兒子又有孫子，孫子又有兒子，子子孫孫一直傳下去，是沒有窮盡的啊！可是這兩座大山呢？再也不會增高了。我們爲什麼挖不平呢！”聽了這話，智叟無言可對。

出自《列子》

240

The Foolish Old Man Removed the Mountains

It's Dogged That Does It

Describing a man of fortitude who is not afraid of difficulties.

THE Foolish Old Man of North Mountain was almost ninety. His house faced two mountains, the Taihang and the Wangwu, which obstructed his way. One day, he called all his family together and said to them, "Let's work together, remove the two mountains and open a road. How do you like it?" Everybody agreed. Only his wife had some doubts. She said, "With the few of you, you can hardly level a small mound. How can you remove two great mountains? Besides, where are you going to put the rocks and earth?" "We'll move the rocks and earth to the shore of the Bohai Sea," the others said.

The following day, the Foolish Old Man and his family began to dig.

Another grey-beard, known as the Wise Old Man, saw them working so hard and said derisively, "How silly you are! At your age, you can hardly pull out a few blades of grass on the mountains. How can you dig up the mountains?"

The Foolish Old Man uttered a deep sigh and said, "How can you be so helplessly foolish. It's true that I'm old and cannot live very long. But when I die, my sons will carry on. When they die, there will be my grandsons, and then their sons and grandsons and on to infinity. High as they are, the mountains cannot grow any higher. Why is it that we cannot flatten them?" The Wise Old Man was not able to answer him.

The Book of Lie Zi

241

嗟 來 之 食
jiē lái zhī shí

喂，來吃吧！ 指帶有侮辱性的施捨。

齊國有一年發生了飢荒。有一個名叫黔敖的富人，在大路旁備了一些食物，用來施捨給飢餓的人吃。一天，有一個餓得不像樣子的人，用袖子遮着臉，拖着破鞋子，跟蹌欲跌地走了過來。黔敖左手拿着吃的，右手端着湯，傲慢地吆喝道："喂，來吃吧！"

那個人抬起頭來輕蔑地瞪了黔敖一眼說道："我就是因爲不吃'嗟來之食'，才餓成這個樣子。我不能接受你這種帶有侮辱性的憐憫。"

黔敖聽了隨即向他謝罪，可是那個人怎麼說也不肯吃，終於餓死了。

出自《禮記》

Relief Food Handed Out in Contempt
Better Die a Beggar Than Live a Beggar

WHEN a famine struck the state of Qi, a rich man named Qian Ao put some food by the roadside and distributed it to those who were hungry. One day, a badly starved man came, his face covered with his sleeve, and walked unsteadily in tattered shoes. With food in his left hand and soup in his right, Qian Ao shouted arrogantly at the man, "You! Eat!"

The man raised his head, stared at Qian Ao in contempt and said, "I've been starved as I am because I don't eat relief food handed out in contempt. I won't accept your humiliating pity."

Qian Ao at once apologized to him, but the man just would not eat his food and eventually died from starvation.

The Book of Rites

暗 渡 陳 倉
àn dù chén cāng

暗中通過陳倉這個地方；形容瞞着別人偷偷摸摸地活動，並達到了目的。

秦朝剛被推翻的時候，項羽、劉邦以及其他參加反秦戰爭的將領，齊集商議怎樣分割領地。項羽自恃勢力強大，佔領長江中、下游和淮河流域一帶肥沃之地。他把最邊遠的巴、蜀和漢中三郡（現四川和陝西南部）劃歸劉邦，而把最富庶的關中（陝西中部）分爲三部份，分別封給三個投降的秦將，以阻擋劉邦回關中的道路。

劉邦對此非常不滿，但懾於項羽的威勢，只得聽從分配，開往漢中。爲了便於防禦和麻痺項羽，他在回漢中的途中，燒毀了在險峻的山崖上用木材架設的通道。

劉邦回到漢中以後，一心想和項羽爭奪天下。他拜才能出衆的韓信爲大將，按照韓信的計劃，先奪取關中，然後向東進發。於是派出幾百名士兵，去修復棧道，表示要從那裏出擊的樣子。可是劉邦和韓信統率的主力部隊却暗地裏越過陳倉（今陝西寶鷄市東面）

攻入咸陽，迅速佔領了全部關中地區。

出自《史記》

Advancing Secretly Along the Chencang Route

Stealing a March Upon

Meaning to attain one's end by clandestine means.

IMMEDIATELY after the Qin Dynasty was overthrown, Xiang Yu, Liu Bang and the other generals who took part in the wars against Qin gathered together to divide the Qin territories. Xiang Yu, being the strongest, took the fertile land of the middle and lower reaches of the Changjiang River, and the Huaihe River valley. The three remote prefectures in Bashu and Hanzhong (today's Sichuan and the southern part of Shaanxi) were given to Liu Bang. The most fertile Guanzhong (central Shaanxi) area was divided into three parts and given to three Qin generals who had surrendered, to block Liu Bang's path to Guanzhong.

Although Liu Bang was profoundly dissatisfied, he had to agree to the arrangement and went to Hanzhong for fear of the powerful Xiang Yu. In order to defend himself and put Xiang Yu off his guard, he burned the plank path along the dangerous cliffs as he withdrew to Hanzhong.

Back to Hanzhong, Liu Bang set his mind on fighting against Xiang Yu for the throne. He made the brilliant Han Xin his chief general and Han Xin's plan was to take Guanzhong first and then march towards the east. A few hundred soldiers were sent to rebuild the plank path to feign that they were to attack from there. Actually Liu Bang and Han Xin were leading their main force stealthily through Chencang (to the east of today's Baoji city in Shaanxi). They stormed into Xianyang and swiftly occupied the entire Guanzhong area.

Records of the Historian

飲 水 思 源
yǐn shuǐ sī yuán

喝水的時候想到水的來源；比喻不忘本。

　　南北朝時代，有個文學家名叫庾信，他奉梁元帝之命出使西魏。在他出使期間，梁朝被西魏滅亡。由於庾信在文學上的聲望，他被西魏留下，並做了大官。庾信在西魏的二十八年間，常常懷念故國和家鄉，在他寫的《征調曲》中有兩句："落其實者思其樹，飲其流者懷其源。"大意是：吃果子的時候，想到生長果子的樹，喝水的時候，想到水的來源。

出自《庾子山集》*

*《庾子山集》　北周庾信（513－581）作。

When You Drink Water, Think of Its Source

This implies that one must not forget to whom one is indebted.

DURING the Southern and Northern Dynasties, Yu Xin, a man of letters, was sent by Emperor Yuandi of the Liang Dynasty to the Western Wei Dynasty as his envoy. While he was serving as an envoy, the Liang Dynasty was subjugated by Western Wei. On account of his literary fame, Yu Xin was asked to serve in the Western Wei court and became a prominent official. During his twenty-eight years' stay in Western Wei, Yu Xin always thought about his old country and home. In a poem he wrote, there are these two lines: "When you eat fruit, think of the tree that bore it. When you drink water, think of its source."

*Collected Works of Yu Xin**

*By Yu Xin (513-581) of the Northern Zhou Dynasty.

與狐謀皮

yǔ hu mòu pí

與狐狸商量借用牠的皮；現大多說作“與虎謀皮”，用來形容不切實際的幻想，即跟壞人商量，要他犧牲自身利益。

從前，有個人想做一件貴重的狐皮袍子，便跑到山裏去找到一隻狐狸，跟牠商量說：“狐狸兄弟，我想借用你的皮做一件袍子，行嗎？”狐狸一聽，嚇得慌忙逃跑了。後來，這個人想辦桌酒席祭祀祖宗，便跑到山坡上跟一隻山羊商量說：“山羊兄弟，我想借你的肉祭祖先，行嗎？”山羊聽了，也嚇跑了。

出自《太平廣記》*

*《太平廣記》 小說總集，宋初李昉（925－996）等編輯。

Asking a Fox for Its Skin

The more often used version today is "Asking a tiger for its skin." This idiom means to ask an evil person to act against his own interests, which is not realistic.

A man wanted to make a robe of the prized fox fur. He went into the hills and found a fox. He said to the fox, "Brother fox, can you lend me your skin so that I can make a robe?" Scared by his words, the fox hurriedly ran away. The same man later wanted to prepare sacrifices for his ancestors. He went to a hillslope and said to a goat, "Brother goat, can you lend me your meat so that I can offer sacrifices to my ancestors?" The goat was also scared by his words and ran away.

Stories Compiled in the Taiping Period*

*A collection of stories compiled by Li Fang (925-996) and others of the early Song Dynasty.

滿 城 風 雨
mǎn chéng fēng yǔ

整個城市都有風雨；比喻一件事發生後，到處議論紛紛。

宋代，有位詩人叫潘大臨。一年秋季，他忽然聽到窗外風雨吹打樹木的聲音，不禁引起了寫詩的興致。當他剛寫好第一句"滿城風雨近重陽"，忽然催收田賦的人闖了進來。詩人的詩興被破壞，這首詩就再也寫不下去了。詩雖然只有一句，但直到現在仍被人們傳誦着。

出自 《冷齋夜話》 *

* 《冷齋夜話》 宋僧人釋惠洪著。

The Whole Town Is Swept by Wind and Rain
Becoming the Talk of the Town

Describing something sensational that has become the talk of the town.

ONE autumn, the wind and rain beating on the trees outside his windows inspired the Song Dynasty poet Pan Dalin to write a poem. When he finished the first line: "As the Double Ninth Festival draws near, the whole town is swept by wind and rain", he was disturbed by a rent-collector who had rushed into his house. As his mood was interrupted, he could not continue. Although the poem has only one line, it has been on everybody's lips ever since.

*Night Talks at Cool Studio**

*By Monk Shi Huihong of the Song Dynasty (960-1279).

實 事 求 是

shí shì qiú shì

根據實證，求索眞相；指從實際出發，正確地處理問題。

　　西漢時，景帝的兒子河間獻王劉德，喜歡讀書。他曾搜集過許多先秦的書籍，並嚴肅認眞地從事研究，受到了人們的讚揚。

　　史學家班固在編著《漢書》時，替劉德寫了傳記。他熱情讚揚劉德研究學問的態度，說他用充份的事實做根據，然後從事實中尋求出正確可靠的結論。

出自 《漢書》

Seeking Truth from Facts

Meaning to proceed from the actual situation and finding correct solutions to problems.

LIU De, Prince Xianwang of Hejian of the Western Han Dynasty, was Emperor Jingdi's son. Fond of studying, he had collected many books written before the Qin Dynasty and studied them conscientiously. He won the praise of many people.

When the historian Ban Gu compiled the *History of the Han Dynasty,* he wrote a biography of Liu De. He warmly praised Liu De's attitude towards learning, saying that he based himself on sufficient facts and then proceeded from these facts to reach the correct and reliable conclusion.

History of the Han Dynasty

竭澤而漁

jié zé ér yú

汲乾了池裏的水提魚；比喻做事不從長遠着眼，只顧眼前利益。

春秋時，晉、楚兩國在城濮地方發生了戰爭。晉文公問大臣狐偃說：“楚強我弱，我們怎樣才能打勝仗呢？”狐偃回答說：“講究禮節的人，不怕麻煩，善於打仗的人，不厭欺詐，我們就用欺詐敵人的戰術吧！”

晉文公把狐偃的話告訴了另一大臣季雍。季雍說：“把池塘的水抽乾了提魚，怎能捉不到呢，但明年就無魚可提了；把山上的樹木燒光了捉野獸，怎能捉不到呢？但明年就無野獸可捉了。現在雖然可以使用欺詐的方法，但以後就不能再用，這不是長遠之計啊！”晉文公採用了狐偃的建議，用欺詐的方法打敗了楚國。但在行賞的時候，首先受賞的是季雍，其次才是狐偃。左右的人疑惑不解，晉文公說：“季雍的意見涉及國家的根本大計，狐偃的話，是臨時變通的辦法，所以首先獎勵季雍是理所當然的。”

出自 《呂氏春秋》

Draining the Pond to Get the Fish

Killing the Goose That Lays the Golden Eggs

Meaning to sacrifice future interests to satisfy present needs.

IN the Spring and Autumn Period, a war broke out between the states of Jin and Chu at Chengpu. Duke Wengong of Jin asked his minister Hu Yan, "Since Chu is strong and we weak, how are we to win?" Hu Yan answered, "People who are particular about etiquette do not spare troubles. Men who are good at fighting a war are never tired of employing deception. Let us use deception against the enemy then!"

Duke Wengong told what Hu Yan said to Ji Yong, another minister. Ji Yong said, "If you drain the pond to get the fish, you surely will be able to get them. But there won't be any fish the next year. If you burn the forest to get the wild beasts, you surely will be able to get them. But there won't be any wild beasts the next year. We can use deception now. But we mustn't use it in the future because it's not a permenant solution." Duke. Wengong of Jin adopted Hu Yan's suggestion, employed deception and defeated the state of Chu. But when the time came to give rewards, he rewarded Ji Yong first and then Hu Yan. People close to the Duke were puzzled. The Duke said, "Ji Yong's opinion concerns the fundamental interests of the country, while Hu Yan's suggestion was a makeshift solution. That's why Ji Yong should be rewarded first."

The Discourses of Lü Buwei

精 衞 塡 海
jīng wèi tián hǎi

精衞鳥用樹枝和石子塡海；比喻不畏艱難，不達目的不止。

傳說上古時代，炎帝的女兒到東海邊去遊玩，忽然海上起了風暴，她不幸被巨浪捲走淹死了。她死後，化做一隻小鳥。這隻小鳥整天"精衞、精衞"地叫着。人們便稱她"精衞鳥"。她恨大海吞噬了她年輕的生命，發誓要把大海塡平。她每天從西山銜來樹枝和石子，然後飛向東海，把它們投進海中。一年又一年地過去，精衞鳥從沒有間斷過自己的工作。後來因爲她的嘴被樹枝和石子磨穿，死去了。

出自《山海經》

Jingwei Fills Up the Sea

The Jingwei bird filling the sea with twigs and pebbles is likened to one who is determined to attain his end in spite of tremendous difficulties.

LEGEND has it that in very ancient times when the daughter of Emperor Yandi was playing on the beach of the East Sea, a storm broke out on the sea and she was carried away by giant waves and drowned. After her death, she became a little bird crying "Jingwei! Jingwei!" all day long. People began to call her the Jingwei bird. She hated the sea that had taken her young life so much that she vowed to fill it up. Every day she picked twigs and pebbles from the Western Hills, flew to the East Sea and dropped them into it. Year after year, the Jingwei bird never stopped her work. She eventually died when her beak was pierced by the twigs and pebbles.

Classic of Mountains and Waters

遠水救不了近火
yuǎn shuǐ jiù bù liǎo jìn huǒ

遠處的水救不了近處的火；比喻緩慢的辦法，滿足不了急迫的
需要。

戰國時期，魯穆公看到鄰邦齊國力量一天比一天強大，担心自
己的國家會被齊國吞併。爲取得大國的幫助，他打算派他的叔叔到
晉國去做官，派他的侄子到楚國去做官。以爲這樣一來，晉國和楚
國都跟魯國有了交情，如果齊國來侵犯，晉、楚兩國一定會來援
助。

魯國大夫犁鉏（音除）不同意這個辦法，他對魯穆公說："假
如有個地方發生火災，你跑到千里以外的海邊去取水來救火，大海
裏的水雖多，但等你把水取來，房子已化爲灰燼了，因爲遠處的水
不能救近處的火。現在晉國和楚國雖然強大，可是離我們太遠，而
齊國就在我們身邊，如果我們不跟齊國友好，一旦有了災難，晉國

252

和楚國是援助不了我們的。"

Water Far Away Cannot Put Out a Fire Nearby

While the Grass Grows the Horse Starves

Meaning a slow remedy cannot meet an urgent need.

DUKE Mugong of the state of Lu during the Warring States Period saw that his neighbouring state Qi was growing more powerful day by day, and he worried that his country might one day be swallowed by Qi. In order to secure the help of the larger states, he intended to send his uncle to the state of Jin and work as an official there and send his nephew to the state of Chu and work as an official there. He thought that when the states of Jin and Chu were on friendly terms with the state of Lu, they would come to his rescue if Qi invaded Lu.

Li Chu, a court official of Lu, disagreed to his plan and said to him, "If a fire breaks out and someone goes to the seaside a thousand *li* away to get water, the house will be reduced to ashes by the time he comes back with water despite of the fact that there is a lot of water in the sea. This is because water far away cannot put out a fire nearby. Although the states of Jin and Chu are powerful, they are too far away. And yet the state of Qi is near. If we are not friendly to the state of Qi, the states of Jin and Chu won't be able to help us if disaster falls."

The Book of Han Fei Zi

聞 鷄 起 舞

wén jī qǐ wǔ

聽見鷄叫聲，就舞起劍來；比喩有志之士及時奮發圖强。

晉朝時，有個叫劉琨的人，在青年時代就有爲國立功的大志。他和他的好朋友祖逖都是管文書的官吏。當時晉朝北方的大片土地都爲異族佔據，國勢已經衰弱。他們倆都懷着共同的報國決心。兩人夜間同睡一床，經常說到深夜。有一天半夜，忽然聽到鷄啼。祖逖用脚踢劉琨，問道："聽見鷄啼了嗎？"原來劉琨也沒睡着。祖逖說："這聲音很激勵人心，我們起來舞劍吧！"兩人一躍而起，抽出寶劍，在鷄啼聲中，興奮地對舞起來。

後來，祖逖、劉琨都成爲晉朝將領。祖逖曾領兵北伐，爲晉朝收復了很多失地。

出自《晉書》

Exercises at Cock's Crow

This is said of people of high aspirations who lose no time to prepare themselves for a great future.

LIU Kun of the Jin Dynasty had great aspirations to render service to his country even when he was very young. He and his good friend Zu Di were both government clerks. With large pieces of its territories in the north occupied by alien nations, the Jin Dynasty was already in a state of decline. Liu and Zu were both determined to render service to their country. They slept in the same bed and often talked far into the night. Late one night, they suddenly heard a cock crow. Zu Di kicked at Liu Kun and asked him, "Did you hear the cock crow?" Liu Kun was also not asleep. "The sound seems to stir people to action. Let's get up and do sword exercise," said Zu Di. So the two jumped out of bed, unsheathed their swords and began to exercise together with excitement to the crow of the roosters.

Later, both became generals of the Jin Dynasty. Zu Di led his army in a northern expedition and recovered many lost territories of the Jin Dynasty.

History of the Jin Dynasty

對 牛 彈 琴

duì niú tán qín

對着牛演奏琴曲；比喻對蠢人講高深的道理，也用來譏笑人講話不看對象。

從前，有個音樂家，叫公明儀，有一天他正在彈琴，看見旁邊有頭牛在吃草。他心想，我來彈幾支曲子讓牠聽聽吧。他先彈了一支高深的樂曲。可是那牛毫不理會，仍然自顧吃草。公明儀想，牛怎能欣賞這種高深的樂曲呢？他又彈了一支曲子，這支曲子彈得一會兒像蚊子叫，一會兒像牛犢叫。這頭牛才搖起尾巴，豎起耳朵，留心地聽起來。

出自 《弘明集》 *

* 《弘明集》 南北朝梁朝僧人釋僧佑作。

Playing the Lute to the Cow

Casting Pearls Before Swine

This alludes to talking about something profound to an un appreciative person, or is used to ridicule someone who wastes his breath on a wrong audience.

255

ONCE when the musician Gongming Yi was playing a lute, he saw a cow munching grass nearby. He thought that maybe he could play some music for the cow. He began to play an exquisite melody, but the cow took no notice of him and continued to munch grass. "How can I expect a cow to understand this kind of profound music?" Gongming Yi realized. So he began to play another melody which imitated the buzzing of the mosquitoes and the cry of a calf. The cow wagged its tail, pricked up its ears and began to listen attentively.

The Hongming Encyclopaedia of Buddhism *

*By Monk Shi Sengyou of the Liang Dynasty (502-557) during the Southern and Northern Dynasties.

對症下藥

duì zhèng xià yào

針對病情用藥;比喻針對問題所在,作有效的處理。

華陀是漢末著名醫學家。一次，州官倪尋和李延兩人都患頭痛發熱病，一道去請華陀診治。華陀仔細地診斷了兩人的病情，開了兩個藥方：倪尋吃通導藥，李延吃發散藥。倪尋和李延按方服藥以後，病都好了。人們問華陀爲什麼兩人患同樣的病却服用不同的藥？華陀解釋說：“倪尋的身體外部沒有病，病是從內部傷食引起的；李延的身體內部沒有病，病是從外部受冷感冒引起的，所以治療方法也就不同。”

出自《三國誌》

Suiting the Medicine to the Illness

Meaning to cope with a problem with effective measures.

HUA Tuo was a famous physician who lived at the end of the Han Dynasty. Once two prefectural officials Ni Xun and Li Yan came to see him together, both complaining of headache and fever. Hua Tuo examined them carefully and wrote out two prescriptions for them: an obstruction-clearing remedy for Ni Xun and a fever-dispersing remedy for Li Yan. After taking Hua Tuo's medicines, both were cured. People asked Hua Tuo why he had given them different medicines when they had the same complaint. Hua Tuo explained, "There was nothing wrong with Ni Xun externally. His illness came from indigestion inside him. Li Yan was all right inside. His illness resulted from cold from the outside. That was why I treated them differently."

History of the Three Kingdoms

圖 窮 匕 見

tú qióng bǐ xiàn

地圖全部展開了，就露出了匕首；一般形容陰謀終於完全敗露。

戰國時，燕國太子丹派荊軻出使秦國，以獻地求和爲名，企圖
伺機行刺秦王。

荊軻和他的助手秦舞陽，帶着燕國督亢地方的地圖，來到秦國。
秦王在咸陽宮召見了他們。荊軻走在前面，秦舞陽跟在後面，當他
們步上宮殿的台堦時，秦舞陽忽然害怕起來，臉色變了，渾身發抖，
引起了秦國官員們的懷疑。荊軻十分鎭定，機智地掩蓋過去。秦王
叫他們把地圖送上去。當秦王打開地圖，翻到最後一部份時，藏
在圖中的一把匕首就露了出來。荊軻迅速抓起匕首，一把抓住秦王
的衣袖，企圖威逼他答應把侵佔別國的領土全部退還。秦王嚇得魂
不附體，扯斷衣袖，倉惶逃走。荊軻擧起匕首，向秦王奮力擲去，
沒有擲中。最後荊軻被當場殺害。

出自《戰國策》

When the Map Is Unrolled the Dagger Is Revealed

Implying that a scheme is exposed.

AT the time of the Warring States, Prince Dan of the state of
Yan sent Jing Ke to the state of Qin under the false pretence
of ceding territory for the sake of peace, to find an
opportunity to assassinate the King of Qin.

When Jing Ke and his assistant Qin Wuyang, carrying a
map of Dukang of the state of Yan, arrived in the state of
Qin, they were received by the King of Qin at the Xianyang
Palace. Jing Ke walked at the front, and Qin Wuyang
followed behind him. As they mounted the steps of the
palace hall, Qin Wuyang was suddenly seized with fear. His
face was drained of colour, and he trembled all over. The Qin
officials became suspicious. Jing Ke remained perfectly calm,
and he cleverly covered him up. The King of Qin asked them
to hand over the map and began to unroll it. When he came
to the end of the map roll, the dagger hidden in it was

revealed. Jing Ke quickly picked up the dagger with one hand and seized the King's sleeve with the other. He wanted to force the King of Qin to promise to return all the territories he had taken from the other states. The King of Qin was so scared that he tore off his sleeve and began to run in panic. Jing Ke raised his dagger and threw it at the King with all his might, but missed him. He was killed on the spot.

Anecdotes of the Warring States

網開三面
wǎng kāi sān miàn

撤掉三面的網；比喻放人一條生路。

古時候，商國的首領商湯有一天到野外去玩，看見一個人張着四面網在捕鳥。捕鳥人祝願說：“願天上飛下來的鳥，地下飛上來的鳥都能進入我的網裏來。”商湯聽見後對捕鳥人說：“你這樣做太殘忍了，鳥兒都要給你捉光了。”於是他命令捕鳥人把網撤掉三面，只留一面。商湯祝願說：“鳥兒啊！你們願意往左飛就往左飛，願意往右飛就往右飛，實在不想活了，就進入我的網裏來吧。”

諸侯聽到這件事後說：“商湯是一位仁慈的王啊！”於是有四十多個部落來歸順他。最後，商湯率領各部落的隊伍滅了夏朝，成了商朝的第一個皇帝。

出自《呂氏春秋》

Leaving Three Sides of the Net Open

Meaning allowing a way out.

IN bygone times, Shang Tang, ruler of the state of Shang, went to the open country one day and saw a man trying to

259

catch birds with a four-sided net. The bird-catcher was
praying, "May birds flying down from the sky and flying up
from the ground all come into my net." When Shang Tang
saw it, he said to the bird-catcher, "Your method is too cruel.
You'll kill all the birds." He ordered the man to remove three
sides of the net. He prayed, "Birds! If you want to fly to the
left, fly to the left. If you want to fly to the right, fly the
right. If you really don't want to live, come into my net."

When the tribe leaders heard about this, they all said that
Shang Tang was a benevolent king. More than forty of them
came over and pledged allegiance. Leading the tribes, Shang
Tang eventually overthrew the Xia Dynasty and became the
first king of the Shang Dynasty.

The Discourses of Lü Buwei

慶父不死，魯難未已
qìng fù bù sǐ, lǔ nàn wèi yǐ

慶父死不了，魯國的災難就不會完結；比喻不除掉禍根，就得
不到安寧。

春秋時，魯國的公子慶父是魯莊公的弟弟。魯莊公死了以後，
子般做了國君，慶父不滿意子般，便殺了子般，另立閔公為國君。
慶父對閔公仍不滿意，又殺死了閔公。慶父這樣專橫殘暴，接連殺
了兩個國君，引起了國內大亂。齊桓公是當時眾諸侯的領袖，便派
大臣到魯國了解情況。大臣回國後向齊桓公報告說："魯國的災難，
都是慶父引起的，不除掉慶父，魯國的災難，是不會結束的。" 後
來，魯國人起來反對慶父，慶父逃到莒國。不久，慶父被押解回魯，
他自知罪惡深重，在途中自殺了。

出自《左傳》

The State of Lu's Troubles Will Not Come to an End If Qing Fu Is Not Removed

Meaning that peace will not come until the trouble-maker is done away with.

PRINCE Qing Fu of the state of Lu in the Spring and Autumn Period was Duke Zhuanggong's brother. When the Duke died, Zi Ban became the ruler of the state. As Qing Fu was not satisfied with him, he had him killed and put Min Gong on the throne. Still not satisfied, Qing Fu killed Min Gong too. Qing Fu's tyranny and atrocity of killing two rulers of the state in succession put the country in a great turmoil. Duke Huangong of the state of Qi, who was then the leader of the princes, sent a minister to find out what was happening in the state of Lu. On his return, the minister told the Duke, "It's Qing Fu who caused all the miseries in the state of Lu. The state of Lu's troubles will not come to an end if Qing Fu is not removed." Later, the people in the state of Lu rose to oppose Qing Fu, and Qing Fu fled to the state of Ju. But before long, he was captured and taken back to the state of Lu. Knowing that he had committed grave crimes, he ended his own life on the way.

Zuo Qiuming's Chronicles

熟 能 生 巧
shú néng shēng qiǎo

熟練了就能產生巧辦法。

　　陳堯咨善射箭。有一天，他在塲地上練習射箭，箭箭都射中了靶子，看的人們都一齊拍手叫好。只有一個賣油的老人，只是略微點了點頭，表示他並不十分驚奇。

　　陳堯咨見他這樣輕視自己，便問這賣油的老人：＂你也會射箭

261

嗎?"賣油老人回答道:"我不會射箭,不過,依我看,你雖然射得很好,但也沒有什麼特別地方,只是手法熟練就是了!"陳堯咨有點生氣了,便說:"你不會射箭,又這麼小看我,真是太不像話了!"老人說:"我是個賣油的,也從斟油上得了一點小經驗,現在請你看一看吧!"

賣油的老人把一個盛油的葫蘆放在地下,把一個銅錢放在葫蘆口上,然後用油勺子將油從錢孔裏瀝下去。油瀝下許多,可是一點也沒有沾在錢孔上。賣油的老人笑着對陳堯咨說:"你看,這也沒有什麼特別的地方,只是手法熟練罷了!"從此以後,陳堯咨再不敢以善射箭而自負了。

出自《歸田錄》*

*《歸田錄》 北宋歐陽修(1007—1072)撰。

Skill Comes from Practice

Practice Makes Perfect

CHEN Yaozi was an excellent archer. One day when he practised at the range, every one of his arrows hit the bull's eye. The on-lookers all applauded for him. Only an old oil-vendor did not appear to be moved very much. He only nodded his head.

Seeing that he had been held in contempt, Chen Yaozi asked the old oil-vendor, "Do you also shoot arrows?" The old man said, "I don't know archery. But, in my opinion, there's nothing special in your shooting good arrows. It is only because you are skilled." Chen became somewhat angry. He said, "You don't know how to shoot arrows. And yet you look down on me. This is really preposterous." The old man said, "I'm an oil-vendor. I've learned something from ladling oil. I can demonstrate it for you, if you like."

The old oil-vendor put the gourd which he used for holding oil on the ground. He placed a copper coin over the

opening of the gourd and began to pour oil into the gourd
with a ladle through the hole in the middle of the coin. He
poured a lot of oil into the gourd without allowing any oil
touching the hole of the coin. Smiling, the old man said to
Chen Yaozi, "You see. There is nothing special. It's only
because I'm skilled." After that, Chen Yaozi never showed
pride again over his archery.

Records After Returning to the Farm*

*By Ouyang Xiu (1007-1072) of the Northern Song Dynasty.

請 君 入 甕
qǐng jūn rù wèng

請老兄鑽進壜子裏去；比喻以整治別人的辦法來整治他自己。

唐代，武則天當皇帝的時候，有兩個殘暴的大臣，一個叫周
興，一個叫來俊臣。他們常用各種嚴厲的刑罰，使人承認有罪。後
來周興被人告發陰謀叛亂。武則天就派來俊臣審理這件案子。

來俊臣假意請周興喝酒。飲酒間，來俊臣用請教的口吻問周興
說：“囚犯不肯認罪，怎麼辦？”周興就得意洋洋地說：“這容
易！你用一隻大壜子，在它周圍燒起炭火來，等到壜子燒熱了，再
把犯人放進去，這樣他便什麼都會招認的。”

來俊臣馬上按照周興所介紹的方法準備了大甕，周圍點起火來
以後，便對周興說：“有人告發你謀反，我奉命來審問你，請老兄
鑽進甕裏去吧！”周興一聽，嚇得魂不附體，急忙跪下叩頭求饒，
當場認罪。

出自《資治通鑑》

Please Step into the Vat

Paying One Back in His Own Coin

Meaning to punish someone with his own method.

DURING the reign of Empress Wu Ze Tian in the Tang Dynasty, there were two cruel ministers, Zhou Xing and Lai Junchen. They used all kinds of atrocious torture to force people to confess to crimes which they had not committed. Later, Zhou Xing was acoused of plotting a rebellion. Wu Ze Tian appointed Lai Junchen to handle the case.

Lai Junchen pretended to invite Zhou Xing to drink. While they were drinking, as if he was trying to learn from him, Lai Junchen asked Zhou Xing, "What would you do if a criminal refuses to admit his crime?" Zhou Xing said complacently. "That's easy. Get a large vat and burn charcoal around it. When the vat is hot, put the criminal in it. He'll confess to anything."

Lai Junchen immediately had a large vat ready and burned charcoal around it. He then said to Zhou Xing, "You've been accused of plotting for rebellion. I'm ordered to question you. Will you please step into the vat?" Zhou Xing was frightened out of his wits. He hurriedly fell on his knees, begged for mercy and confessed to his crimes.

History as a Mirror

鄭人爭年

zhèng rén zhēng nián

鄭人爭論誰的年齡大；比喻進行無謂的爭論。

鄭國有兩個人爭論誰的年齡大。一個人說："我和帝堯同一年生。"另一個人說："我和黃帝同一年生。"這兩個人都吹噓自己比對方生得早，吵吵嚷嚷，爭論不休。後來，有一個人過路，了解

264

到他們爭吵的原因，就問他們：「傳說中的堯和黃帝是哪一年生的，你們誰能答得出來？」這兩個人瞠目而視，原來誰也不知道。

出自《韓非子》

The Quarrel over Seniority

Implying a meaningless quarrel.

TWO men from the state of Zheng had a quarrel over the question of who was the senior of the two. One man said, "I was born in the same year when Emperor Yao was born." The other said, "I was born in the same year the Yellow Emperor was born." Each of them boasted that he was born earlier than the other. They quarrelled noisily and endlessly. A passer-by who learned what they had been quarrelling about asked them, "Can you tell me in what years the legendary Emperor Yao and Yellow Emperor were born?" The two were dumbfounded because neither of them could answer.

The Book of Han Fei Zi

鄭人買履
zhèng rén mǎi lǚ

鄭國人買鞋；比喻心眼死，不知變通。

有個鄭國人，想去買雙新鞋子。他在家裏先用尺子把腳量了量，記下尺碼。可是由於急於趕路，把尺碼忘在家裏了。他到了市上，走進鞋店，不見了那尺碼，就對店伙說：「我忘了帶尺碼，不曉得要多大的鞋，等我回家拿了尺碼來再買。」說完，拔腿就跑。等他從家裏再趕回市上，天已晚了，鞋店關門了。他白白忙了一陣，也没有買到鞋子。有人問他：“你身上不是長着脚嗎，爲什麼不用脚試一試？”買鞋的人說：“我不相信我自己的脚。”

出自《韓非子》

A Man from Zheng Buys Shoes

This alludes to a man with a one-track mind who does not know how to be flexible.

A man from the state of Zheng intended to buy a new pair of shoes. He measured his foot at home and wrote down its size. As he was in a hurry, he left what he had written at home. When he got to the market and walked into a shoemaker's shop, he could not find what he had written. He said to the shop assistant, "I've forgotten to bring the measurement. I don't know what size of shoes I should buy. I must go home and get it." After saying so, he immediately ran back. When he came back to the market, it was already very late and the shop had closed. Seeing that he did not get his shoes, somebody said to him, "Don't you have a pair of feet? Why didn't you try them on?" "I cannot trust my feet," said the man.

The Book of Han Fei Zi

賠了夫人又折兵

péi lé fū rén yòu zhé bīng

賠了夫人又打了敗仗；比喻想佔便宜，反而受到雙重損失。

三國時，東吳孫權想從蜀劉備手中索還荆州。大將周瑜想了一條計策，假借將孫權的妹妹嫁給劉備，誆騙劉備到東吳，乘機把他扣留，作爲索取荆州的人質。劉備按照軍師諸葛亮的計謀行事，到東吳後施展了種種詭計，居然和孫權的妹妹成婚，之後，又把她帶走逃回。周瑜帶兵追趕，被諸葛亮設下的伏兵打敗。蜀軍士兵嘲笑說：「周郎妙計安天下，賠了夫人又折兵。」

出自《三國演義》

Losing Both the Lady and the Soldiers
Throw the Helve After the Hatchet

This describes someone who intends to profit at other people's expense but suffers two-fold losses instead.

SUN Quan of the Kingdom of Wu in the east intended to retake Jingzhou from Liu Bei of the Kingdom of Shu. Zhou Yu, the chief general of Wu, devised a ruse: They were to trick Liu Bei into coming to the Kingdom of Wu on the pretext of giving Sun Quan's younger sister to him in marriage and take him as a hostage to force him to return Jingzhou to the Kingdom of Wu. Liu Bei followed his military adviser Zhuge Liang's stratagem, used one ruse after another and eventually succeeded in actually marrying Sun Quan's sister and taking her back with him to the Kingdom of Shu. Zhou Yu pursued him with his soldiers but was defeated in an ambush laid by Zhuge Liang. The Shu soldiers ridiculed him, saying, "General Zhou Yu has a good plan to conquer the country. He lost both the lady and his soldiers."

Tales of the Three Kingdoms

樂 不 思 蜀
lé bù sī shú

快樂得連蜀國都不懷念了；比喻樂而忘返或樂而忘本。

三國時代，蜀國的君主劉備死後，由他的兒子劉禪繼位。劉禪昏庸無能。魏國大將軍司馬昭攻破蜀國後，劉禪投降了。司馬昭勒令劉禪從蜀國的成都遷往魏國的洛陽居住。有一天，司馬昭設宴欸待劉禪。宴會上，司馬昭命人為他表演蜀國的歌舞節目。蜀國原來的官吏看了都十分難過，甚至落下淚來。唯獨劉禪却有說有笑，毫無傷感之情。事後，司馬昭問劉禪：「你還想不想蜀國呢？」劉禪回答說：「我住在這裏很快樂，不再想蜀國了。」

出自《三國誌》

Being So Happy as to Forget the State of Shu

Implying that one is so happy as to forget to return or forget one's past.

WHEN Liu Bei, the King of the state of Shu during the period of the Three Kingdoms, died, the throne was succeeded by his son Liu Chan, a stupid ruler. When the state of Shu was overran by the army led by Sima Zhao, the chief general of the state of Wei, Liu Chan surrendered himself. He was forced by Sima Zhao to leave Chengdu in the state of Shu and live in Luoyang in the state of Wei. One day, Sima Zhao entertained him at a banquet and had the songs and dances of the state of Shu performed at the feast. The former officials of Shu all felt very sad, and some even shed tears. Only Liu Chan was talking and laughing cheerfully, feeling no sadness at all. "Do you still miss Shu?" Sima Zhao asked him after the banquet. "I am so happy here that I've forgotten about the state of Shu," answered Liu Chan.

History of the Three Kingdoms

餘 音 繞 樑

yú yīn rào liáng

餘音繞着屋樑；形容歌聲優美，給人以流連回味。

春秋時代，韓國有個名叫娥的有名歌唱家。有一次她去齊國，路上斷了糧，她便以歌唱求食。她走後，人們覺得她那優美的歌聲環繞着屋樑三天不絕，好像她還沒有走一樣。

出自《列子》

The Music Lingers Around the Beams

A Thing of Beauty Is a Joy Forever

Describing good music that lingers in the air.

A famous singer named E of the state of Han in the Spring and Autumn Period ran out of food when she was on her way to the state of Qi. She begged for food from place to place by singing. After she had left one place, her beautiful voice seemed to be lingering around the beams of the house for three days, as if she was still there.

The Bood of Lie Zi

磨 杵 成 針
mó chǔ chéng zhēn

把鐵杵磨成細針；比喻只要下苦功夫，事情一定能辦成。

唐代大詩人李白，小時候經常逃學。有一次，他從書房裏逃出來了，跑到大路邊去玩，看見一位老婆婆正一心一意地在一塊石頭上磨一根鐵棒槌。李白很奇怪，過去問她：“老婆婆，這是幹什麼？”老婆婆說：“磨針做衣服。”李白笑着問道：“老婆婆，這麼大的鐵棒怎能磨成一根針呢？”老婆婆望望李白說：“鐵棒大，我天天磨呀，還不怕它變不成針。”李白想：“對！做事只要有恆心，就什麼都能做好。讀書，不也一樣麼？”他拔腿轉身，再回到書房裏，把那些讀不懂的書本打開來，仔細閱讀，此後李白再沒有逃過學。

出自《潛確類書》*

* 《潛確類書》 明陳仁錫（1581－1636）撰。

Grinding an Iron Pestle into a Needle
Little Strokes Fell Great Oaks

Meaning that there is nothing that cannot be accomplished

270

by preseverance.

WHEN he was a child, Li Bai, the great poet of the Tang Dynasty, often played truant. Once having slipped out of the classroom he loitered by the roadside and saw an old granny diligently grinding an iron pestle on a stone. Being curious, Li Bai asked her, "Granny, what are you doing this for?" The old woman said, "I'm going to grind it into a needle to sew cloth with."

Li Bai laughed. "How can you hope to grind this big pestle down to a needle?" The granny looked at Li Bai and said, "Although the pestle is big, it will become a needle if I grind it day after day." Li Bai thought, "She's right. There is nothing that cannot be accomplished by preseverance. The same is true with learning." He turned round and immediately returned to the classroom and began to read carefully the books that he had not understood. He never played truant again.

Qianque Encyclopaedia*

*Compiled by Chen Renxi (1581-1636) of the Ming Dynasty.

諱 疾 忌 醫
huì jí jì yī

因怕醫治而不説出自己的病； 比喻因怕批評而掩飾自己的過
錯。

春秋時，有個著名的醫生，叫扁鵲。有一次，他路過齊國，見
齊王氣息不好，就對齊王說他有病，這病在皮膚裏，不重，如不趕
快治，就會重起來。齊王不信。等扁鵲走後，齊王說："醫生就是
喜歡向那些沒有病的人炫耀本領，圖取名利。五天後，扁鵲又去見
齊王，告訴齊王說他的病已進入到肌肉和血脈裏，如再不治，會更
加重。齊王仍不信。又過五天，扁鵲又去見齊王，說病已進入腸胃
裏，如不治就來不及了。齊王仍不理睬。再過五天，扁鵲見到齊
王，不再說話，回頭就走。齊王很奇怪，派人去追問他爲什麼不再
提他的病了，扁鵲說："齊王的病已深入到骨髓裏去了，再也沒法
治了。"不久，齊王果然遍體疼痛，急忙派人去找扁鵲，但已找不
到了。不多日，齊王就病故了。

出自《史記》

Refusing to Admit One's Illness for Fear of Treatment

This describes a man who tries to gloss over his mistake for fear of criticism.

THERE lived in the Spring and Autumn Period a doctor famous for his healing skill. He was known by the name of Bian Que. Once when he was passing through the state of Qi, he saw that the Duke of Qi looked pale. He told the Duke that he was ill and his illness was only in the skin and therefore not serious. But Bian Que added, if he did not receive treatment immediately, it would become serious. The

272

Duke would not believe him. After Bian Que had gone, the Duke of Qi said, "Doctors like to treat healthy people in order to show off their skill and gain money and fame from it." Five days later, Bian Que came to see the Duke again and told him that his illness had gone into his muscles and blood and that it would become more serious if not treated at once. The Duke still would not believe him. Five more days passed and Bian Que again came to see the Duke and told him that the illness had already gone into the internal organs and that it would be too late if he did not have it treated by a doctor. The Duke still paid no attention. Another five days passed and when Bian Que saw the Duke, instead of speaking to him, he turned round and walked away. The Duke was puzzled. He sent someone after him and asked him why he made no mention of the Duke's illness. Bian Que said, "The Duke's illness has gone into the marrow. There's no way of curing it now." Before very long, the Duke of Qi began to feel pain all over his body. He hurriedly sent for Bian Que, but could not find him anywhere. The Duke died in a few days.

Records of the Historian

樹 倒 猢 猻 散

shù dǎo hú sūn sàn

樹倒了，爬在樹上的猢猻也就一哄而散了；比喻主子一旦垮台，僕從們就失去了依附。

南宋初年，曹咏投靠了竊據宰相職務的秦檜，做了大官，許多人都爭先恐後地去諂媚奉承。唯獨曹咏的妻兄厲德斯不理睬他。曹咏對此異常不滿，利用權勢對他進行威脅。但厲德斯不屈服。秦檜死後，那些依附秦檜的人紛紛垮台，曹咏也被貶到新州。厲德斯寫了《樹倒猢猻散賦》寄給曹咏。他把秦檜比做樹，把曹咏等人比做猴子。這是一篇富有妙趣的諷刺文章，曹咏看了，氣得要死。

出自《說郛》*

* 《說郛》 明陶宗儀作。

When the Tree Falls the Monkeys Scatter

Rats Desert a Sinking Ship

Meaning that when the master falls from power, his hangers-on lose their support.

EARLY in the Southern Song Dynasty, Cao Yong became a high official after he threw in his lot with Qin Hui who unjustly occupied the post of Prime Minister. Many people vied with each other to fawn on Cao Yong. Only his wife's brother Li Desi refused to have anything to do with him. Cao was displeased with him and often bullied him. But Li Desi would not yield. After Qin Hui died, all his followers fell from power and Cao Yong was banished to Xinzhou. Li Desi wrote a prose poem — entitled *When the Tree Falls the Monkeys Scatter* and sent it to Cao Yong. It was a satirical work full of cutting jests, in which he compared Qin Hui to a tree and Cao Yong and his like to a pack of monkeys. Cao Yong almost died from anger after reading it.

A Collection of Stories and Notes*

*Compiled by Tao Zongyi of the Ming Dynasty (1368-1644).

黔驢技窮
qián lú jì qióng

貴州驢子本領拙劣；比喻無計可施。

　　貴州人向來不養驢子；有個好奇的人，却在外地買了一頭，用船載了回來。可又派不了什麼用塲，就把牠放在山下，讓牠自己去尋食。有一天，來了一隻老虎，一看驢子比自己還要高大，就認爲一定是個怪物，便不敢暴露自己，只好躲在密密的樹叢裏偷看。後來，又有一天，老虎正在打量這驢子，忽然驢子大叫了一聲，老虎以爲是咬牠來了，嚇得趕快跑開。過一會，沒有什麼動靜，老虎再走近看看驢子，覺得也沒有什麼特別的地方，就是牠那宏大奇特的叫聲，也似乎並不包含什麼企圖。老虎再走近些，覺得驢子也沒有什麼可怕。於是老虎走近驢子身邊，靠牠、擠牠、用前腳撲牠。驢子惱火了，用後腿一踢。這時候，老虎看透了驢子，牠想："原來就只這麼一手！"於是猛撲過去，把驢子掀倒，咬斷牠的喉管，吃了牠的肉。

出自《柳河東集》

The Guizhou Donkey Has Exhausted Its Tricks

At One's Wit's End

This is compared to a man of limited skills.

DONKEYS were not bred in Guizhou. A man of curiosity bought one from another place and took it to Guizhou by boat. But once it was there the man could make no use of it. So he set the donkey free at the foot of a mountain and let it fend for itself. One day a tiger came. Seeing the donkey was even larger than itself, the tiger thought that the donkey must be a monster, and did not care to reveal itself. It only peeped at the donkey from behind a dense grove. One day, as the tiger was watching the donkey, the donkey brayed. The tiger took fright and fled, thinking that the donkey was coming to bite it. After a while, when the tiger saw that nothing had happened, it returned and came in for a closer look at the donkey. The tiger decided that there was nothing special about the donkey and even its loud braying did not seem to express a particular intention. The tiger came closer and still did not see anything frightful about the donkey. So the tiger came still closer, shoved and jostled it and clawed at it with its fore-paws. The donkey lost its temper and kicked out with its hind legs. "So that is all it can do," thought the tiger, who had by now saw through the donkey. It leaped on the donkey, fell it to the ground, severed its throat and

276

devoured its flesh.

濫竽充數
làn yú chōng shù

　　拿着竽（古樂器）湊數；比喻沒有本領的人冒充有本領，或以次貨冒充好貨。

　　齊宣王喜愛聽吹竽，他那個吹竽的樂隊，就有三百人；他常叫這三百人一齊吹奏。有個南郭先生，本來不會吹竽，看到了這個賺錢的機會，便請求參加這個吹竽隊。齊宣王把他編在吹竽大隊裏，並給他很高的薪水。每逢吹竽，南郭先生就混在樂隊裏面湊數。這樣一天天地混過去，沒有露過破綻。

　　等到齊宣王死了，他的兒子湣王接替了王位。這位新王不喜歡大家一齊吹竽，他要叫那些吹竽的人，一個個地吹給他聽。南郭先生聽了這個消息，感到再也混不下去，就偷偷地逃掉了。

　　　　　　　　　　　　　　　出自《韓非子》

Passing Oneself Off as a Player to Make Up the Number

This describes a man who is unfit for a given job or a poor substitute.

KING Xuanwang of the state of Qi was fond of listening to the *yu* flute. He had an orchestra composed of three hundred *yu* players. He often asked them to perform together. A man named Nanguo did not know how to play the *yu*. He applied to join the orchestra because he saw it was a good chance to make money. The King made him a member of the orchestra and paid him a high salary. Nanguo passed himself off as a player to make up the number. Day after day he muddled along without being detected.

After the death of King Xuanwang, the throne was succeeded by his son King Minwang. The new king did not like the performers to play in unison and asked each of the players to play a solo for him. When Nanguo heard the news, he knew he could not continue any longer, and quietly took himself off.

The Book of Han Fei Zi

臨 渴 掘 井

lín kě jué jǐng

臨到口渴的時候才去掘井；比喻事先不準備，臨時才動手。

春秋時，魯昭公被逐出國，逃亡到了齊國。齊景公對他說：
"你正是年輕有爲的時候，怎麼就把國君的位置丟了，這是什麼原
因呢？"

魯昭公說："早些時候，人們都對我很好，有很多人經常鼓勵
我，而我沒有親近他們。也有很多人經常勸誡我，我也沒有聽信他
們，因此，真正愛護我的人一個也沒有了。奉承我、欺騙我的反倒
很多。這樣我就好比秋天的蓬草似的，表面上枝葉似乎還好看，但
根莖都已枯萎，秋風一起，就被連根拔掉了。"

齊景公聽了，覺得頗有道理，便把這番話轉告給大臣晏子，並
且說："要是現在有可能讓昭公回魯國去，他會成爲一個賢明的國
王吧！"晏子說："不會。涉水過河而溺水的人，多半是因爲事先
沒有探明河水的情況。迷路的人也多半是因爲事先沒有問清路徑。
等到他溺水以後才去探水，迷路以後才來問路，不是已經晚了嗎！
這好像臨到戰亂已經爆發了的時候，才去鑄造兵器，遇到喉嚨乾渴
得很的時候，才去掘井。"

出自《晏子春秋》

Not Sinking a Well Until One Is Thirsty
Making One's Cloak When It Begins to Rain

***Meaning making no preparation beforehand and doing
nothing until the last minute.***

DURING the Spring and Autumn Period, Duke Zhaogong of
the state of Lu was banished from his country and sought
refuge in the state of Qi. Duke Jinggong of Qi asked him,

"You're young and have a great future. Why is it that you have lost sovereignty?"

Duke Zhaogong of Lu said, "In the past, people were all good to me. Many people often encouraged me, but I kept a distance from them. There were also people who admonished me, but I didn't listen to them. Therefore, I lost all those who really loved me. There were instead many who flattered me and deceived me. As a result, I was like a grass in autumn. Although its leaves still looked beautiful, its stem and root had already withered. It was uprooted when the autumn wind blew."

Duke Jingong thought there was truth in what he said. He repeated it to his minister Yan Zi and said, "If Duke Zhaogong is able to return to the state of Lu, he probably will become a wise king." Yan Zi said, "I don't think so. Many people were drowned while wading across a river because they didn't bother to find out about the depth of the river beforehand. Many people lost the way because they did not bother to ask their way. Isn't it too late to do so when they are being drowned or when they have lost their way? This is like making weapons when the war has broken out and sinking a well when one is parched with thirst."

Anecdotes of Yan Zi

孺 子 可 教

rú zǐ kě jiào

這孩子可以教育；讚揚青少年有成材的希望。

張良謀刺秦始皇沒有成功，逃到下邳隱藏起來。一天，張良在一座橋上遇到一位老人。老人見到張良時故意把鞋子扔到橋下並對張良說："小伙子，到橋下替我把鞋撿上來。"等張良把鞋撿上來後，老人又說："替我穿上。"張良便跪在地上替他穿上。老人滿意地笑着走了。不一會，老人回轉來對張良說："你這個孩子可以教育啊！"他告訴張良五天後到橋上來和他相會。

五天後，天一亮，張良就來到橋上，但老人已經先到了。他責備張良來晚了並叫他五天後再來。第二次，張良在雞叫時來到橋上，但老人又先到了。這次老人大發脾氣，怪他來晚了，叫他五天後再來。這次，張良不到半夜就來了。等了一會，老人才到。老人非常高興，當即交給張良一本書並告訴他，讀了這部書將來大有用處。張良回家一看，原來是部兵法書，他日夜攻讀，後來成了一位著名的軍事家。

出自《史記》

A Youth Worth Teaching

This idiom is used to praise a promising youth.

AFTER Zhang Liang failed in his attempt to assassinate the First Emperor of Qin, he went into hiding in Xiapei. One day, he met an old man while crossing a bridge. When the old man saw Zhang Liang he purposely took off a shoe and threw it down from the bridge. He said to Zhang Liang, "Young man, go under the bridge and pick up my shoe for me." When Zhang Liang returned the shoe to him, he said to

Zhang Liang, "Put it on for me." Zhang Liang kneeled down and put his shoe on for him. With a satisfied smile, the old man began to walk away. Before he was quite far away, he turned back and said to Zhang Liang, "You're a young man worth teaching." He then told Zhang Liang to wait for him at the bridge five days later.

After five days, Zhang Liang came to the bridge as soon as it was daybreak. The old man was already there. He reproached Zhang Liang for having arrived too late and told him to come again after five more days. The second time, Zhang Liang was at the bridge at cock's crow, only to find the old man was again already there. The old man was angry and blamed him for having come too late. He told Zhang Liang to come again after five more days. This time, Zhang Liang came to the bridge before midnight, and the old man did not come until he had waited for him for a while. The old man was very pleased. He gave Zhang Liang a book and told him that reading that book would greatly benefit him in the future. When Zhang Liang returned home, he found the book was about military strategy. He studied it day and night and later became a famous military strategist.

Records of the Historian

螳 臂 擋 車
táng bì dāng chē

螳螂用前腿阻擋車子；比喻做事自不量力。

齊莊公有一天乘車出去打獵，看見一隻綠色的小昆蟲舉起兩隻前腳，向馬車輪子直撲過來。齊莊公很奇怪， 就問馬車夫： "這是什麼蟲啊？" 馬車夫回答道： "這是螳螂。這種蟲，只知道前進，不知道後退，從不估量自己的力量，總是逕直地去攻擊敵人。" 莊公聽了，深有感觸地說： "牠要是人的話，一定會成爲天下無敵的勇士啊！"然後他命令馬車夫從螳螂身邊繞道而過，不要碾着牠。

出自《莊子》

A Mantis Trying to Stop a Chariot
Throwing Straws Against Wind

Implying that one is trying to do beyond one's ability.

ONE day when Duke Zhuanggong of the state of Qi went out hunting on a chariot, he saw a green insect rushing straight at the wheel of the chariot with its two forelegs raised. Puzzled, the Duke asked his driver, "What is this insect?" "This is a mantis," the driver answered. "This insect knows only to advance and not to back off. It always pounces straight at the enemy without considering its own strength." The Duke was deeply moved. He said, "If it were a man, it would become an invincible hero." He then ordered the driver to make a detour so that the chariot would not crush the mantis.

The Book of Zhuang Zi

螳 螂 捕 蟬

táng láng bǔ chán

螳螂捕蟬，比喻貪圖眼前利益，不顧後患。

　　吳王要去攻打楚國，他和臣子們說："誰敢來勸阻，我就殺了他。"　有個侍從官的兒子想要勸阻，但又不敢去。清早，他拿了彈弓和泥丸在後花園遊玩，一連三天如此，露水沾濕了他的衣服。

　　吳王知道後問他："你為什麼這樣自尋苦惱，把衣服都弄濕了！"少年回答道："早晨，我在花園裏的樹上看見一隻蟬，牠在高處鳴叫着，喝着樹葉上的露水，却不知道螳螂就在牠後邊。那隻螳螂彎着身子想去捕蟬，却不知道黃雀在牠的旁邊。黃雀伸長脖子要去啄那隻螳螂，却不知道我在後面正用彈弓瞄準了牠。這三個傢伙都一心一意追求眼前的利益，却不顧身後的禍患。"吳王明白他比喻的含義，就取消了攻打楚國的打算。

出自《說苑》*

*《說苑》　晋朝劉向（公元前77－公元前 6 ）編。

The Mantis Stalking the Cicada

This describes someone who covets gains before his eyes in disregard of future troubles.

THE King of Wu intended to launch an attack against the state of Chu. He said to his court officials, "Whoever tries to stop me will die." A young retainer wanted to advise the King not to do so but dare not. Early in the morning, he came to the rear garden, carrying a catapult and some pellets. He looked here and there and explored everywhere until his clothes were wet with dew. He did this on three mornings in a run.

When the King learned about it, he said, "Why do you look for trouble? Your clothes are wet." The young man asnwered, "In the morning, I saw a cicada on a tree in the garden. It chirpped high above and drank the dew on the tree leaves, not knowing that a mantis was stalking behind it. Bending its back, the mantis was trying to catch the cicada, but it did not know that a siskin was near. As the siskin was stretching its neck to get at the mantis, it did not know that I was aiming at it with my catapult from behind. The three creatures all covet gains before their eyes without being aware of danger behind. The King of Wu saw what he meant and cancelled his plan to attack the state of Chu.

*The Garden of Stories**

*A book chiefly of ancient historical stories compiled by Liu Xiang of the Western Han Dynasty. (77-6 B.C.)

覆 水 難 收
fù shuǐ nán shōu

倒出來的水,難以收回;比喻事情已成定局,無法挽回。

古時候,有個人叫姜太公。在他未做官前,生活十分貧困。他的妻子嫌他窮離開了他。

後來,姜太公受周文王的聘請,做了丞相。他的妻子知道了,想和他和好。姜太公端來一盆水,潑在地上,叫她把水收回到盆裏來,他的妻子收了半天,只收了些泥漿。姜太公對她說:"妳已經離開了我,不可能再言歸於好。這好比水潑在地上難以收回一樣。"

出自 《拾遺記》 *

* 《拾遺記》 誌怪小說集,東晉王嘉作。

Spilt Water Cannot Be Recovered

No Use Crying over Spilt Milk

Meaning what is done cannot be undone.

LORD Jiang was very poor before he became a high official. His wife left him on account of his poverty.

Later, he was appointed by King Wenwang of the Zhou Dynasty as his Prime Minister. When his wife learned about it, she was regretful and wanted to reunite with him. Jiang spilt a basinful of water on the ground and told his wife to recover it. His wife tried for a long time, but all she could recover was some mud. Jiang said to his wife, "As you have left me, it's impossible for us to make it up. It's like spilt water that can't be recovered."

Collection of Lost Stories*

*A collection of stories of gods and ghosts by Wang Jia of the Eastern Jin Dynasty (317-420).

覆巢無完卵
fù cháo wú wán luǎn

鳥巢翻了，鳥蛋也就不會完整了；比喻整體已經覆滅，個體也就不能倖存。

東漢時，有個叫孔融的人，很有才華。他對當時權勢很大的丞相曹操很不滿意，時常拿話諷刺他。有一次，曹操要發兵去攻打劉備，孔融不同意，勸曹操停止出兵，曹操不聽。孔融曾在背地裏發過幾句牢騷。有個人平時和孔融不和，就向曹操報告說："孔融一向輕視你。"曹操聽到後，十分生氣，立即下令逮捕孔融。逮捕孔融的這一天，孔融的兩個兒子正在下棋，大的九歲，小的八歲，看見官差來抓他父親，却一點不驚慌。孔融要求官差留下這兩個孩子，他的兒子說：" 誰見過鳥巢翻了，還會有完整的鳥蛋呢？" 他倆從容地跟着父親一同被抓走了。後來，孔融和他的兩個兒子都被曹操殺了。

出自《三國誌》

When the Nest Is Overturned No Egg Stays Unbroken

In the Same Boat

Meaning when the whole is destroyed the part cannot expect to survive.

KONG Rong of the Eastern Han Dynasty was a talented man. Disapproving the presumptuous Prime Minister Cao Cao, he often satirized him. Once when Cao Cao intended to mobilize his forces and start an attack on Liu Bei, Kong Rong disagreed with him and tried to persuade him out of it. Cao Cao refused to listen to him. Kong Rong voiced his discontent behind Cao Cao's back, and his words were relayed to Cao Cao by someone who was not on friendly terms with him. "Kong Rong always speaks of you in contempt," said the man to Cao Cao. Cao Cao became very angry and ordered the immediate arrest of Kong Rong. On the day when a few wardens came to arrest Kong Rong, his two sons, one aged nine and the other eight, were playing chess. They did not appear fluttered at all. Kong Rong begged the wardens to leave the two children behind. His sons said, "When the nest is overturned, no egg stays unbroken." Unhurriedly they followed their father to the prison. Later, Kong Rong and all the family were killed by Cao Cao.

History of the Three Kingdoms

雙 管 齊 下
shuāng guān qí xià

兩枝筆同時並用；比喻同時做兩件事情。

唐代著名畫家張璪，擅長畫松樹，他能夠一隻手握住兩枝筆同時繪畫。一枝筆畫蒼翠的樹枝，一枝筆畫彎曲的樹幹，都畫得生動逼真。因此，當時人們稱讚他的畫是“神品”。

出自《圖畫見聞錄》 *

* 《圖畫見聞錄》 宋郭若虛撰。

Painting with Two Brushes at the Same Time

Meaning to do two things simultaneously.

ZHANG Zao, a famous painter of the Tang Dynasty, was good at painting pines. He could hold two brushes in one hand, painting the dark green branches with one brush and the crooked tree trunk with the other at the same time. All his pictures were vivid and lifelike. People, therefore, praised his pictures as "divine creations".

*Record of Information on Paintings**

*By Guo Ruoxu of the Song Dynasty (960-1279).

懷 安 喪 志
huái ān sàng zhì

沉浸於安樂之中，使人意志衰退。

春秋時，晉國公子重耳在國內遭受迫害，逃往國外。初出奔時，重耳懷有歸國繼位、振興晉國的大志。但當他在齊國避難時，齊桓公把女兒姜氏嫁給了他。從此，重耳留戀於安樂的生活，一躲就是七年。重耳的舅父子犯和其他幾個跟隨他的人都十分憂慮，便商議如何勸他離開齊國。姜氏得知後對重耳說：「我知道你有大志，要離開這裏到別處去，這很好。」重耳說：「沒有這回事啊！」姜氏勸勉他說：「你走吧。迷戀享受，安於現狀，容易使人意志衰退，現在你的隨從要護送你回國，你要聽從他們的意見。」重耳不聽，姜氏就和子犯商量，用酒把重耳灌醉，載上車子離開齊國回國。日後，重耳做了晉國的國王。

出自《左傳》

An Easy Life Saps One's Will

PRINCE Chong Er of the state of Jin in the Spring and Autumn Period fled abroad in order to avoid persecution at home. While abroad, he at first harboured the great ambition to come home one day to succeed the throne and rebuild the state of Jin. But while he sought refuge in the state of Qi, Duke Huangong of Qi gave him his daughter Jiang in marriage. Chong Er began to settle down to a peaceful and happy life, and seven years passed quickly. Chong Er's uncle Zi Fan and a few others who came with him were very worried. They discussed how to make him leave the state of Qi. When Jiang heard about it, she said to Chong Er, "I know you have your great ambition. I think it is very good that you should leave here and go somewhere else." Chong Er said, "I don't have such a plan." Jiang advised him, saying, "Go. One's will is easily undermined if one immerses oneself in pleasure and is satisfied with things as they are. Your followers want to escort you back to your own country now. You must listen to their opinion." Chong Er turned a deaf ear to her. After holding a discussion with Zi Fan, Jiang gave

Chong Er a great deal of wine to drink until he was drunk. He was then taken onto a carriage which took him back to his own country. Later, Chong Er became the sovereign of the state of Jin.

Zuo Qiuming's Chronicles

鷄 鳴 狗 盜
jī míng gǒu dào

善於模仿鷄叫和裝做狗去偷東西；比喻微末的技能。

　　戰國末，齊國有個貴族叫孟嘗君，他養着數千帮閑的門客。秦昭王仰慕孟嘗君的名聲，約請他訪問秦國。秦國的相國嫉妒他，勸秦昭王把他殺掉，免得他回國後，對秦不利。秦昭王把孟嘗君囚禁起來。孟嘗君派人到秦昭王的妃子那裏求救。這個妃子要孟嘗君拿一件貴重的白狐皮袍子作爲禮品。可是孟嘗君僅有的一件白狐皮袍子已送給秦昭王了，這使他很爲難。這時，門客中一位會偷東西的人說他能弄到那件白狐皮袍。當天夜裏，這個人裝做狗，潛入秦宮中的庫房把那件白狐皮袍子偷了出來。妃子得到皮袍之後，就勸說秦昭王把孟嘗君釋放了。

　　孟嘗君被釋放後，料到秦王會後悔，就急忙逃走了。當到達關卡時，正是半夜。根據關上的規定，要到鷄叫時才准進出。這時，門客中一個會學鷄叫的人，“喔喔”地叫了幾聲，引起附近的鷄也跟着叫了起來。守關的人聽到鷄叫，以爲天已破曉，就打開城門讓他們出關。等到秦昭王派兵追來的時候，孟嘗君已離開秦境很遠了。

出自《史記》

Crowing Like a Cock and Snatching Like a Dog

This is a synonym of people who know small tricks.

PRINCE Meng Chang, a nobleman of the state of Qi at the end of the Warring States Period, provided food and lodgings for several thousand of his hangers-on. Admiring his fame, King Zhaowang of Qin invited him to come to the Qin capital for a visit. The Prime Minister of Qin was jealous of the Prince. He urged the King to have the Prince killed lest he should do harm to the state of Qin when he returned to his own country. When the Prince was locked up in prison, he sent someone to a concubine of the King's asking her to save his life. The concubine in return asked for a precious robe of white fox fur as a gift. The Prince had only one such robe and he had given it to the King. As he did not know what to do, one of his hangers-on who was a smart thief told him that he could get the robe. That night, the man feigned the barking of a dog, made his way into the storeroom of the Qin palace and stole the robe. When the concubine had the robe, she persuaded the King of Qin into setting the Prince free.

After he was released, the Prince knew that the King of Qin would change his mind. He was therefore in a hurry to make his get-away. It was midnight when he reached a checkpost. According to the rules, no one was allowed to pass the checkpost before cockcrow. "Cock-a-doodle-doo...." another one of Prince Meng Chang's hangers-on who knew how to imitate the crow of a cock began to demonstrate his skill. He was echoed by all the roosters in the vicinity. When the guards at the checkpost heard the crow of the roosters, they thought it was daybreak. They opened the city gate and allowed Prince Meng Chang and his followers to pass. By the time the soldiers dispatched by King Zhaowang arrived at the checkpost, the Prince and his followers were already far away from the Qin border.

Records of the Historian.

驚弓之鳥
jīng gōng zhī niǎo

被弓箭嚇怕了的鳥；比喻受過驚恐的人，遇到一點動靜就非常害怕。

魏國有個著名的射手叫更贏。有一天，他跟魏王到郊外遊玩，看到鳥在天空飛翔，更贏對魏王說：「我不用發箭，只拉一下弓就可以把天空的鳥射下來。」國王說：「你的技術有這樣高明嗎？」一會兒，一隻大雁正從東方飛來，更贏拉開弓，對準大雁輕輕碰了一下弦，大雁立刻落到他們跟前。魏王贊許地說：「你射箭的技術真高明呀！」更贏說：「這是一隻負傷的雁。牠叫得那樣淒厲，飛得那樣倦乏，可以看出，牠的傷口還沒有長好。牠聽到了弦音，就以為自己又被射中，從天上掉下來了。」

出自《戰國策》

A Bird Startled by the Mere Twang of a Bow-String
Once Bitten, Twice Shy

This describes a person who is easily frightened because of a traumatic experience.

GENG Lei was a famous archer of the state of Wei. One day while he was on an excursion outside the city with the King of Wei, he saw a bird circling in the sky. He said to the King, "I don't have to use an arrow. I'll just pull the bow-string and the bird will fall from the sky." "Do you have that marvellous skill?" asked the King. Presently they saw the wild goose flying from the east. Geng Ying twanged the string of his bow and indeed the wild goose at once dropped to the ground in front of them. "You're really a wonderful archer," said the King with approval. Geng Lei said, "This is a wounded wild goose. From its desolate cry and tired flight, you can see its wound has not yet healed. When it heard the twang of my bow-string, it thought it was again hit by an arrow, and fell from the sky."

Anecdotes of the Warring States

鷸蚌相爭、漁翁得利
yù bàng xiāng zhēng, yú wēng dé lì

鷸和蚌互相爭執；比喻雙方不和，讓第三者得到了好處。

一隻河蚌張開蚌壳，在河灘上晒太陽。有隻鷸鳥正從河蚌身邊走過，就伸嘴去啄河蚌的肉。河蚌急忙把兩片壳合上，把鷸嘴緊緊地鉗住。鷸鳥用盡力氣，怎麼也拔不出嘴來。河蚌和鷸鳥就爭吵起來。鷸鳥說："一天、兩天不下雨，沒有了水，你總是要死的！"河蚌說："假如我不放你，一天、兩天之後，你也別想活！"

河蚌和鷸鳥吵個不停，誰也不讓誰。這時，恰好有個打魚的老頭兒，從那裏經過，就把牠們一起捉去了。

出自《戰國策》

The Fight Between the Snipe and the Clam

Two Dogs Fight for a Bone, and a Third Runs Away with It

This means that it is the third party that profits from a tussle.

A clam opened its shell and was basking in the sun on a river flat. A snipe passed by and pecked at it. The clam clamped down on the bird's beak and held it fast. Hard as it tried, the snipe could not free its beak from the calm. The two began to quarrel. "If it doesn't rain in a day or two, there'll be no water and you'll be a dead clam.'," said the snipe. "Don't think you can live if I don't let you go for a day or two," retorted the clam.

As they quarrelled on and on and neither of them would give in, an old fisherman came by. He caught both of them.

Anecdotes of the Warring States

附錄
Appendices

英文索引
English Index

302

303

漢語拼音索引
Chinese Phonetic
Alphabet Index

307

312

引用書目
Bibliography

Anecdotes of Confucius
Anecdotes of the Kaiyuan and Tianbao Reigns
  by Wang Renyu
Anecdotes of the States
Anecdotes of the Warring States   by Liu Xiang (77-6 B.C.)
Anecdotes of Yan Zi
Biography of the Governor of Southern Branch
  by Li Gongzuo (c.770-c.850)
Book of Han Fei Zi, The   by Han Fei (280-233 B.C.)
Book of Huai Nan Zi, The   by Liu An (179-122 B.C.)
Book of Lie Zi, The   by Lie Yukou
Book of Mencius, The   by Men Ke (Mencius, 372-289 B.C.)
Book of Mo Zi, The   by Mo Di (c.468-376 B.C.)
Book of Rites, The
Book of Xun Zi, The   by Xun Kuang (c.313-238 B.C.)
Book of Zhuang Zi, The   by Zhuang Zhou (369-286 B.C.)
Classic of Mountains and Waters
Collected Jokes   by Handan Chun (220-280)
Collected Works of the Earl of Loyalty   by Liu Ji (1311-75)
Collected Works of Liu Zongyuan   by Liu Zongyuan
  (773-819)
Collected Works of Yu Xin   by Yu Xin (513-581)
Collection of Lost Stories   by Wang Jia (?-c.390)
Collection of Stories and Notes, A   by Tao Zongyi
Commentaries on Calligraphy of Different Dynasties
  by Zhang Huaiguan
Confucian Analects

313

Confucian Discourses   by Yang Xiong (77-6 B.C.)
Discourses from the Zhanyuan Study   by Bai Ting
Discourses of Lü Buwei, The   by Lü Buwei (?-235 B.C.)
Famous Paintings in History   by Zhang Yanyuan
Forests of Arts and Mountains of Learning   by Hu Yingling
    (1511-1602)
Garden of Stories, The   by Liu Xiang (77-6 B.C.)
Historical Legends   by Luo Mi
History as a Mirror   by Sima Guang (1019-86)
History of the Han Dynasty   by Ban Gu (A.D. 32-92)
History of the Jin Dynasty   by Fan Xuanling (579-648)
History of the Later Han Dynasty   by Fan Ye (398-445)
History of the Northern Dynasties   by Li Yanshou
History of the Song Dynasty   by Tuotuo (1314-55)
History of the Three Kingdoms   by Chen Shou (233-297)
Hongming Encyclopaedia of Buddhism, The   by Monk Shi
    Sengyou
King Wuwang's Expedition Against King Zhou
Leisurely Talks at Shengshui   by Wang Pizhi
Narrative Poems   by Meng Qi
New Discourses   by Liu Xiang (77-6 B.C.)
New Social Anecdotes   by Liu Yiqing (403-444)
New Views   by Huan Tan (? B.C.-A.D. 56)
Night Talks at Cool Studio   by Monk Shi Huihong
Nirvana Sutra Yiwen Encyclopaedia, The   by Ouyang Xun
    (557-641)
Notes Taken during Intervals of Ploughing in South Village
    by Tao Zongyi
Notes Taken on Quiet Nights   by Yu Wenbao
Outlaws of the Marsh   by Shi Nai'an
Poems from Jiannan   by Lu You (1125-1210)
Poems of Different Dynasties Reviewed by the Shaoxi Fishing
    Hermit   by Hu Zai
Qiangque Encyclopaedia   by Chen Renxi
Random Talks Recorded in Residual Ink   by Sun Yun

Records After Returning to the Farm   by Ouyang Xiu (1007-1072)

Records of the Historian   by Sima Qian (145-   B.C.)

Selected Writings   by Xiao Tong (501-531)

Stories of Supernatural Beings   by Niu Qiao

Sutra of One Hundred Parables

Talks at Luyuan Garden   by Qian Yong

Tales of the Three Kingdoms   by Lou Guanzhong (c.1330-1400)

Zuo Qiuming's Chronicles   by Zuo Qiuming

中國歷史年代簡表
A Chronology of
Chinese Dynasties

夏		約公元前21世紀——公元前16世紀
商		約公元前16世紀——公元前11世紀
周		約公元前11世紀——公元前221年
	西周	約公元前11世紀——公元前770年
	東周	公元前770年——公元前221年
	春秋	公元前770年——公元前476年
	戰國	公元前475年——公元前221年
秦		公元前221年——公元前207年
漢		公元前206年——公元220年
	西漢	公元前206年——公元24年
	東漢	公元25年——公元220年
三國		公元220年——公元280年
	魏	公元220年——公元265年
	蜀	公元221年——公元263年
	吳	公元222年——公元280年
晉		公元265年——公元420年
	西晉	公元265年——公元316年
	東晉	公元317年——公元420年
南北朝		公元420年——公元589年
	南朝	公元420年——公元589年
	宋	公元420年——公元479年
	齊	公元479年——公元502年

梁	公元502年——公元557年
陳	公元557年——公元589年
北朝	公元386年——公元581年
北魏	公元386年——公元533年
東魏	公元534年——公元550年
西魏	公元535年——公元557年
北齊	公元550年——公元577年
北周	公元557年——公元581年
隋	公元581年——公元618年
唐	公元618年——公元907年
五代十國	公元907年——公元979年
宋	公元960年——公元1279年
北宋	公元960年——公元1127年
南宋	公元1127年——公元1279年
遼	公元916年——公元1125年
金	公元1115年——公元1234年
元	公元1271年——公元1368年
明	公元1368年——公元1644年
清	公元1644年——公元1911年

Xia	c. 21st century — 16th century B.C.
Shang	c. 16th century — 11th century B.C.
Zhou	c. 11th century — 221 B.C.
Western Zhou	c. 11th century — 770 B.C.
Eastern Zhou	770-221 B.C.
Spring and Autumn Period	770-476 B.C.
Warring States Period	475-221 B.C.
Qin	221-207 B.C.
Han	206 B.C. — A.D. 220
Western Han	206 B.C. — A.D. 24
Eastern Han	25-220
Three Kingdoms	220-280
Wei	220-265
Shu	221-263
Wu	222-280
Jin	265-420
Western Jin	265-316
Eastern Jin	317-420
Southern and Northern Dynasties	420-589
Southern Dynasties	420-589
Song	420-479
Qi	479-502
Liang	502-557
Chen	557-589
Northern Dynasties	386-581
Northern Wei	386-534
Eastern Wei	534-550

318

Western Wei	535-557
Northern Qi	550-577
Northern Zhou	557-581
Sui	581-618
Tang	618-907
Five Dynasties and Ten Kingdoms	907-979
Song	960-1279
Northern Song	960-1127
Southern Song	1127-1179
Liao	916-1125
Kin	1115-1234
Yuan	1271-1368
Ming	1368-1644
Qing	1644-1911

漢語拼音發音指南
Guide to Chinese Phonetic Alphabet

請注意以下幾點：

q 發英文中ch的聲音，如cheer, chimney, chin。

x 發英文中sh的聲音，如she, shell, shoe。

z 發英文中ds的聲音，如reads, records, seeds。

c 發英文中ts的聲音，如dots, products, students。

*   *   *   *

中國普通話裏有四種聲調，每個字都有一種聲調，即音調的升降。如：

第一聲(一)，高而平；

第二聲(／)，升；

第三聲(∨)，由降而升；

第四聲(＼)，降。

聲調符號標在主要母音上邊，如這個主要母音是 i ，則不標。

聲調在漢語中很重要，同音的字由於聲調不同，字義也就不同。

如：

mā	má	mǎ	mà
媽	麻	馬	罵
yī	yí	yǐ	yì
一	移	椅	譯

Watch out for these letters:

q sounds like *ch* in "*ch*eer", "*ch*imney", "*ch*in".

x sounds like *sh* in "*sh*e", "*sh*ell", "*sh*oe".

z sounds like the final *ds* in "rea*ds*", "recor*ds*", "see*ds*".

c sounds like the final *ts* in "do*te*", "produc*ts*", "studen*ts*".

***   ***   ***

Every Chinese character has a tone which is actually the contour of the rise or fall in pitch during pronunciation. There are four tones in *putonghua* (common speech), shown by the following marks:

— 1st tone, high and level;

╱ 2nd tone, rising;

∨ 3rd tone, falling-rising; and

╲ 4th tone, falling.

The tone mark is placed above the main vowel; when the main vowel is "i", the dot is omitted.

The tones are extremely important. Characters which have the same sound (that is, are spelled the same way in the phonetic alphabet) may have different meanings, and this is indicated by the tone. For example:

ma	ma	ma	ma
mother	hemp	horse	scold

yi	yi	yi	yi
one	move	chair	translate

Chinese Phonetic Alphabet	International Phonetic Alphabet	Chinese Phonetic Alphabet	International Phonetic Alphabet	Chinese Phonetic Alphabet	International Phonetic Alphabet	Chinese Phonetic Alphabet	International phonetic Alphabet
b	[p]	s	[s]	ê	[ɛ]	ian	[ian]
p	[p']	zh	[tʂ]	er	[ər]	in	[in]
m	[m]	ch	[tʂ']			iang	[iaŋ]
f	[f]	sh	[ʂ]	ai	[ai]	ing	[iŋ]
d	[t]	r	[ʐ]	ei	[ei]	iong	[yŋ]
t	[t']			ao	[au]	ua	[ua]
n	[n]	y	[i]	ou	[əu]	uo	[uɑ]
l	[l]	w	[w]	an	[an]	uai	[uai]
g	[k]			ang	[aŋ]	ui, uei	[uei]
k	[k']	a	[a]	eng	[əŋ]	uan	[uan]
h	[x]	o	[o]	ong	[uŋ]	un, uen	[uən]
j	[tɕ]	e	[ə]	ia	[ia]	uang	[uaŋ]
q	[tɕ']	i	[i]	ie	[iɛ]	ue	[yɛ]
x	[ɕ]	u	[u]	iao	[iau]	uan	[yan]
z	[ts]	u	[y]	iu, iou	[iəu]	un	[yn]
c	[ts']	-1	[ɿ] [ʅ]*				

[ɿ] used after z, c, s; [ʅ] used after zh, ch, sh, r.